Conducting School-Based Functional Behavioral Assessments

The Guilford Practical Intervention in the Schools Series

Kenneth W. Merrell, Series Editor

Helping Students Overcome Depression and Anxiety: A Practical Guide
Kenneth W. Merrell

Emotional and Behavioral Problems of Young Children:
Effective Interventions in the Preschool and Kindergarten Years
Gretchen A. Gimpel and Melissa L. Holland

Conducting School-Based Functional Behavioral Assessments:
A Practitioner's Guide
T. Steuart Watson and Mark W. Steege

Conducting School-Based Functional Behavioral Assessments

A Practitioner's Guide

T. STEUART WATSON
MARK W. STEEGE

THE GUILFORD PRESS
New York   London

© 2003 The Guilford Press
A Division of Guilford Publications, Inc.
72 Spring Street, New York, NY 10012
www.guilford.com

Printed in Canada

This book is printed on acid-free paper.

Last digit is print number: 9 8 7 6 5 4 3

Library of Congress Cataloging-in-Publication Data
Watson, T. Steuart.
    Conducting school-based functional behavioral assessments : a practitioner's guide /
T. Steuart Watson, Mark W. Steege.
        p. cm. — (The Guilford practical intervention in the schools series)
    Includes bibliographical references (p.   ) and indexes.
    ISBN 1-57230-854-0 (pbk. : alk. paper)
    1. Behavioral assessment of children—Handbooks, manuals, etc.   2. Problem children—
Behavior modification—Handbooks, manuals, etc.   3. School psychology—Handbooks,
manuals, etc.   I. Steege, Mark W.   II. Title.   III. Series.
    LB1124.W38 2003
    370.15′3—dc21
                                                                              2003000715

To those who have knowingly and unknowingly contributed their expertise to the work in this book, thank you. To my family: I appreciate all the sacrifices you have made during the completion of this book. A special dedication to my late grandmother, Marie Craven Salley: thanks for the lessons.

—T. S. W.

Writing this book has been like running a marathon: tense anticipation at the start, a dogged determination during months of drafts and revisions, and a mix of relief and exhilaration at the finish. I dedicate this book to my incredible support team—my wife, Lisa, and sons, Matt and Dan. Without your love, patience, encouragement, and understanding I would never have been able to begin, much less complete, "the race." You're the greatest.

—M. W. S.

About the Authors

T. Steuart Watson, PhD, is Professor and Coordinator of the School Psychology Program at Mississippi State University. He received his doctoral degree in school psychology with a minor in applied behavior analysis from the University of Nebraska–Lincoln. In 1998, Dr. Watson was awarded the Lightner Witmer Award from Division 16 of the American Psychological Association for outstanding research by a young scholar. Dr. Watson is currently active in several lines of research, including direct behavioral consultation, functional analysis and treatment of habits and tics, and evaluating the effects of olfactory stimuli on learning. He is the coeditor of the *Handbook of Child Behavior Therapy*, the forthcoming *Comprehensive Encyclopedia of School Psychology* and *Proven Practice: Prevention and Remediation Solutions for Schools*, a nationally refereed journal. He is also the coauthor of *Crime in the Schools: Reducing Fear and Disorder with Student Problem-Solving*.

Mark W. Steege, PhD, is Professor of School Psychology and Director of the Graduate Program in School Psychology at the University of Southern Maine. His educational background includes a degree in psychology from Iowa State University and graduate degrees in school psychology from The University of Iowa. After completing his PhD in 1986, he completed postdoctoral work as a pediatric psychologist within the College of Medicine at The University of Iowa. He joined the faculty at the University of Southern Maine in 1989, where he continues to conduct research on the application of applied behavior analysis (ABA) methodologies with persons with developmental disabilities. He also serves as Supervising Psychologist to the Margaret Murphy Center for Children, an ABA-based program serving children with autism and other developmental disabilities. Dr. Steege has authored numerous articles and book chapters on the subjects of functional behavioral assessment and single-case experimental design. A member of the Program Approval Board (National Association of School Psychologists), he has served two terms on the editorial board of the *Journal of Applied Behavior Analysis*. He also has been a member of the editorial board, and is currently Associate Editor of *Proven Practice: Prevention and Remediation Solutions for Schools*.

Preface

The information contained in this book represents many thousands of hours spent in schools with a wide variety of students trying to improve some aspect of their educational experience. It is our fervent hope that you, the reader, will be able to use this information in a meaningful manner in your daily practice. You will probably notice that the tone of this book is rather conversational. This was done on purpose. This book is not meant to be a reference text that one consults periodically for the answer to some arcane question. Rather, it is meant to be used by the school-based practitioner whose job is to conduct functional behavioral assessments (FBAs); hence the title. We wrote like we talk to colleagues, teachers, and other support personnel. We believe that most readers talk similarly and will be able to better relate to our message without having to sift through a terminologically and technologically thick manual that requires several other books just to understand the information.

This book, as you will see, is replete with case examples to illustrate the points we are attempting to make. All of these case examples are based on actual cases taken from those we have encountered in our own practice. The names, locations, dates, and other identifying information have been changed in all case examples. We believe that, although your cases will be different, you will be able to identify and see children from your own practice in the examples we provide.

All of the information contained in this book is malleable. That is, the forms can be used "as is" or they can be modified to fit your specific needs. One of the wonderful aspects of FBA is its dynamic and flexible nature that allows you to fit the procedure to the individual student, not the other way around—as is typically done in more traditional, standardized assessments. You can use as many of the procedures as you wish with an individual case and determine which procedures are needed based on the information that you collect as the process unfolds.

We are extremely indebted to a number of people without whom the completion of this work would not have been possible. First, to our families who sacrificed our presence and attention on many occasions. Their belief and interest in this project gave us the strength to persevere through many long days and nights of writing and phone conversations. Second, to the many graduate students, children, teachers, parents, and other support personnel who have assisted us in developing the procedures and forms we have presented, a most heartfelt thank you is offered. Third, special thanks goes to Chris Jennison at The Guilford Press and Kenneth W. Merrell, the editor of this series, for approaching us about writing a book on FBA. There are many distinguished scholars doing work in this area, and we feel honored that they chose us for this most important work. We hope that our efforts have not let them down. A final thank you is offered to the reader of this book. Thank you for entrusting us with guiding the direction of your FBAs. We will consider this book a resounding success only if you tell us that the information contained herein has helped you become more competent in conducting FBAs and has improved the educational experiences of children.

T. STEUART WATSON
MARK W. STEEGE

Contents

1

Introduction to Functional Behavioral Assessment

Once in possession of a set of terms we may proceed to a kind of description of behavior by giving a running account of a sample of behaviors as it unfolds itself in some frame of reference. This is a typical method in natural history. . . . It may be classified as a narration. . . . From data obtained in this way it is possible to classify different kinds of behavior and to determine relative frequencies of occurrence. But although this is, properly speaking, a description of behavior, it is not a science in the accepted sense. We need to go beyond mere observation to a study of functional relationships. We need to establish laws by virtue of which we may predict behavior, and we may do this only by finding variables of which behavior is a function.

—B. F. SKINNER (1938, p. 8)

Students who display interfering behavior in the classroom challenge the resources of schools, social service agencies, and their families. An inordinate amount of time, energy, and resources are expended attempting to develop strategies to address the behaviors exhibited by these students and to make them more successful in the classroom. When students are referred to school-based teams because of problematic behavior in the classroom, the multidisciplinary team[1] often discusses what action to take regarding the behavior of the individual in crisis. Invariably, in an urgent attempt to resolve the immediate crisis, the team discusses the inappropriateness and severity of the problem behavior and develops a set of procedures for responding to the individual when the problem behavior recurs, instead of arranging environmental conditions to prevent it from occurring. Too often, what has been lost in this process is a comprehensive analysis of the conditions that contribute to the occurrence of problem behavior.

---

[1]School-based assistance teams are often referred to as multidisciplinary teams, transdisciplinary teams, student support teams, teacher support teams, and functional behavioral assessment teams. Regardless of the name, their purpose is roughly the same, and we use these terms interchangeably throughout the book.

1

INTERFERING BEHAVIOR

Throughout this guide, we will be using the term "interfering behavior" to refer to those behaviors that have historically been referred to as "maladaptive," "inappropriate," "dysfunctional," "disruptive," "challenging," and "problematic." We prefer this term for several reasons: (1) it is consistent with the language of the Individuals with Disabilities Education Act (IDEA); (2) it conveys that the behavior is interfering in some way with the individual's social, emotional, behavioral, and/or academic development or that of his/her peers; (3) it makes no prior assumptions about the appropriateness/inappropriateness or other qualities of the behavior; (4) it does not convey that some behaviors result in a "bad" adaption, because any behavior that is functional is by definition adaptive (that is why we dislike the term "maladaptive"); and (5) it does not convey that some behaviors have the "wrong" function as does the term "dysfunctional."

THE "GOOD OLD DAYS"

Prior to the introduction of functional behavioral assessment methodologies, interventions to treat severe behavior problems in people with disabilities typically involved a process wherein team members conducted informal interviews and observations of the referred individual and, based on these findings, identified specific interventions. The selection of interventions was often a personal decision, with practitioners implementing preferred interventions or procedures with which they were very familiar. Practitioners typically used one or more of the following processes in selecting interventions:

• A member of the team reviewed the research literature and chose an intervention that had been demonstrated to be effective with individuals who displayed similar problems behaviors. For example: " I conducted a comprehensive review of the literature regarding interventions used to address oppositional–defiant behavior. I recommend that we consider implementing a treatment package that includes the following components: (1) guided compliance training, (2) behavioral contracting, (3) cognitive-behavioral counseling twice weekly, (4) family therapy once weekly, (5) differential reinforcement of other behavior (DRO), and (6) differential reinforcement of incompatible behaviors (DRI)." Or "I just heard about a study conducted in Portland where they found dill pickles were effective in reducing problem behaviors. Apparently gherkins were more effective than sliced. Let's try dill pickle therapy using gherkins with Stevie."

• The team chose an intervention that had been implemented and was thought to have been effective with another individual who displayed similar problem behaviors. For example: "Remember Billy. Billy displayed very similar behaviors. We used time-out with Billy and it seems to help. Let's try time-out with Sue."

• The team used a brainstorming session to collaborate in the design of what they hoped to be an effective intervention. For example: "We need to consider all of our options. Let's get creative here and use our collective resources to come up with a plan that really meets Stevie's needs." One hour later: "OK, we need to narrow this down to two or three reasonable procedures. Let's convene in 2 weeks and get some closure on this issue." Two weeks and 1 hour later: "OK, we've been discussing some very compelling options, but we're no closer to an intervention plan today than we were 2 weeks ago. Let's agree to disagree on the utility of facilitated communication and sensory integration procedures. I recommend that we continue with the current interventions of time-out and physical restraint and study this issue further."

THE SHIFTING SANDS OF TREATMENT APPROACHES

In the early 1980s, a dramatic shift in the conceptualization of problem behaviors and the development of functional behavioral assessment methodologies emerged. The "new thinking" of that era gave consideration to the environmental etiology of problem behaviors as a basis for the rational selection of treatment procedures (Mace & Roberts, 1993). Interventions were to be based on the *function* rather than merely the form of the behavior. This meant, for example, that interventions addressing behaviors maintained by negative reinforcement (e.g., escape from tasks) would be different than interventions focusing on behaviors maintained by positive reinforcement (e.g., social attention). The following examples illustrate the difference between addressing the form versus the function of behavior:

> Chris, a 7-year-old student diagnosed with an emotional disability engages in shouting, swearing, and throwing of materials when asked to complete science lab worksheets.

> Arlene, a 12-year-old student with a diagnosis of mild mental retardation displays high-pitched vocalization, as well as throwing work materials when teachers work directly with her peers within the classroom.

> Felix, a 14-year-old with a diagnosis of autistic disorder exhibits inappropriate verbalizations and throwing of objects in a variety of settings, times of day, and with various peers and staff members.

A review of these examples indicates that the *form* of interfering behaviors exhibited by Chris, Arlene, and Felix are very similar (i.e., all three individuals engage in inappropriate vocal behaviors and throw objects/materials) although not identical. Despite the similarity in form, the *function* of the interfering behaviors may be very different in each of the cases. For example, the results of comprehensive functional behavioral assessments indicated that for Chris interfering behaviors were motivated by negative reinforcement (i.e., escape from and/or avoidance of difficult tasks) whereas Arlene's behaviors were motivated by positive reinforcement (i.e., access to staff attention). Felix's behaviors were motivated by automatic positive reinforcement (i.e., the sensory consequences produced by the occurrence of these behaviors). Again, in each of these examples, the target behaviors were similar in form but the motivation (i.e., function) for each person was strikingly individualized.

Given that interventions matched to the function of behavior typically result in more effective and efficient outcomes compared to interventions based on the form of behavior, the intervention developed for each individual should be distinctly different from the interventions developed for the others. For instance, intervention for Chris might involve manipulating task difficulty, escape extinction, and teaching a more appropriate response to signal that assistance or a brief break is needed; for Arlene, treatment might involve providing attention contingent upon the absence of the behaviors for increasingly longer periods of time (DRO), attention extinction, and teaching a more appropriate means of obtaining adult attention; for Felix, intervention might consist of providing the opportunity for increased sensory stimulation through more appropriate behaviors and teaching new behaviors that result in sensory activation. It is important to note that although completing a functional behavioral assessment may lead to the identification of a *single function* of a specific behavior (e.g., negative reinforcement only as opposed to positive reinforcement and automatic reinforcement), in many cases a specific behavior may be motivated by *multiple functions*.

The team has a number of resources available to assist them in choosing interventions, among them some type of intervention manual (e.g., *The PreReferral Intervention Manual* [PRIM])[2] in which behavior is categorized according to topography (e.g., hitting, out-of-seat behavior, swearing, refusing to do work). Once a target behavior is selected, the team simply locates that behavior in the manual and chooses from among 50 listed interventions—that's right, 50 possible interventions for each target behavior! There are no guidelines on which intervention is likely to be most effective, nor are there guidelines on how to select interventions for a particular student. Quite obviously, function is not considered in these types of publications. Thus, their helpfulness is limited by their lack of attention to the function of behavior as well as their lack of creativity in intervention design (e.g., reinforce an opposite behavior). Too often the processes described above lead to the selection of ineffective interventions that, at best, result in no changes in problem behaviors but oftentimes lead to an increase in the frequency, intensity, and/or duration of problem behaviors. The results of these hastily developed and premature interventions are often ineffective programming, an escalation in the intensity of the original problem behavior, and/or the display of related but more severe forms of the problem behavior.

A more thoughtful and systematic approach for addressing these challenging behaviors is *functional behavioral assessment (FBA)*. Although the basic principles of functional behavioral assessment have been in existence for several decades in related professions (e.g., applied behavior analysis, behavior modification, and developmental disabilities; see Chapter 2 for a more in-depth discussion), it was not until the passage of Public Law 105-17 did the term become meaningful for most school psychologists and other school-based practitioners. Because of its relative "newness" within the educational domain, we will attempt to accomplish several goals in this brief introductory chapter:

---

[2]First published in 1988. Available from McCarney & Cummins-Hawthorne Educational Services, P.O. Box 7570, Columbia, MO 65205.

- Provide a definition and description of FBA
- Provide a clear and convincing rationale, beyond the obvious legal implications, for conducting FBAs in the schools
- Describe some of the most common errors associated with FBA
- Discuss the traditional view of behavioral treatment in the schools and contrast that with treatments based on function
- Provide an overview of types of FBA methodologies

WHAT IS FUNCTIONAL BEHAVIORAL ASSESSMENT?

Behavior does not occur in a vacuum. Rather, behavior occurs in reaction to a complex array of interacting variables (environmental, individual, biological, and instructional, to name a few). Only by identifying the relationships between the unique characteristics of the individual and the contextual variables that trigger and reinforce behavior can we begin to truly understand human behavior and work in concert with the person and those in his/her environment to develop interventions that lead to socially significant and meaningful behavior change. *Identifying these relationships is the core of functional behavioral assessment.*

This book is intended to be a resource that provides school-based practitioners with conceptual models and applied procedures for assessing problem behaviors that interfere with a student's personal, academic, and social development and functioning. All of the procedures and models that are presented in this book are designed to assist the practitioner in understanding *why* an individual displays a behavior in a particular setting at a particular time. Our models of functional behavioral assessment follow a problem-solving process demonstrating how an array of assessment methodologies can be used to understand the whys of behavior and design and evaluate positive behavioral support interventions. Thus, functional behavioral assessment is not one specific methodology. Rather it is an amalgamation of techniques that have the same purpose: *identifying the variables that control a behavior and using that knowledge to design individualized interventions.*

THE NEED FOR OBJECTIVE AND INDIVIDUALIZED BEHAVIORAL ASSESSMENTS (OR, THE COMMON ERRORS COMMITTED DURING FUNCTIONAL BEHAVIORAL ASSESSMENTS)

Decisions regarding the development and evaluation of interventions with students who exhibit problem behaviors should be based on objective and accurate information. Failing to do so often results in ineffective programming. Consider the following scenario:

As a member of the student assistance team (SAT), the school psychologist was asked to provide comprehensive assessment to develop a positive behavioral support plan with an adolescent with autism who exhibited aggressive behaviors (i.e., hair pulling, hitting, biting others). When the school psychologist asked school staff to offer an example of an occurrence of aggressive behavior, a educational technician reported an incident in which she had asked the student to complete a series of math worksheets, saying "Jerry, it is time to do your math. These are math worksheets. I'm sure that you can complete these worksheets. Do you want help or can you do these all by yourself?" She reported that Jerry immediately jumped up out of his chair, lunged toward the education technician, grabbed her by the hair, and wrestled her to the floor. This resulted in a three-person physical restraint that lasted 44 minutes. The educational technician stated that the reason Jerry engaged in aggressive behavior was his clear and obvious dislike for math worksheets. Some practitioners may stop at this level of information gathering because (1) they have a firsthand description of the sequence of events that led to the physical restraint, (2) it is a reasonable hypothesis that Jerry reacted in such an aggressive manner because of either poor skills in math or a dislike for math, and/or (3) they are being pressed by the team or other school personnel to quickly design an intervention plan because of the potentially dangerous nature of the aggressive behavior. While on the surface this may appear to be an accurate conclusion, the results of a subsequent *comprehensive* FBA indicated otherwise. The educational technician's error in this case was an *error of association* (see the accompanying box).

To conduct a functional behavioral assessment, one must gather more than just one report of a single incident using more than one method. The educational technician had prematurely concluded, based on this one incident, that the trigger for Jerry's aggressive behavior was indeed math worksheets. Having some knowledge of the various functions of behavior, she further stated that it appeared that his aggressive behavior was motivated by "escape from and/or avoidance of math worksheets." Quite reasonably, she also stated that she did not want to introduce math worksheets in the future out of fear of an aggressive response. After interviewing the educational technician, the school psychologist conducted a comprehensive FBA that included interviews with other staff, direct observations, ongoing data collection of aggressive behavior and related variables (i.e., antecedents and consequences), and a brief functional analysis. Data from the various sources demonstrated that aggressive behavior was unrelated to math worksheets. Instead, aggres-

---

In the case of Jerry, the educational technician made an *error of association*. In this example, math worksheets were *associated* with the occurrence of aggressive behavior but were not functionally related. That is, the math worksheets were not the antecedent that acted as a trigger for Jerry's aggressive behavior. The association of two variables (e.g., math worksheets and aggressive behavior) does not necessarily mean that there is a functional relationship between those variables. This is similar to the research adage of "correlation does not mean causation."

sion was found to be triggered by excessive verbal instructions and reinforced by the cessation of verbal instructions. Had an intervention been implemented based on the premature (and incorrect) hypothesis that math worksheets were the antecedent for aggressive behavior, it is highly unlikely that such an intervention would have been effective. Manipulating the math sheets in some way without altering the length of verbal instructions would have been ineffective and may have resulted in any combination of the following consequences:

- Ineffective treatment for Jerry
- Increased risk of potential physical danger to Jerry, the educational technician, and other staff because the aggressive behavior would likely have continued, perhaps worsened, and resulted in additional physical restraints
- A more restrictive placement for Jerry
- Decreased confidence in functional behavioral assessment from the SAT

The error committed by the educational technician was only one type of error that can occur within the FBA process. Each of these errors leads to inaccurate results and include (1) recency error of perception, (2) primacy error of perception, (3) error of inaccurate functional behavioral assessment, (4) error of misplaced precision, and (5) error of association. These errors often occur during interviews with staff regarding previous occurrences of interfering behavior. With the *recency error of perception*, interviewees report the most recent occurrence of a behavior and attribute its occurrence to variables that were present during the incident. This error is illustrated by the following example:

Jaime was a student in a fourth-grade regular education class. He was referred to the SAT because of frequent disruptive outbursts in class that sometimes included swearing and minor property damage. During the initial stages of the FBA process, the school psychologist interviewed the classroom teacher. She indicated that she thought his outbursts were the result of an abrupt transition from a relatively unstructured, highly physical activity (e.g., recess or gym class) because the most recent episode had occurred within the first 20 minutes after gym class. In fact, she reported that she believed most of his outbursts had occurred after gym or recess. Again, based on what is known about some children's difficulty in making transitions from one activity to another, particularly from an unstructured situation to a more structured classroom environment, the teacher's initial hypothesis was quite reasonable. Just to be certain, however, the school psychologist decided that a more comprehensive functional behavioral assessment was necessary in order to validate the teacher's hypothesis and to accurately identify some of the temporally proximate (see the accompanying box) triggers of Jaime's outbursts. The school psychologist conducted several direct observations of Jaime in his classroom, including those times immediately after lunch recess and gym and at other randomly selected times. In addition, the teacher agreed to keep track of Jaime's outbursts using a time-based scatterplot and an antecedent checklist. When combined, these data revealed two findings that were significant for understanding Jaime's outbursts and for planning intervention: (1) on occasion, his outbursts occurred after recess or gym, but only infrequently; (2) more than 65% of Jaime's out-

> Events that occur close in time to a challenging behavior are said to be *temporally proximate*. In the vast majority of functional behavioral assessments, one should look first at these events to determine what is triggering and maintaining the target behavior. Having said that, however, we acknowledge that events that occur more removed in time, *temporally distant events (TDEs)*, may also have a profound impact on school behavior. We discuss these temporally distant events in Chapter 10 and provide examples and procedures for determining when and how to check for TDEs that may be operating relative to a specific behavior.

bursts occurred immediately after his teacher issued a negative comment regarding either the quality or quantity of his academic work output.

The *primacy error of perception* is similar to the recency error of perception except in this case interviewees report the initial occurrence of interfering behavior and attribute its cause to variables that were present at that time. Both types of errors can result in very misleading information about the topography and function(s) of interfering behaviors. For example:

> Sheryl was an eighth-grade junior high student receiving special services for children diagnosed with specific learning disabilities. In addition to her diagnosed learning disabilities in math and reading, her social skills were quite poor. More specifically, she often threatened her classmates with physical harm although she had not yet reached the point of physical aggression. When a member of the SAT interviewed one of her teachers about the verbal aggression, the teacher was quite certain that she knew the reason behind Sheryl's verbal aggression: teasing from classmates regarding her sometimes poor academic performance. To support her hypothesis, the teacher recalled the first time she directly witnessed Sheryl threatening a classmate, which was about 10 weeks prior to the interview. The student had teased Sheryl about her inability to read a selected paragraph, and Sheryl responded by threatening to beat her up if she didn't stop teasing her. The teacher concluded by saying that, although she didn't always hear what was going on, she was convinced that the teasing was the reason behind Sheryl's verbally aggressive behavior. Although the initial incident as described by the teacher may indeed have been accurate, it may or may not have reflected what was currently happening to prompt and maintain Sheryl's verbal threats. Hence, more functional behavioral assessment was indicated to determine the extant cues that trigger (antecedents) and the consequences that maintain Sheryl's verbal threats.

The *error of misplaced precision* is illustrated in the following case example:

> A preschooler with autism was receiving intensive in-home applied behavior analysis service. A comprehensive data collection system was used to record the frequency of each of several problem behaviors (e.g., self-injury, aggression, tantrums, stereotypy). For example, staff used a tally mark system (i.e., ⦀⦀ ⦀) to record each occurrence of the

specified problem behaviors. This data-recording procedure yielded the rate of occurrences of problem behavior per day. During a program evaluation, a consulting psychologist noted that the recording of the frequency of all problem behaviors resulted in imprecise measures of several of the behaviors. For example, the length of the tantrum behaviors varied considerably, from a few seconds to several minutes. Thus, a frequency count of one tantrum that lasted 5 seconds is not equivalent to one tantrum that lasted 28 minutes. Moreover, the tally system offered no information about the contextual variables associated with each of the problem behaviors. In this example, the data-recording procedures were not matched to the dimensions of each behavior. Comprehensive individualized functional behavioral assessment procedures that included frequency, duration, and performance-based behavioral recording procedures were developed. Additionally, an individualized scatterplot data-recoding form was developed that resulted in the identification of controlling variables. This is an example of the *error of misplaced precision* because, although there was great concern and care for recording the frequency of several behaviors, the effort put forth on collecting frequency data would have been more beneficial if it had been placed on gathering more relevant data.

The *error of inaccurate functional behavioral assessment* is demonstrated in the following case example:

A student with a history of social emotional and learning difficulties was referred for psychological evaluation regarding oppositional and defiant behaviors (e.g., refusing to comply with teacher requests and refusing to complete assignments). Based on informal interviews and anecdotal observations, the school psychologist concluded that problem behaviors were motivated by social attention (i.e., the attention the student received from the one-on-one teacher assistant whenever problem behavior occurred). Based on that conclusion, a "time-out procedure" to address problem behavior was implemented for several weeks. During that time, the frequency and duration of oppositional and defiant behaviors increased markedly. A second referral to the school psychologist led to a more comprehensive FBA. This time, the school psychologist conducted an assessment that included a structured interview, direct observations, and brief functional analysis procedures. The combined assessment results indicated that problem behavior was motivated by avoidance or termination of academic tasks, not social attention. The time-out intervention, while designed to reduce problem behavior, was actually serving to reinforce and strengthen oppositional and defiant behaviors because academic tasks were terminated contingent upon oppositional or defiant behavior so that the student could be placed in time-out. Based on the results of the more comprehensive FBA, a positive behavioral support plan incorporating antecedent modification and functional communication training was developed. The revised procedure, which was based on the results from an accurate FBA, resulted in a significant decrease in problem behaviors and a marked increase in task participation, task completion, and task accuracy.

A central theme to identifying and correcting the errors depicted in each of these scenarios is the need to closely examine objective behavioral assessments. In each case, behavioral assessment procedures were used to record behaviors and to systematically identify controlling variables. A conclusion drawn from these examples is that an anecdotal report (i.e., interview data) alone is often an inadequate method for understanding complex behavioral interactions. Moreover, not all behavioral assessment methods are suitable for recording and evaluating all forms of behavior. When FBAs of interfering behavior are conducted, an individualized assessment process that takes into account the characteristics of the individual, the behaviors exhibited, and the environments in which these behaviors occur must be implemented. Thus, we do not recommend a "cookie-cutter" approach to FBAs. Although we acknowledge several critical components that must be included in every FBA (e.g., direct observations of behavior), the timing and extent of these and other components will likely be different for each student.

THE "NOT SO GOOD OLD DAYS": INTERVENTION MOMENTUM AND PREMATURE IMPLEMENTATION

Despite almost 2 decades of research demonstrating the utility of using a functional approach for determining the most effective treatment, school-based teams do not always engage in productive discussions during meetings, as the following example illustrates. Unfortunately, this meeting did not occur 20 or 15 years ago or even 10 years ago. In sad truth, this meeting occurred within the last couple of years.

Recently, I (Steege) attended a SAT meeting at a middle school. I was invited to the meeting by the parent of Chris, a student whom the team would be discussing. The purpose of the meeting was to discuss interfering behaviors that Chris had been exhibiting for several weeks. Participants at the meeting included the parent, the special education case manager, Chris's mainstream teachers, the school psychologist, a behavior specialist, an educational technician, an occupational therapist, and the principal. The meeting began with introductions of all team members. Next, the special education case manager began to describe several "behavioral incidents" over the past few weeks in which Chris displayed "silly disruptive behaviors." The team spent approximately 2 minutes discussing the target behavior(s) and less than 1 minute addressing possible antecedent, individual, or consequence variables. Several minutes were devoted to a discussion of possible diagnoses (e.g., Asperger's disorder, oppositional–defiant disorder, nonverbal learning disability, obsessive–compulsive disorder, and attention-deficit/hyperactivity disorder). The team members spent approximately 40 out of the 60 minutes of the meeting discussing the advantages and disadvantages of various intervention strategies that could be used to address these behaviors. The discussion about interventions focused on strategies that would change Chris's behaviors. Toward the end of the meeting, the team agreed to implement four or five of the strategies and "see how Chris responds to these changes." Because of my role as "invited guest" and not having worked with this team before, I spent the majority of my time observing the collaborative problem-solving process as it unfolded. On a positive note, the team members were respectful of each other's opinions and suggestions and appeared to be working very hard to develop fair and equitable strategies to reduce occurrences of "silly disruptive behaviors."

Throughout the meeting, I kept track (yes, I love to collect data) of the number of specific strategies that were suggested. This team identified 22 specific intervention strategies (time-out, response cost, a token economy program, social skills training, individual counseling, group counseling, self-esteem building activities, peer tutoring, peer mentoring, one-on-one educational technician support, life space interviewing, brief walks around the school to reduce anxiety, brief walks to stimulate attending, several sensory integration techniques, among others). This is a classic case of a team developing *intervention momentum*. Intervention momentum occurs when members of the team begin to suggest (oftentimes in rapid-fire motion) strategy after strategy after strategy. It's the snowball effect—or, for folks from warmer climates, it's the tidal wave effect. A team member's idea sparks an idea in another team member, whose suggestion triggers the offering of a strategy by another team member, and so on. This type of brainstorming can often be quite valuable in identifying creative and effective interventions. However, it is a much more effective and efficient process when it occurs *after* a comprehensive FBA has been conducted and the team members have a full understanding of all the variables associated with the behavior(s) of concern. This case example also illustrates another classic situation that often occurs within school and agency setting, namely, *premature implementation*. Premature implementation occurs when team members, usually out of a sense of urgency to act or to be "helpful," frantically identify and implement intervention strategies that are preceded by little if any forethought. Premature implementation, although meeting an immediate need to "do something," may in fact do nothing, or—in a worst-case scenario—may actually complicate the situation and result in an increase in the problem behavior.

The Solution: Conduct a comprehensive FBA, use the results of the FBA to design individually tailored interventions, and objectively evaluate the effectiveness of the intervention.

EMPIRICAL SUPPORT FOR FUNCTIONAL BEHAVIORAL ASSESSMENT

Since the early 1980s, there has been a dramatic and steady increase of research supporting, demonstrating, and validating a wide range of FBA procedures. A central theme of this research is that the understanding of behavior needs to be conducted on an individualized basis. Numerous school-based FBA studies have shown that individual topographies of problem behavior may be maintained by various forms of reinforcement across populations of students (Radford, Aldrich, & Ervin, 2000). A recent study by Kennedy, Meyer, Knowles, and Shukla (2000) clearly illustrates this point. We have summarized the Kennedy et al. study in the accompanying box.

Kennedy et al. (2000) investigated the behavioral functions associated with stereotypy (body rocking, object manipulation, tapping objects, head weaving, hand waving, among others) of five students with autism who attended age-appropriate public school placements that ranged from a full-time general education class to a self-contained special education class. Stereotypic behavior has historically been referred to as "self-stimulatory behavior," implying that sensory consequences are reinforcing and maintaining the behavior. For example, hand flapping is often considered to be a form of self-stimulatory behavior, with the explanation that the movement of the hand in front of the face produces visual stimulation that is reinforcing to the individual. The above authors conducted functional behavioral assessments of a range of stereotypic behaviors, most of which might be classified as self-stimulatory. FBAs showed that stereotypy served multiple operant functions, including positive reinforcement (i.e., access to social attention) and negative reinforcement (i.e., termination of demanding tasks), and occurred in the absence of environmental reinforcement (presumably from perceptual or sensory reinforcement). Kennedy et al. demonstrated that just because a behavior looks like it serves self-stimulatory purposes does not necessarily mean that that is the function of the behavior. They found that one cannot presume the function of behavior based on the form of the behavior. They next developed tailored interventions with each student, interventions that were based on the results of the FBA. For example, for a student whose stereotypic behavior was motivated by both negative reinforcement (i.e., the occurrence of behavior revisited in the termination of a difficult task) and positive reinforcement (i.e., social attention), he/she was taught to raise his/her right hand to request attention and to sign "break" to indicate a request to terminate difficult tasks. The intervention resulted in a marked increase in functional communication skills and a decrease in stereotypic behaviors.

The findings of Kennedy et al. (2000) are consistent with previous research that has demonstrated that interventions based on the function of behavior rather than the form of behavior result in meaningful behavior change (e.g., Carr & Durand, 1985; Steege, Wacker, Berg, Cigrand, & Cooper, 1989; Steege et al., 1990; Wacker et al., 1990). Basically, the body of research from 1982 to the present in the area of FBA clearly demonstrates that the identification of the function(s) of problem behavior is critical to the design and successful implementation of positive behavioral support interventions.

BRIEF OVERVIEW
OF FUNCTIONAL BEHAVIORAL ASSESSMENT PROCEDURES

FBA goes beyond merely identifying and describing problem behavior. The FBA process is an investigative endeavor that also focuses on identifying and evaluating the variables that trigger and maintain behavior. The results of an FBA are then used as the basis for designing individually tailored intervention plans. There are three forms of FBA:

1. Indirect functional behavioral assessment
2. Direct descriptive functional behavioral assessment
3. Functional behavioral analysis

Indirect functional behavioral assessment involves a variety of methods, including review of records, behavior-rating scales, social skills ratings, adaptive behavior assessments, informal interviews, and semistructured interviews. The primary purposes of indirect FBA procedures are to (1) identify and describe behavior and (2) generate *hypothesized* functional relationships (i.e., the identification of antecedent, individual, and consequent variables that are associated with the targeted interfering behavior). Indirect FBA procedures are typically used as the first step in conducting an evaluation of interfering behaviors. In the vast majority of cases, this should not be the only step of an FBA. As discussed earlier, interviewees often unintentionally report biased and erroneous information. Teams that base an FBA solely on interviews risk conducting inaccurate and invalid (and perhaps illegal) assessments that result in ineffective interventions. The next step in conducting an FBA involves direct observation and recording of behaviors.

Direct descriptive functional behavioral assessment involves the collection of observational data on the occurrence of behavior and contextual variables within the context of natural environments. These assessments involve observing and recording the specified target behavior and relevant environmental events. Direct observation of target behaviors and causal conditions within the natural environment is a procedure school-based practitioners can use that allows educational teams to construct applied interventions that are clearly indicated by the assessment data (Skinner, Rhymer, & McDaniel, 2000). There are a variety of direct descriptive FBA methods. Selection of the method typically depends on several factors including the topography of the behavior and the skills/resources of those who are conducting the assessment. At the most basic level, direct descriptive FBA involves identifying and describing the behavior, designing an appropriate behavior-recording procedure, and observing and recording the behavior and associated antecedent and consequence variables. Although valuable for identifying these potential relationships, information gathered from both indirect FBA and direct descriptive FBA are only *suggestive* of functional relationships because they do not systematically isolate and manipulate environmental variables (McComas & Mace, 2000).

In order to *confirm* hypothesized functional relationships, it is necessary to conduct a more precise assessment in which an experimental or functional behavioral analysis is conducted. There are two types of functional behavioral analysis: (1) brief functional behavioral analysis and (2) extended functional behavioral analysis.

Note: We have seen several examples of *one-page* FBA forms designed by practitioners and/or school district personnel. These forms are completed using interviews often conducted during a team meeting. This does not represent a best-practices approach to conducting an FBA. The one-page "quick" and oftentimes "dirty" approach should be viewed as only the start of the hypothesis-testing approach.

FUNCTIONAL BEHAVIORAL ANALYSIS

It is important to note the slight change in terminology: from *functional behavioral assessment* to *functional behavioral analysis*. Functional behavioral assessment refers to the broad range of assessment methodologies (i.e., indirect, direct, and experimental assessments) that are used to identify the variables that trigger and maintain problem behavior. Functional behavioral analysis refers to an assessment model in which environmental events are systematically manipulated and examined within single-subject experimental designs. (McComas & Mace, 2000).

Both brief and extended functional behavioral analysis procedures involve the observation of behavior and the direct manipulation of antecedent and/or consequence variables for the purpose of empirically determining the motivating function of a behavior. Extended functional analysis procedures (i.e., Iwata, Dorsey, Slifer, Bauman, & Richman, 1982/1994) involve multiple assessment trials of several minutes (e.g., up to 30 minutes) for each assessment condition (e.g., five trials of academic demand, five trials of social attention, five trials of alone) typically within an alternating treatments design. The brief functional analysis model incorporates the same general assessment methodologies as the extended functional analysis, except the number and duration of assessments of sessions is limited (e.g., 8–10 sessions from 10 to 15 minutes each).

Steege and Northup (1998) described a brief functional behavioral analysis procedure in which the assessment is conducted within two to three phases: (1) standard assessment, where potential maintaining variables are evaluated; (2) confirmatory assessment, where the results of the initial assessment are replicated; and (3) contingency reversal, where the identified function of problem behavior is provided contingent on appropriate behavior. Over the past 20 years, extensive research has validated the experimental rigor and clinical utility of functional behavioral analysis procedures. Suffice it to say, these procedures are clearly evidence based and have emerged as the "gold standard" for conducting FBAs.

The need for comprehensive, rigorous, and objective assessment of behaviors is obvious. There are a wide range of FBA methodologies available to practitioners. A common question at workshops is "Is one method absolutely better than the others?" We can answer that with an emphatic "NO!" There is no one best FBA procedure or set of procedures. In our application of FBAs across a wide range of individuals, referral issues, and settings, our methodologies have taken many forms. The particular form depends on the individual being assessed, the target behaviors, the setting, and the amount of training and experience in behavior analysis of teachers, support staff, parents, etc. To address the full range of presenting issues, practitioners need to be well trained and experienced in a wide range of assessment methodologies. In short, it is naive to expect that we can assess all behavioral issues with a single method (i.e., the standard battery approach) or a "shotgun" approach (use of every FBA procedure every time in hopes that we get the requisite information). Either of these approaches, which are probably often utilized in practice, are at the very least *inefficient* and likely *ineffective*. Instead, practitioners need a well-stocked arsenal of assessment methods from which they can choose. With these tools in hand, practitioners will be able to:

- Match the assessment process to the referral issues
- Conduct assessments that result in accurate, reliable, and valid data
- Design effective and realistic interventions that result in meaningful improvements in the student's academic, behavioral, and social functioning

To reiterate, this book will not tell a practitioner *which* particular FBA method to use in a given situation. Nor will it give a formulaic approach that can be applied to all FBAs conducted in a district. Rather, it will equip the practitioner with information and skills that will facilitate improved decision making throughout the FBA process.

In the following chapters, we offer a brief review of the empirical and legal support for conducting FBAs and an overview and description of FBA procedures.

2

Genesis of
Functional Behavioral Assessment

What a long strange trip it's been.
—GRATEFUL DEAD

During a workshop that we were conducting on functional behavioral assessment, a special educator asked, "Just when did all of this focus on function of behavior and functional behavioral assessment start? I've been in this business 18 years and have never even heard of it." Undoubtedly, many educators and psychologists are in a similar position of being unfamiliar with function and functional behavioral assessment as it applies to behavior. With the recent passage of Public Law 105-17, these and related terms have been introduced into the everyday vocabulary of professionals providing psychological services to children in educational settings. Despite the recent appearance of functional behavioral assessment as an educational practice, however, the notion that all behaviors serve some purpose (FUNCTION) actually has a lengthy history, dating back to the work of E. L. Thorndike (1898) and B. F. Skinner (1938), among others.

The purpose of this short chapter is to provide a very general overview of that history because we believe that school practitioners need to be able to relate to others the relative "un-newness" of functional behavioral assessment and that it is not merely another bandwagon onto which educational reform/legislation has hopped. We also think it is important to know why the focus on function is so very crucial for understanding the reasons children behave the way they do and for remedying problematic academic and social behaviors.

To get at the roots of function, let's begin with the work of Edward L. Thorndike, who coined the term *law of effect* (1898; see the accompanying box). Although the work of Thorndike did not directly influence the development of research specifically related to function, it is a predecessor to some of the concepts that Skinner used to understand human behavior. Without our going into undue detail in the present context, we note that

---

LAW OF EFFECT

Briefly, the law of effect states that behaviors that result in satisfying consequences are "stamped in" or tend to recur and those that result in "annoying" consequences are "stamped out" and tend not to recur.

Thorndike observed over a series of trials that the behavior of cats was influenced by the consequences (escape from a box and access to food) of their behavior. That is, behaviors that resulted in escape from the box (i.e., pulling a wire or pressing a lever), and hence access to food, increased over time, whereas other behaviors that did not result in escape from the box (i.e., clawing and biting at the box) decreased. In addition, each cat spent less time in the box with each succeeding trial before it exhibited the behavior that allowed it to escape. Thus, not only were the cats learning behaviors that resulted in positive consequences, but they were exhibiting the behaviors in a more efficient fashion. Thorndike's experiments were a simple yet elegant illustration of the powerful effects that consequences can have on responding.

John B. Watson, who is known as the father of behaviorism, asserted that all behaviors were the result of environmental events and that psychologists should study overt behaviors and their environmental determinants and not the internal urges/drives that dominated the field of psychology at the time. Almost everyone is familiar with Watson's most famous experiment in which he conditioned a fear response in an 11-month-old infant to demonstrate the effects that environmental events can have on the development of "emotions" (J. B. Watson & Rayner, 1920). Watson's psychology was appropriately called "stimulus–response" because of the focus on the relationship between the presentation of a stimulus and the resulting response. Watson, like Ivan P. Pavlov earlier, illustrated the behavior-eliciting effects of certain stimuli. When behavior is a function of (or caused by) a stimulus that *preceded* it, the behavior is called a *respondent behavior*. The accompanying example (see box on p. 18) illustrates the principle of respondent behavior.

In the early 1930s, Burrhus Frederic Skinner, who was heavily influenced by Charles Darwin in addition to Pavlov, Thorndike, and Watson, began studying the effects that consequences have on behavior as well as the stimuli that evoke behavior. Skinner primarily used rats in his laboratory and analyzed the effects that different schedules of reinforcement have on behavior. One of Skinner's most important findings was that behavior was a function of (i.e., was caused by) the consequences that followed it. For instance, Skinner's data indicated that if lever pressing was positively reinforced with food (i.e., lever presses were immediately followed by a food pellet), lever pressing increased. In this example, lever pressing is *operant behavior* because it is controlled by the consequences that followed it. If food is no longer presented after lever pressing, then lever pressing will decrease in frequency until it is no longer exhibited. The accompanying example (see box on p. 19) illustrates how the principle of operant conditioning works in the classroom to produce interfering behavior.

A REAL-LIFE EXAMPLE OF RESPONDENT BEHAVIOR

On a cool spring day, little Mackenzie, age 4, was playing on the swingset in her backyard, swinging, laughing and singing, and pumping her legs so that she would go ever higher in the air. Unbeknownst to her, a nasty wasp had entered the area and had pinpointed her as a target for its mildly poisonous but painful stinger. Mackenzie visually detected the wasp just as it landed on her leg and inserted its stinger into her calf muscle. The wasp had inflicted a painful stimulus on Mackenzie and, like most children her age when they are hurt, she began crying and screaming and running from the aversive stimulus (the wasp).

Several days later, Mackenzie was once again playing on the swingset in her backyard. And once again, a wasp was flying around the swingset, perhaps looking for potential targets. Mackenzie saw the wasp and immediately jumped from the swing and ran away screaming and crying; essentially exhibiting the same behavior as during her first encounter with a wasp. This encounter was different in at least one important aspect, however. This time Mackenzie exhibited the same behavior without being stung. This is an extremely critical point because Mackenzie had not received a consequence for this encounter with the wasp yet she exhibited behavior as if she had indeed been stung. In this case, we say that her crying, screaming, and running behaviors were *respondent behaviors* because they resulted from, or were caused by, the presentation of a stimulus (i.e., the wasp).*

---

*This story was told here with the permission of Mackenzie Watson.

From these two examples, we see that behavior can be caused by events that precede it (i.e., respondent conditioning) and by events that follow it (i.e., operant conditioning). In some instances, behavior is a function of both respondent and operant conditioning. In such instances, the behavior may be referred to as "two-factor" behavior. To illustrate two-factor learning, let's return to Mackenzie from the respondent conditioning example (see the accompanying box on p. 20).

One of the obvious criticisms of Thorndike's and Skinner's work is that they used animals—and not humans—to scientifically study behavior. Certainly the behavior of humans is much more complex than that of cats or rats because humans can think, reason, talk, develop morals, make laws, etc. Or is it? Beginning in the early-to-middle 1950s and throughout the 1960s, applied researchers began using Skinner's principles to solve problems presented by humans. One early study examined the effects of using positive reinforcement on cooperation in children ranging in age from 7 to 12 years (Azrin & Lindsley, 1956). It was found that, even in the absence of instructions to cooperate, positive reinforcement was effective for developing and maintaining cooperative behavior. Likewise, discontinuing reinforcement for cooperative behavior resulted in elimination of cooperation. In perhaps one of the most interesting early behavior modification studies, Flanagan, Goldiamond, and Azrin (1959) demonstrated that stuttering could be instituted in otherwise fluent speakers by making escape from mild shock contingent upon nonfluent speech. That is, stuttering was negatively reinforced because it resulted in the termination of a

A REAL-LIFE EXAMPLE OF OPERANT BEHAVIOR

Barry is a third-grade student who is well liked by his peers and his teachers. He gets along well with everyone in his class, has a wonderful personality, and does well academically . . . except in math. For some reason, he has always had difficulty with even basic math concepts like addition and one digit by one digit multiplication computations. Despite his difficulty, his grades and standardized achievement scores have never been sufficiently low to warrant consideration for special education testing. Until the current school year, Barry was a model student in terms of classroom behavior. His teacher noted that recently his behavior has been getting progressively worse, especially during math instruction and while doing worksheets. What typically happens is that the teacher will either begin a lesson on math or assign a worksheet to be completed at his desk which results in Barry either complaining loudly that he can't do the work, running around the classroom, or being openly defiant of her. Quite obviously, the teacher is concerned about why he is engaging in this behavior and why it has gotten progressively worse. In talking with the teacher, we discovered that her most common reactions to Barry's behaviors were to first ignore them and, if they did not cease, to send him to the principal's or the counselor's office, or to a desk in the hall. As a result of these disciplinary practices, Barry often fails to complete his assignments, which in turn worsens his grade in math. The trigger, or antecedent, for these behaviors is fairly obvious: math worksheets or any type of math instruction. What is not so well understood is why, especially after being punished for engaging in these behaviors, Barry's behavior has not only persisted but actually worsened. In looking more closely at the behavior, we see that all of the consequences for Barry's behavior result in him being able to AVOID or ESCAPE his math assignments. Thus, we say that Barry's behaviors are *negatively reinforced* because whenever he is sent out of the room, whether to the principal, counselor, or a desk in the hall, each of these consequences result in him not having to do his math or listen to math instruction. In essence, these behaviors are "working" for Barry because they result in him not having to do math. A simple concept? Most definitely. Well understood by most in the school system? Definitely not. It does not matter whether a person intends for a particular consequence to be a punishment or not, as in the case of Barry's teacher. What matters is the effect the consequences have on behavior. In this example, Barry's behaviors are caused by the consequences that follow the behavior and are *operant behaviors*.*

*This story was told here with the permission of Barry (a pseudonym but a real kid).

painful stimulus. Please remember that this study was conducted more than 40 years ago when different ethical standards were in place for experimental studies using human subjects. Putting that consideration aside for the moment, we note that this study was a powerful demonstration of the effects that consequences have on human behavior.

In another study, Azrin (1960) used contingent rest breaks (a form of negative reinforcement because the person got to take a break from working) to increase work output by 50%, despite reports that the individual had reached his/her physical limit. (*Does this type*

A REAL-LIFE EXAMPLE OF TWO-FACTOR LEARNING

Recall that Mackenzie exhibited running, crying, and screaming behavior when she observed a wasp (respondent behavior). This behavior resulted from her being stung by a wasp some days earlier. The most immediate result of her running, crying, and screaming was avoiding another sting from a wasp (the operant element). Thus, we can say that these behaviors were negatively reinforced and are controlled partly by their consequences (avoidance of a sting) and partly by the stimuli that precedes them (sight of the wasp).

---

of procedure ring a bell for anyone trying to increase the amount of work that a student produces in class? If not, it certainly should!) Ayllon (1960) and Ayllon and Azrin (1965, 1968) used basic reinforcement procedures such as a token economy and desirable activities (e.g., going for a walk, watching a movie, and attending a music session) to modify the psychotic and social behaviors of patients in a mental hospital ward. Baer and Sherman (1964) and Baer, Peterson, and Sherman (1967) demonstrated that imitative behaviors of young children and children with mental retardation could be altered using social reinforcers. The effects of time-out from positive reinforcement (a procedure that is alive and well today and is considered to be one of the most effective, nonintrusive means for changing a variety of behaviors) were experimentally investigated by Holz, Azrin, and Ayllon (1963) and Azrin (1961). Their findings influenced the development of proper use of time-out and the ancillary procedures that are often used to augment the effects of time-out. Even cigarette smoking, which is considered to be one of the most difficult behaviors to modify, was significantly decreased by using stimulus control (Azrin & Powell, 1968) and punishment (Powell & Azrin, 1968) procedures.

In the studies cited above, the common thread was that each used procedures derived from Skinner's principles of operant conditioning. Collectively, the science of behavior change that grew from these and numerous other studies was known as *behavior modification*. Although function was not specifically addressed, there was tacit acknowledgment and demonstration that consequences exert tremendous influence on human behavior.

In 1968, Bijou, Peterson, and Ault were among the first applied researchers to conduct what would later become known as descriptive functional analyses to derive interventions. They argued that, instead of merely answering the question "How?," applied psychology should concern itself with answering the question "Why." In a layperson's language, "why" is synonymous with "function." In other words, the science of human behavior could only advance when the individual's interactions with the environment were clearly delineated so that the "purpose" or function of the behavior could be discerned. To that end, Bijou and his colleagues advocated that an A-B-C (i.e., *antecedent–behavior–consequence*) system *be used when one is directly observing and recording behavior and they demonstrated the procedure using a case example. From these relatively humble beginnings, the A-B-C procedure has become the basis for functional behavioral assessments/analyses. This recording procedure has persisted for almost 4 decades, a testament to its applied value and its usefulness for helping to understand the "whys" of human behavior.*

Throughout the 1970s and early 1980s, applied researchers continued to refine existing techniques and develop new strategies for changing human behavior, all of which were based on operant principles. These techniques were applied to a wide range of human problems across a wide span of settings, particularly educational settings. In 1977, Carr published a seminal article on identifying the "motivation" for self-injurious behavior (SIB). Carr reviewed the extant studies on SIB and concluded that, across studies, one of five hypotheses consistently emerged to explain SIB, with four of the five actually having an empirical basis. These four hypotheses were as follows: (1) SIB is maintained by some type of socially mediated *positive reinforcement*; (2) SIB is maintained by some type of socially mediated *negative reinforcement*; (3) SIB is maintained by the *sensory stimulation* produced by the behavior; and (4) SIB is the by-product of an *aberrant physiological process*, that is, due to some biological or genetic disorder. Although Carr further described a step-by-step methodology for determining the motivation (i.e., function) of SIB, he did not directly utilize the methodology he proposed.

Taking the mantle from Carr, Iwata and colleagues (1982/1994) published the first study using an experimental method for determining function in nine participants with self-injurious behavior (SIB). The methodology they employed was essentially the same methodology that Carr (1977) had laid out previously. Without going into undue detail we note that, Iwata et al. systematically exposed participants to several experimental conditions designed to test each of the motivational hypotheses for SIB presented by Carr. To test the first (social attention) hypothesis, the experimenter provided a verbal reprimand and brief phsyical touch contingent upon SIB. To test the second (negative reinforcement) hypothesis, the experimenter terminated the presentation of a difficult academic task contingent upon SIB. To test the third (sensory stimulation) hypothesis, the experimenter placed the participant in a therapy room alone without any toys or other materials. An unstructured play condition was included to act as a control condition. Iwata et al. found idiosyncratic functions across the nine participants. That is, for four of the participants it appeared that the function of SIB was automatic reinforcement (i.e., sensory stimulation). For two of the participants, the function of SIB appeared to be escape from academic task demands. One participant's SIB seemed to be maintained by social attention. Three of the participants had high levels of SIB across all experimental conditions, perhaps suggesting that their SIB was maintained by multiple functions.

Since Iwata and associates' seminal publication, literally hundreds of studies utilizing some type of functional behavioral assessment have been published in the professional literature. A great portion of these studies, admittedly, have very little applied value. That is, they were conducted using very lengthy and complex experimental functional analysis procedures, in settings that could best be described as contrived, and with participants with little or no decision-making or ambulatory ability. However, many studies have been conducted in applied settings using the natural consequences found in the environment with normal functioning participants that have extended the ecological validity of functional behavioral assessment. A review of those studies is far beyond the scope of this chapter and book. Readers who are interested in a bibliography of the functional behavioral assessment/analysis studies that have been conducted in educational settings are referred to Ervin and Ehrhardt (2000).

In part because of the vast amount of empirical literature that has accumulated on deriving interventions based on function since the early 1980s and partly because of the philosophical movement away from punishment-based interventions that were sometimes present in behavior modification programs, basing interventions on function has become best practice in the field of applied behavior analysis and, through federal legislation, has worked its way into the special education arena via the Individuals with Disabilities Education Act (IDEA). Many would say that its appearance in education is long overdue, whereas others would maintain that it is merely another bandwagon that, if given enough time and left to its own devices, will run its course and be replaced by something else. We agree with both of these positions. We agree that it is long overdue because it took almost 15 years and a plethora of research before education "caught on" and embraced functional behavioral assessment as a way of designing maximally effective interventions. We also agree that it is possible that, in another 15 years, there will have been sufficient scientific and technological advances in the understanding of human behavior that functional methodology may be replaced by something more effective (we are not sure what it will be but are willing to acknowledge the possibility). Until other, more effective means of understanding and changing human behavior become available, it behooves all educators to become familiar with the rationale behind functional behavioral assessment and the associated terminology, procedures, and methodology to help ensure a better educational experience for the children they serve each day.

During the past 20 years, advances within the fields of applied behavior analysis, special education, developmental disabilities, and school psychology have established innovative technologies that are designed to improve our understanding of what problem behavior looks like, where and when it occurs, what might trigger it, and how to use this information to design behavioral support plans and document behavior change (Steege & Northup, 1998; Shapiro & Kratochwill, 2000; Steege, Brown-Chidsey, & Mace, 2002). Paralleling these technological advances have been legislative, regulatory, and legal decisions that have emphasized and, in some cases mandated, individualized assessment and intervention services for persons with disabilities. For example, in the late 1980s, the Association for Behavior Analysis and the National Institutes of Health both endorsed the use of FBA procedures to evaluate problem behavior, with the results used to design behavioral interventions with person who display problem behavior. More recently, the IDEA Amendments of 1997 required that school districts conduct FBAs and provide positive behavioral support interventions in cases where students are disciplined for problem behaviors. In addition, several states mandate that whenever restrictive interventions are used within school settings on a regular basis, it is required that the educational team examine the school environment to determine factors that may be contributing to the students behavior problems and develop plans for teaching prosocial behaviors (Jones & Jones, 1998). Finally, several states (e.g., Minnesota, Florida, California, Utah, Washington, New York, and Maine) have developed laws or regulations requiring that FBAs be conducted and used as the basis for designing individualized behavioral programs (O'Neill et al., 1997).

A LOOK AHEAD

Next, Chapter 3 describes the basic principles upon which functional behavioral assessment is based. Some of the topics that are addressed include:

- The three functions of behavior
- Antecedents
- Consequences
- Basic operant principles
- Indirect methods of functional behavioral assessment
- Direct methods of functional behavioral assessment
- Brief and extended functional behavioral analysis

Each of these topics will be discussed in sufficient detail and will lay the foundation for what we cover in the remaining chapters.

A Special Note

Before continuing, we would like to briefly describe the conceptual model to which we adhere that guides all of the activities associated with our FBAs. This is called the AIBC model:

A: *A*ntecedent variables are those stimuli that precede and "trigger" behavior.
I: *I*ndividual variables (e.g., observed individual differences, prior learning, affect, medical conditions) are those personal characteristics of the individual that contribute to the occurrence of the behavior.
B: *B*ehavior is the response exhibited by the person.
C: *C*onsequence variables are those events that occur contingently after a behavior and serve to strengthen and maintain the behavior.

Within this model, human behavior is considered to be the result of an interaction among variables that are both within an individual and surrounding that individual (i.e., antecedents and consequences). To gain a complete understanding of a student's behavior, the team needs to carefully consider each of these variables. The following chapters show you how to assess each of these variables in order to understand human behavior and then design positive behavioral supports to change behavior.

Good luck!

3

Legal Aspects
of Functional Behavioral Assessment

The temptation to form theories based on insufficient data is the bane of our profession.
—SHERLOCK HOLMES (by Sir Arthur Conan Doyle)

Implementation of FBAs and positive behavior support plans has proven to be an onerous task for many school districts. From our collective professional experiences and reading of the literature in these areas, it seems that there are three primary sources for the asperity associated with FBAs and behavior intervention plans (BIPs). First, much of the difficulty may lie in the lack of clear direction provided by the IDEA. At times the language is ambiguous and allows for great latitude in interpretation of the law and the requirements for adherence. Second, perhaps some of the difficulty is attributed to the lack of appropriately trained school district personnel. We will discuss the skills that we think are necessary for conducting not only legally defensible FBAs but also "best-practice" FBAs. Each of these requires specific skills and a knowledge base that are not typically present in most educational systems. And, third, it may be that school districts and administrative personnel are unaware of their legal obligations to perform FBAs and design behavior plans that focus on positive instead of aversive consequences and the implications of not doing so. For instance, a pilot survey was conducted at a state university using 130 teachers and administrators enrolled in the Educational Leadership Program. Surprisingly, or perhaps not, 40% of the respondents indicated no knowledge of FBAs; 46% were unaware of how their district determined which students needed an FBA. All respondents indicated that their districts provided no additional training for becoming acquainted with FBAs. This last finding is not that alarming given that 40% did not even know about FBAs! And, finally, 50 of the respondents were unaware that the law *required* an FBA in certain instances as specified by the reauthorization of the IDEA (Dieterich & Villani, 2000).

Subsequent chapters will, we hope, adequately address the first two obstacles. Thus, this chapter is intended to provide a brief overview and our opinion regarding some of the major legal issues and challenges related to FBA and positive behavior support plans. This is by no means an exhaustive treatment nor definitive legal treatise on the topic of FBAs and BIPs. There are several other sources that offer a more in-depth treatment of the legal aspects of FBAs. In an attempt to clarify what must be done according to the law, we will, however:

- Examine the pertinent sections of IDEA that are related to FBAs and BIPs
- Provide discussion of representative due process and/or administrative hearing decisions
- Discuss relevant case law
- Review Office of Special Education Programs (OSEP) policy statements

It is extremely important for readers to remember that we are not attorneys and are not rendering expert opinions on matters of law and that our opinions are not legally binding. Furthermore, special education law is a complex and fast-changing field. It is complex because there are many different laws that govern the provision of services—laws that at times seem to contradict one another. Another reason behind this complexity is that different courts have yielded different rulings on the same issue. Thus, a school district's legal obligation may sometimes depend on the U.S. district court's jurisdiction in which it resides. A third reason for the complexity of special education law is related to the hearing process. In some states procedural matters may be heavily weighted, whereas in other states procedural issues are largely discarded. Hearing officers often have considerable leeway in interpreting state rules, regulations, and guidelines as they apply to individual cases. Hence, the decisions provided by hearing officers may at times seem inconsistent with case law regarding a particular issue (see the accompanying box).

The format we have chosen for this chapter is to present each topic as a question that has probably been asked of you by an administrator in your school district. Within the discussion of each topic, we will integrate information as appropriate from each of the bulleted points above.

When does the law require that we conduct an FBA?

Although there are circumstances under which an FBA *must* and *should* be conducted (see Chapter 10), the law states that:

- The team must address through a BIP any need for positive behavioral strategies and supports (614(d)3(B)9i).
- In response to disciplinary actions by school personnel, the individualized education program (IEP) team must within 10 days meet to develop an FBA plan to collect information; this information should be used for developing or reviewing and revising an existing BIP to address such behaviors (615(k)(1)(B).
- In addition, states are required to address the in-service needs of personnel (includ-

ILLEGAL FBAS 101: AN INTRODUCTION

Drasgow and Yell (2001) reported that as of August 2000, 3 years since the reauthorization of IDEA, 14 state-level due process hearings had occurred that involved issues regarding FBA. The primary disputes ranged from school districts simply not conducting an FBA when one was clearly warranted (11 out of the 14 cases) to parents asserting that the district had completed an inadequate FBA (3 of the 14 cases). There is no excuse for a district abrogating its legal and educational obligation to conduct FBA procedures that are *required* by law. Thus, let's focus on the those cases where districts were charged with conducting inadequate FBAs. In *Independent School District No. 2310 (MN)*, the district was found by the hearing officer to have conducted an inadequate FBA because it used limited data sources (i.e., a 1-hour observation by the school psychologist during a class party). In *Bonita Unified School District*, a "handwritten, fill-in-the-blank" document was used that was deemed to be insufficient for subsequent behavioral planning. Needless to say, the school districts lost each of the three cases in which the adequacy of the FBA procedures was questioned. Among the 14 overall cases, the hearing officer ruled in favor of the parents in 13 cases. Although not precedent setting in a legal sense, the results of these due process hearings indicate a relative consensus that an adequacy standard exists for conducting FBAs. Perhaps the most meaningful implication for school practitioners is that they must conduct *adequate* and not *exemplary* FBAs.

ing professionals and paraprofessionals who provide special education, general education, related services, or early intervention services) as they relate to developing and implementing positive intervention strategies (653(c)(3)(D)(vi)).

Although neither the IDEA Amendments of 1997 (IDEA, 1997) nor federal regulations identify specific "problem behaviors" that would result in an FBA, Drasgow, Yell, Bradley, and Shriner (1999) compiled a list of types of behaviors that probably should trigger an FBA based on their review of administrative hearings and court cases:

- Behaviors that preclude the teacher from teaching
- Behaviors that prevent other students from learning
- Noncompliance
- Verbal aggression/abuse
- Physical aggression/abuse
- Property destruction

Again, this list leaves a great deal of latitude to the school-based team to determine which behaviors trigger the FBA process. Historically, the U.S. Congress has given IEP teams a rather wide berth to make individualized decisions for students with disabilities, which brings us to the next question.

Do I conduct FBAs only for children with disabilities,
or do I have to use FBAs with children in regular education?

The answer to this question becomes a bit more dicey. For children with disabilities whose behavior falls within any of the above-listed categories, FBA is clearly warranted. But what about those children who are in regular education but exhibit the same behaviors. Our opinion here is twofold: (1) it is simply good practice to conduct an FBA for children in regular education when the same or similar behavior of a student in special education would result in an FBA; (2) if someone on the school staff suspects that the student *may* have a disability that is contributing to his/her interfering behaviors, then IDEA protection falls to that student who is *suspected* of having a disability. Let's take a look at an example to illustrate this second point:

> Divinia is a fifth-grade student who engages in a variety of behaviors that her teacher, Ms. Presley, has generically labeled as "odd." For instance, Divinia often speaks in very hushed tones punctuated by loud giggles, meows in class, yells obscenities at the teacher, scratches herself to the point of drawing blood, and calls other students names. All of these behaviors occur during class and often interfere with academic instruction or related activities. Ms. Presley has sent her to the principal's office on a number of occasions for these and other behaviors because she was unable to teach with these behaviors occurring. In response, the principal, Mr. Martin, has suspended Divinia both in and out of school on several occasions. She is coming dangerously close to being suspended for more than 10 days because of these behaviors. Ms. Presley was overheard one day in the teacher's lounge telling the speech pathologist, a member of the building's teacher support team, that surely Divinia had some type of "emotional problem" that was causing these behaviors to occur. The speech pathologist correctly informed Ms. Presley that because she suspected that Divinia was suffering from an emotional problem, she should make a referral to the building's teacher support team for an FBA and positive behavioral intervention before any further disciplinary action was taken against Divinia.

In addition, there is case law that has addressed issues related to this question and gives some very solid guidance. In *Hacienda La Puente Unified School District v. Honig* (1992), the Ninth Circuit ruled that the protections offered by the IDEA (in this case, the "stay-put" rule) extended also to those children who had not been previously identified by their Local Education Agency (LEA) as having a disability. Although other courts supported this decision, *Rodiriecus L. v. Waukegan School District No. 60* (1996) provided some limitations to the protections offered by the *Honig* case. The court ruled that in order for the stay-put rule to apply to students without identified disabilities, the LEA must have reasonably suspected that the student had a disability or that a school official must have known that the student had a disability.

The IDEA has provided some concrete guidance on this issue as well. The law states that in order for students without an identified disability to be afforded the same protections as a student with a disability, the LEA must have known that the student had a disability before the behavior occurred [(20 U.S.C. § 1415 (k)(8)(A)]. If any of the following four circumstances exist, the LEA is considered to have known that the student had a disability:

- The parent expressed concern in writing to the LEA that the student is in need of services [20 U.S.C. § 1415 (k)(8)(B)(i)].
- The student's behavior or performance has demonstrated that he or she needs those services [20 U.S.C. § 1415 (k)(8)(B)(ii)].
- The parent has requested a nondiscriminatory evaluation [20 U.S.C. § 1415 (k)(8)(B)(iii)].
- The student's teacher or other school personnel expressed their concern regarding the student's behavior or performance to the LEA's special education director or other personnel [20 U.S.C. § 1415 (k)(8)(B)(iv)].

Both case law and the IDEA seem to protect students without disabilities if their behavior or performance (we take performance to mean either academic or behavioral performance) would reasonably indicate that a disability is present. For children whose behavior is of sufficient concern that teachers conference with parents, make repeated referrals to the principal's office or school counselor, or engage in other disciplinary procedures, an FBA should be conducted to protect the school district from legal action should the parents question what may seem to be excessive disciplinary action taken against their child. It never hurts anyone to conduct an FBA and implement positive behavioral supports. All it takes is time and effort, although both are sometimes in short supply for certain students.

We would be remiss if we did not mention that LEAs may document they had no knowledge of a disability if they have met both of the following criteria:

- Performed an appropriate evaluation and determined that the student did not have a disability or determined that an evaluation was unnecessary
- Provided proper notification to the student's parents of its determination [34 C.F.R. § 300.527(c)]

In cases where the above two criteria are met, the LEAs may proceed with their normal disciplinary procedures.

Must we conduct an FBA before suspending a student receiving special services for less than 10 cumulative days in a school year?

This one is easy. The answer is NO, you *musn't*, but you probably should. The only thing magical about the number 10 is that the IDEA gives us this criterion. If you notice that a student is exhibiting behavior that is consistently disruptive and that has either already resulted in some type of disciplinary action or out-of-school suspensions, it is wise to go ahead and conduct the FBA even though the 10-day rule has not yet been met. There is one notable exception to this rule, however, and that is if the school anticipates a change in placement. If the school is considering any type of discipline-based change of placement, then an FBA *must be conducted* and a positive BIP implemented prior to the change in placement. If a BIP was already in place, it must be reviewed prior to the change in placement [20 U.S.C. § 1415 (k)(1)(B)(ii); 34 C.F.R. § 300.520 (b)(1)(ii)]. The law is not really clear as to what constitutes a "review" of the behavior plan. It is our position that a review must explore and attempt to resolve the following questions to be legally defensible:

- Is the behavior plan tied to the results from the functional behavioral assessment?
- Is the plan primarily proactive in nature and not merely intended to eliminate an undesirable behavior?
- Are there data to show that the plan has actually been implemented as intended (i.e., treatment integrity)?
- Are there data to show the effectiveness or ineffectiveness of the plan (most likely if there is a review of the behavior plan prior to a possible change in placement, the plan has been judged to be ineffective)?
- If the plan was deemed ineffective, is there evidence that the team modified the plan at least once in an attempt to change the behavior in the current environment?
- Are there data to show that the modified plan was not working?

Answering the above questions not only provides substantial legal protection to the school district, it also ensures that the student is getting appropriate educational services.

Is it really important that the positive behavior intervention be implemented as indicated on the IEP? (This roughly translates to: Is it enough for us to just have this plan on the IEP with no evidence of implementation?)

We just love the easy questions, and this is another one of those. NO! It is not enough merely to have documented that a positive BIP was designed. If school-based teams do not implement positive behavioral supports and do not have evidence indicating that they have done so, they are guilty of failing to provide a "free and appropriate public education" (FAPE). FAPE is one of the cornerstones of the original IDEA (Public Law 94-142) and stresses that education must be individualized to meet the unique needs and challenges of the student with a disability. Failure to implement this individualized plan denies the student of an "appropriate" education. Therefore, school districts should develop some mechanism to demonstrate that they are indeed addressing interfering behaviors identified on the IEP. This mechanism should involve at the very least all of the following:

- Some type of intervention checklist (i.e., procedural integrity or treatment integrity)
- A means to graphically illustrate student performance
- Evidence that the plan has been modified based on the student's performance

If there is no one in our school district qualified to conduct FBAs, what do we do then?

There are actually several options here. The first is to train school-based teams of personnel to conduct FBAs [after all, the IDEA mandates that "states are required to address the in-service needs of personnel (including professionals and paraprofessionals who provide special education, general education, related services, or early intervention services) as they relate to developing and implementing positive intervention strategies" (653(c)(3)(D)(vi))]. The second option is to contract with someone on a case-by-case basis who does have expertise in conducting FBAs. And a third option is to hire someone whose sole responsibility is to conduct FBAs. There are a number of advantages and disadvantages associated with each of these options, which means that each district must decide on which is most workable for it. Some very small school districts, for example, may find it more economically feasible and realistic to hire a qualified person on a case-by-case basis. A larger district, on the other hand, may receive such a large number of referrals that training school-based teams or hiring a full-time behavior specialist, or several, can best meet their needs. We believe that all of these are viable options and are consistent with the IDEA, which states that:

> Either before or not later than 10 days after taking a disciplinary action described in 615 (k)(1)(a) if the LEA did not conduct [an FBA] and implement a [BIP] for such a child before the behavior that resulted in the suspension described in 615 (k)(1)(a), the agency must convene an IEP meeting to develop an assessment plan to address that behavior[;] or . . . if the child already has a behavioral intervention plan, the IEP team must review the plan and modify it, as necessary, to address the behavior [Section 615(k)(1)(b)].

As stated, the IEP team (which can be combined with the teacher support team) must meet to develop an "assessment plan" and not necessarily conduct the FBA themselves. We take this to mean that it is the responsibility of the IEP team to make certain that all rules and regulations are followed and that all procedural safeguards are in place.

Must we conduct an FBA prior to holding a manifestation determination review?

This is one of those situations where two hearing officers have yielded two very different conclusions. The first case involved a student with a disability who was discovered to possess drugs and drug paraphernalia at school. The Connecticut hearing officer ruled that it is not necessary to conduct an FBA prior to a manifestation determination review [*In re: Student with a Disability*, 20 IDELR 113 (SEA CT 1999)]. Conversely, a California hearing officer, citing Section 1415(k)(4), concluded that the information gained during an FBA is necessary for an appropriate manifestation determination. A hearing officer in Minnesota reached a similar conclusion as the above Connecticut hearing officer did in determining that information gained during an FBA was not required for a manifestation determination review. Given these conflicting outcomes, what is the correct answer? Although there is probably no single correct answer, the OSEP does provide some guidance on this issue. In its training overheads, the OSEP makes no link between an FBA and a manifestation determination review. In fact, Section 1415(k)(4) makes no reference whatsoever to using FBA data to assist in the manifestation determination review. Thus, it appears that IEP teams are free to conduct a manifestation determination review prior to conducting an FBA without legal repercussions. Do remember, however, that the language regarding the relationship between an FBA and a manifestation determination review is quite imprecise and is subject to varying interpretations, as evidenced by the differing conclusions reached by the hearing officers.

We often remove students to an interim alternative educational setting (IAES) and then conduct an FBA; is this legal?

Probably not. If the behavior that resulted in the removal to an IAES involved weapons or drugs, then the LEA has the authority to do so for purposes of safety for a period of up to 45 days without an *order* from an independent hearing officer. In such cases, the FBA process would involve indirect assessment procedures. In our collective experiences, however, most of the school districts that place students into an IAES prior to conducting an FBA are doing so without justifiable concerns for safety. In cases where safety is not an issue and the student has already been placed into an IAES without benefit of an FBA or a BIP, then the district would be considered to have made a change in placement without first adhering to the requirements of accommodating the student's interfering behaviors in the least restrictive setting. Furthermore, as we indicated earlier, failing to address a student's interfering behaviors before making a change in placement denies the student of an appropriate education.

If a student has already been suspended, can we conduct a "post hoc FBA"?

The obvious answer is "Well, sort of." You can conduct an FBA, but it would certainly not be a best-practices approach. There may be circumstances in which the student has been suspended, and previously collected data (e.g., student attendance records, detentions served, discipline referrals, recordings of specific interfering behaviors, etc.) may be useful. In addition interviews with key informants (e.g., teachers, guidance staff, administrators, family members, etc.) could also yield valuable information. Because the student is not present within the natural educational setting, however, direct observations and recordings of behaviors and related contextual variables cannot be conducted. Thus, the assessment is limited to recording reviews and interviews. In these types of situations, in which the practitioner is limited only to indirect FBA procedures, we recommend labeling the report as a "Preliminary Functional Behavioral Assessment."

We have a student with a disability who is having difficulty on the bus; must we conduct a bus FBA?

The short answer is—YES. IDEA does not relieve a district of the responsibility for conducting an FBA merely because a student is riding school-sponsored transportation. If disciplinary decisions are being made with regards to a student with a disability that involves his/her transportation, then an FBA must be conducted in the setting where the interfering behavior is occurring—on the bus! This may be more difficult than it sounds even with the use of indirect assessment procedures like the ones we have described in this book and video technology, which would allow for a modified (i.e., removed in time) direct descriptive assessment. Two recent cases that we were involved with highlight many of the issues that are covered not only in this chapter but throughout the book:

> Jack was an 18-year-old male with multiple disabilities including cerebral palsy, severe mental retardation, and blindness. He was attending a self-contained class for students with multiple disabilities in a small rural school. Jack engaged in mild SIB during the day but especially on the bus. In an attempt to modify his bus-related SIB, the school district modified the seat in several ways, made certain his protective helmet was in place prior to getting on the bus, and had him strapped upright to the seat with a harness that buckled in the back. Jack's mother requested that the district not use the harness because that was not teaching him to sit in the seat without banging his head on the glass window (in our opinion Jack's mother was absolutely right in this case). In other words, she was asking for a more proactive approach. Because of the size of this school district, it contracted with consultants to provide their FBA services. The problem was that district policy did not allow nonemployees to ride the bus! Therefore, how was the district going to conduct the FBA? Could it use videotapes to record Jack's behavior? Possibly, but videotapes might not capture all of the stimuli that could be functionally related to Jack's SIB (e.g., rough roads, comments from others, bumps in the road). In this particular case, the solution involved getting special permission from the school board to allow the consultants on the bus to complete the FBA that was required by law. Allowing the consultants to ride the bus and directly observe Jack's behavior also served to prevent the mother from filing a threatened suit against the district for not adhering to the IDEA and failing to provide her son with the appropriate accommodations.

The next case was a bit different in that it did not involve a student with an identified disability but rather a student for whom school personnel *suspected* that she had a disability.

> LaTarsi was a 5-year-old female kindergarten student who had been warned by the principal several times not to "stand up" on the bus while it was in motion. Concurrently, her teachers noted on an internal written progress form that she was "slow in her schoolwork and would probably need to be tested for special education at some point" and that "she had difficulty remembering classroom rules." After being written up once more by the bus driver for standing up while the bus was moving, the principal removed LaTarsi from her class and swatted her buttocks seven to nine times with a wooden paddle to "try and help her remember to remain seated on the bus." Whether or not you personally or philosphically agree with corporal punishment, there are two issues involved here: (1) LaTarsi was suspected of having a disability as evidenced by the written note of the teacher, and thus IDEA protections extend to her as if she indeed had been diagnosed with a disability; (2) the principal engaged in a very negative behavior reduction technique without first conducting an FBA and trying a more positive, proactive approach. In a school board hearing regarding the mat-

ter, the principal was demoted and transferred and the school was ordered to perform an FBA and implement a positive behavior support plan.

Both of these cases, although a bit extreme, highlight the necessity of performing FBAs for "on-bus" behavior. Positive proactive behavioral intervention strategies do not need to cease at the schoolhouse door; they can be extended to any part of the student's educational experience.

Does FBA apply to extended day programs and summer school?

Yes and yes, the requirements to conduct an FBA extend to after-school programs as well as summer school programs. Part of the reason this is so is because a school day is defined as "any day, including a partial day, that children are in attendance at school for instructional purposes" (34 C.F.R. §§ 300.9, 300.519–300.529). Furthermore, neither IDEA nor any supporting regulations define a "school year." Thus, the school year does not merely encompass the traditional 9-month school calendar. A recent U.S. district court decision (in the Eastern District of New York) affirmed that "summer school education for struggling students is intrinsically related to the ability to receive a free appropriate public education" (LIH v. New York City Board of Education, 2000). Therefore, students with disabilities or suspected of having a disability are afforded the same protections under IDEA during these two activities as they are during the regular school day and school year.

SUMMARY

As stated previously, we are not attorneys and are not rendering expert opinions on matters of law. Practitioners who have legal questions or predicaments need to seek the services of a legal professional. Quite obviously, the above questions do not represent *all* of the issues that arise when FBAs and BIPs are addressed. They are instead a sampling of cases across a wide range of domains to give you a "feel" for the legal landscape. Perhaps the best advice we can give regarding FBAs and BIPS is this: *If you think an FBA might be needed (for best-practice purposes or for legal purposes) go ahead and do it without spending undue time trying to determine exactly how much (or how little) you and your school district must do to stay out of legal hot water.* Conducting an FBA and implementing a positive intervention certainly carries no harm and provides students with state-of-the-art educational services. In the end, who knows—You might just make a significant difference in the lives of the kids with whom you interact.

4

Basic Principles
of Functional Behavioral Assessment

The external variables of which behavior is a function provide for what may be called
a causal or functional analysis. We undertake to predict and control the behavior of
the individual organism. This is our "dependent variable"—the effect for which we are
to find the cause. Our "independent variable"—the causes of behavior—are the external conditions of which behavior is a function. Relationships between the two—the
"cause–effect relationships" in behavior—are the laws of a science. A synthesis of
these laws expressed in quantitative terms yields a comprehensive picture of the
organism as a behaving system.

—B. F. SKINNER (1953, p. 35)

ANTECEDENTS AND CONSEQUENCES

At its most basic level, FBA is a rather simple concept. The purposes of all activities within
the FBA domain are to determine under what conditions a behavior is most likely to occur
(*antecedents*) and what happens in the environment as a result of the behavior and main-
tains that behavior (*consequences*). As is the case with most subjects, however, FBA can
become quite complex and onerous. When one must sometimes consider the possibility
that establishing operations (see Chapter 10) are impacting school behavior, the methodology becomes more unwieldy and the margin of error increases.

When an evaluator is conducting an FBA, it is critical that he/she differentiate among
antecedents and consequences that are *associated* with interfering behavior and those
variables that are *functionally related* to interfering behavior (see the accompanying box).
Essentially, a functional relationship is a *cause → effect* relationship. Put another way,
events can be viewed as being either *molar* or *molecular* in nature. A molar event refers to
associated relationships while molecular events are those that are functionally related to
interfering behavior. Casual, anecdotal observations tend to yield information regarding
molar variables. Perhaps the best example of a molar event is the widely held notion that
odd behavior occurs more frequently during a full moon. That is, although there may be an

34

An *antecedent* is any event or stimulus that occurs before a behavior occurs. For any behavior there may be one or numerous antecedents. The dual purpose of an FBA is to first *identify* these antecedents and then determine which are directly related to *triggering* the target behavior.

A *consequence* is any event or stimulus that occurs after a behavior. Again, there may be many things that happen after a behavior. The purposes of an FBA are to identify what actually happens after the target behavior and then determine which one or combination of these events are maintaining (i.e., reinforcing) that behavior.

association between some behaviors and the lunar cycle, the moon is not *causing* behavior. A more systematic analysis of behavior typically uncovers the molecular variables that trigger and/or reinforce behavior. For example, consider the case of a student who frequently engages in disruptive behavior when the teacher provides verbal instruction. At a molar level, we might say that verbal instructions serve as an antecedent to disruptive behavior. Further assessment showed that it was the length of verbal instructions that triggered disruptive behavior and not verbal instructions per se. This is an important distinction because of the direct implications for intervention. If the school staff merely altered the content of the verbal instruction without altering length, there would likely be a minimal effect on the disruptive behavior. As it turned out, the staff reduced verbal instructions to one to three word cues which eliminated disruptive behavior and prompted the student to participate in instructional programming. Identifying these molecular influences on behavior requires considerable knowledge, time, expertise, a degree of experience with FBA, and skill in observing behavior.

Before discussing methodology or FBA procedures, we think it is essential that the same basic terminology be understood and used by everyone who is conducting and talking about FBAs. You will have noticed by now that we highlight words in italic that we think are especially important. Words or concepts of even greater import get their own box with a more in-depth description. Therefore, the first section of this chapter will describe some of those vital principles of functional behavioral assessment. As the book progresses, however, we hope to introduce more complex topics and procedures associated with FBAs.

THE FUNCTIONS OF BEHAVIOR

We presented a 2-day workshop on FBA at a recent National Association of School Psychologists (NASP) convention. We began the workshop by posing what we thought was a very simple question: *"How many functions of behavior are there?"* A number of hands were raised, and one person sitting in the front row was called on to answer. He answered,

"Thousands." The one word answer was quite a shock and served as a prompt for us to quickly modify the opening hour of our presentation. Mistakenly, we had assumed that this question was one to which everyone knew the answer. Therefore, to avoid any misunderstandings and incorrect assumptions, we are going to begin by discussing the *three functions* of behavior:

- Social attention, access to activities, and access to tangibles (stuff) (positive reinforcement)
- Escape or avoidance of aversive (unpleasant) stimuli/situations (negative reinforcement)
- Sensory stimulation and cognitively mediated events, both positive and negative

Within each of these categories are a number of subcategories. Before looking at the various possibilities within each, however, let's discuss them in a very broad sense. The first set, social attention and access to activities and tangibles, is referred to as *positive reinforcement*. Humans, by their very nature, are social beings. Thus, attention from others is often a powerful positive reinforcer for behavior. Let's take a look at two examples whose circumstances are probably familiar to most readers to illustrate the power of social attention as a positive reinforcer:

Kent is a seventh grader of average-to-above average ability. His daily classroom performance and test grades do not reflect his true potential, according to his teachers. In fact, they often report that Kent is quite annoying in the classroom. When asked to describe what he does that is so annoying, his teachers uniformly report that he makes numerous wisecracks each day in response to lecture material or class discussions. His teachers feel that he spends more time thinking about what he is going to say than in listening to either the lecture or doing his work. On a side note, they do report that his comments are often quite funny and evoke at least mild chuckles from classmates. Direct observations of Kent's behavior confirm the teacher's reports of his wisecracking behavior, the inherent humor in what he says, and—perhaps most importantly— the response of his classmates: laughter or groans.

In this example, the response from his classmates (i.e., laughter or groans) is positively reinforcing Kent's wisecrack remarks. Thus, his wisecracking has increased in frequency and is likely to continue for as long as his peers respond in this manner. Let's now look at the other example:

Teresa is a 5-year-old who had moved from her mother's home to live with her grandmother. The move was considered by many adults around Teresa to be quite traumatic, as her mother was being investigated for child neglect and endangerment and her grandmother lived over a thousand miles away from her mother. Shortly after the move, Teresa began kindergarten. During the first few days, Teresa cried when she entered the classroom. The teacher, Ms. Rob, who was a very competent, loving, nurturing teacher took extra care to make sure that Teresa felt safe in her new environment by greeting her with a hug in the morning and a hug whenever she cried. This was a strategy this particular teacher had successfully used on new kindergarteners for more than 20 years. In addition, Ms. Rob often paired Teresa with a classmate when she noticed Teresa becoming tearful during a class activity or at a media center. In this particular case, however, Teresa's crying did not abate within a couple of days. In fact, her crying became worse in terms of intensity (louder) and duration (longer crying periods). To the teacher's dismay, Teresa's behavior even took a turn for the worse as she began to behave in an aggressive manner toward the teacher and her classmates. When she exhibited aggressive behavior, Ms. Rob removed her from the classroom to the assistant principal's office, where the assistant principal talked to her to discover what she was so "angry about" or "afraid of."

In this example, social attention from the teacher and peers, and possibly from the assistant principal, seems to be the function maintaining Teresa's crying. What is not clear at this point is whether it is the teacher's attention, the peer's attention, the assistant principal's attention, or any combination that are functional for Teresa's crying.

The second function, escape or avoidance of unpleasant events or painful stimulation, is called *negative reinforcement*. Humans find some activities fun and enjoyable and other activities boring, painful, too difficult, or otherwise aversive in some way. Activities that are sufficiently unpleasant without having any, or minimal, reinforcing value are those that we tend to shy away from. Most adults, for instance, do not engage in behaviors that they do not find fun in some way (perhaps one of the best examples is exercising). Below is an example of how negative reinforcement operates in the classroom:

> Creed is an 8-year-old male who exhibited disruptive behavior (e.g., throwing materials, yelling at the teacher, climbing on desks, running out of the room) throughout the day. His teacher, Ms. Timmerman, had not noticed a pattern to his behavior and noted that his outbursts seemingly occurred at random times. She tried every trick in her disciplinary bag from a "corner time-out" to keeping him in the classroom during recess. As the number of incidents began to pile up during the day, she resorted to sending Creed to the principal's office where corporal punishment had been administered on multiple occasions. Ms. Timmerman, in a somewhat bewildered tone, offered the observation that Creed's behavior had not gotten any better. After conducting some FBA using a time-based scatterplot and the A-B-C recording form, the school practitioner noticed that Creed's outbursts did indeed have a pattern. In fact, almost all of his outbursts occurred when writing was part of the assignment. He used a pencil to fill in ovals on his spelling tests without incident, but any time he was required to actually produce written work, regardless of the subject matter, an outburst occurred. Thus, the antecedent was identified (i.e., assignments that required writing) as was the consequences (i.e., all of the consequences implemented by the teacher resulted in his either completely avoiding or escaping the assignment). As a result, Creed learned through numerous interactions in the classroom that anytime an assignment was given that involved writing, a disruptive outburst allowed him to either escape or avoid that assignment. Thus, his outbursts were being *negatively reinforced*. In addition, his grades were suffering in some subjects because he was not producing the required written work.

One component of the third function, *automatic reinforcement*, is typically regarded as behavior that, when performed, results in some type of physiological sensation. One example of this is a young girl who twirls her hair because the sensations produced by having the hair in her hands and by the feeling in her scalp is positively reinforcing. Thus, this type of automatic reinforcement is called *automatic positive reinforcement*. Conversely, there are some behaviors that, when performed, result in the lessening of painful or aversive physiological stimulation. For instance, scratching an area on your arm that itches reduces the "amount" of itch. Thus, scratching has been *automatically negatively reinforced* because that behavior (i.e., scratching) resulted in the person reducing an itching sensation. In both examples, the behaviors were not socially mediated behaviors; they did not require the presence of anyone else to be either positively or negatively reinforced. This point is critical for understanding the experimental conditions associated with an extended functional analysis, because an "alone" condition is often included to determine if the student will perform the behavior without anyone or anything present. Performance of the behavior while alone points to the possibility of an automatic reinforcement component. It is also important to note that the types of behaviors that are most likely to be maintained by some type of automatic reinforcement are self-injurious behaviors (SIBs), stereotypies, and certain habits (e.g., thumb sucking, nail biting, hair pulling/twirling).

The foregoing discussion addressed those behaviors that have social or sensory consequences. But what about behaviors that *do not appear* to be related to these functions and appear to be related to "private events" such as thoughts and feelings? For example, consider the case of an adolescent who exhibits bullying behavior within the school setting. As part of an FBA for bullying behavior, team members report that these behaviors are motivated by power and control. Issues of power and control suggest cognitively mediated events. From our perspective, placing the emphasis on cognitively mediated events is a molar level of analysis. As stated earlier, a molecular level analysis involves identifying how these variables serve to directly reinforce bullying behavior. A molecular analysis would involve asking questions such as the following:

- How might power and control impact this student's opportunity to receive attention from others?
- How might these behaviors impact this student's ability to obtain tangibles?
- How might these behaviors impact this student's ability to avoid social and/or academic situations?
- How might these behaviors result in the student's increased perception of self-esteem?

Assessing the bullying behaviors from this angle allows a more precise delineation of the observable variables that are serving to maintain bullying. Consider the case of Steve, an 11-year-old male who bullies his male peers in the hallway during class changes. He typically bullies them by bumping into them, calling them names, and using verbal threats. The interdisciplinary team to which he was referred conducted interviews with Steve and his victims and concluded, prematurely and incorrectly, that the primary function of his bullying behavior was to gain power for himself and control over his peers. A closer look yielded a remarkably different picture. Careful observations indicated that a small circle of friends provided both immediate and delayed positive reinforcement for Steve's bullying by laughing at him (immediate social reinforcement) and by talking at length about his bullying several hours after the event (delayed social reinforcement). In addition, the observations indicated that the victims exhibited behavior that Steve reported in an interview to be reinforcing (e.g., looking scared, moving away from him, avoiding him in the hallway). Steve also reported that he "liked" the reputation of being a "tough guy" and was especially pleased when he overheard someone say that about him. Thus, the molecular analysis indicated a much clearer picture than the molar analysis of *why* Steve was engaging in bullying behavior. In this case, the molecular analysis resulted in a deeper understanding of the critical issues that reinforced bullying behavior and consequently identified the specific variables to be addressed in interventions.

FBA DECISION TREES

Before discussing the basic elements involved in an FBA, we think it is important to understand the deductive process that best embodies school-based functional behavioral assessment. We have included "decision trees" (see Figure 4.1) that we use to help in our understanding of human behavior, but also for explaining and describing the process and results of the FBA to parents and school personnel.

KEY ELEMENTS OF FUNCTIONAL BEHAVIORAL ASSESSMENT

FBA involves a range of assessment strategies that are used to identify the antecedents and consequences that set the occasion for problem behaviors and maintain them (Horner, 1994). It is also a process of gathering information that can be used to maximize the effectiveness and efficacy of behavior support plans. O'Neill et al. (1997) specified that a functional behavioral assessment is complete when:

- The behavior is defined operationally
- The behavior can be predicted to occur
- The function of the behavior is defined

As Drasgow and Yell (2001) have noted, the above criteria are also necessary for a legally defensible FBA. In addition to these three criteria, for a complete functional behavioral assessment we would add a fourth:

- A positive behavior support plan is (1) designed based on the results of the assessment procedures, (2) implemented with a high degree of integrity, (3) periodically evaluated to determine whether the intervention is being successful or not, and (4) modified as needed based on the results of the evaluation or changes in the environment.

FBA procedures are used to determine not only the variables associated with the occurrence of maladaptive behavior (i.e., stimuli that occasion and/or reinforce problem

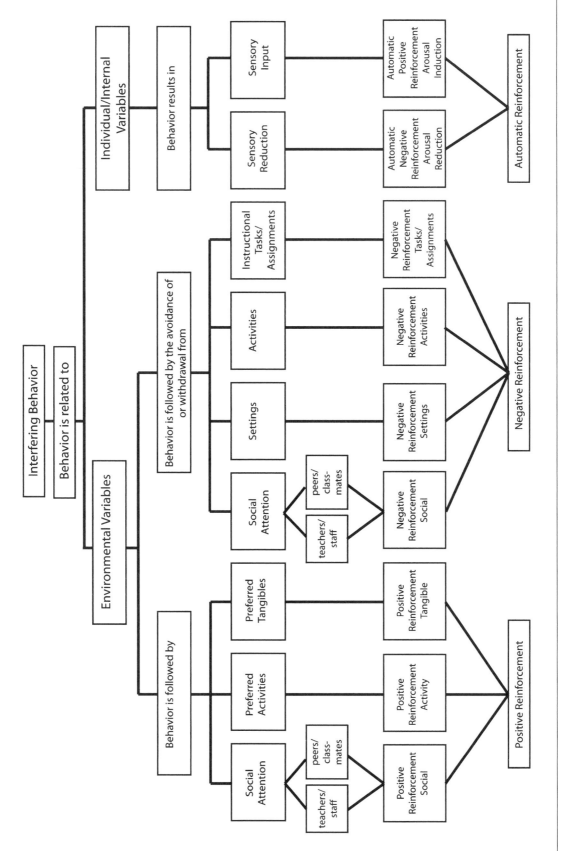

FIGURE 4.1. Functional behavioral assessment: Identifying the function(s) of interfering behaviors. Based on O'Neill et al. (1997).

behavior) but also the variables that are associated with appropriate behaviors. The results of a complete FBA are then used as the basis for designing individually tailored intervention plans. By identification of the stimuli that are likely to trigger and maintain appropriate responding as well as inappropriate responding, behavior supports can be planned that take this information into account and modify the environment such that the stimuli associated with appropriate behavior occur more frequently than the stimuli associated with problem behavior.

Although many activities and procedures may be considered to be a functional behavioral assessment, there are three categories of FBA into which all procedures fall:

- Indirect FBA
- Direct descriptive FBA
- Functional behavioral analysis

Indirect Functional Behavioral Assessment

Indirect methods involve a variety of procedures including:

- Review of records
- Behavior rating scales
- Adaptive behavior scales
- Interviews
- Social skill assessments
- Assessment of academic skills
- Semistructured interviews

The primary purposes of indirect FBA are to:

- Identify the behaviors that interfere with the students academic or social development
- Describe interfering behaviors in clear, unambiguous terms
- Identify environmental variables that appear to trigger interfering behavior
- Identify environmental variables that occur after an interfering behavior has occurred and that appear to serve to reinforce the behavior
- Identify possible individual differences that may contribute to the occurrence of interfering behavior
- Identify possible replacement behaviors
- Identify possible interventions

Review of Records

Many students with whom school practitioners come into contact have mountainous cumulative folders. Unfortunately, much of the information contained in these folders is either irrelevant for FBA or the relevant information is buried among the scree. Therefore, it is wise to be selective and purposeful about the type of information that one is attempting to cull from such folders. You may find the *School Archival Records Search* (SARS) (Walker, Block-Pedego, Todis, Severson, & Pedego, 1991) a useful tool for systematically collecting and synthesizing information found in a student's cumulative folder. See Chapter 5 for a more in-depth discussion of what to look for during a record review.

Behavior Rating Scales

There are a multitude of parent, teacher, and student self-report versions of behavior rating scales available. Although most of these won't be particularly useful for identifying function, they can help to identify behaviors of concern and perhaps identify *functionally equivalent behaviors* (see the accompanying box).

Adaptive Behavior Scales, Academic Assessments, and Social Skills Assessments

You may be asking, "Why adaptive behavior, academic, and social skills assessments? I thought these were part of a traditional standardized assessment. Don't these deal primarily with personal living, social, communication, leisure, vocational, community living, and self-help skills?" *Precisely!!* Many problem behaviors are directly related to specific skill deficits. By assessing these skill domains, one may identify critical variables related to interfering behavior. For example, some problem behaviors are often directly related to communication skill delays. In such cases, teaching functionally equivalent communication skills eliminates the targeted problem behaviors. Moreover, in schools, problem behavior is often motivated by avoidance of or termination of academic assignments or tasks. Modifying academic tasks often results in an increase in active participation within academic situations *and* a decrease or elimination of problem behavior. Teaching prosocial behaviors is often a critical component of a positive behavioral intervention. Finally, social skills deficits are often directly related to the occurrence of interfering behaviors. In short,

---

FUNCTIONALLY EQUIVALENT BEHAVIORS

These are behaviors that look different but have the same function. For example, a boy may call out in class, walk around the room, bother his neighbors, and quietly make rude remarks to the girls because of the attention those behaviors gain him. Even though they are very different behaviors, they all serve the same function. Identifying functionally equivalent behaviors is especially important in the FBA process because intervening with one behavior may have positive effects on all the other behaviors, thus precluding the need for designing separate interventions for each of the behaviors. The trick is to identify the one behavior that, when reduced or eliminated, will result in the reduction of functionally equivalent inappropriate behaviors.

assessment of adaptive behavior, academic skills, and social skills is often an essential component of the comprehensive FBA process.

Interviews

One of the most frequently used types of indirect FBA methods involves either clinical or semistructured interviewing. Every school practitioner is probably familiar with conducting some type of clinical interview with teachers, parents, and/or the referred student but may be less familiar with semistructured interviews associated with ascertaining function. Sattler's (2001) book is an excellent resource that includes three chapters covering issues related to (1) clinical assessment interview techniques, (2) interviewing children, parents, teachers, and families; (3) reliability and validity of interview procedures; (4) self-evaluation of interviewing; and (5) advantages and disadvantages of different interview techniques. Interviews can be valuable sources of information during the FBA process. Several semistructured interviews are available that have been demonstrated to be quite useful in helping to identify salient antecedents and consequences. Two of the most promising semistructured interviews are the Functional Assessment Interview Form (FAIF) provided in O'Neill et al. (1997) and the Functional Assessment Informant Record—Teacher (FAIR-T) provided in Edwards (2002) (see also Figure 6.10).

As with other forms of assessment, it is important to conduct reliable and accurate behavioral interviews. A couple of the main advantages of semistructured interviews are that they are designed to decrease subjective responding by interviewees and to increase accuracy of secondhand information. In subsequent sections of this book, we have included examples of semistructured interview forms that we have found to be effective when conducting functional behavioral assessments.

Direct Descriptive Functional Behavioral Assessment

Direct descriptive FBA provides data on the occurrence of the behavior within the context of the natural environment in which it occurs (e.g., classroom, home, cafeteria, media center) and also on the environmental events that surround it (McComas & Mace, 2000). This procedure involves all of the following:

- Generating an operational definition of the behavior
- Determining an appropriate behavior-recording procedure
- Observing and recording the behavior
- Observing and recording the associated antecedent and consequent variables

One of the primary advantages of direct observation of target behaviors and related conditions/events within the natural environment is that school practitioners and educational teams can use the data to construct applied interventions that are clearly indicated by the observational data (C. F. Skinner, Rhymer, & McDaniel, 2000).

There are a variety of direct descriptive FBA methods. The selection of the most appropriate method typically depends on several factors including the topography of the behavior and the skills and/or resources of those who are conducting the assessment. Each method of assessment is conducted by observing and recording behavior as it occurs in the *natural* environment. At the most basic level, direct descriptive FBA involves identifying and describing the behavior, designing appropriate behavior-recording procedures, and observing and recording the behavior and associated antecedent and consequent variables.

Note: These procedures are particularly useful for assessing low-incidence behaviors, behaviors difficult to observe due to unpredictable occurrence, and those behaviors that are dangerous to the individual or others.

There are four basic ways of conducting a direct FBA:

1. Anecdotal record keeping (e.g., McComas & Mace, 2000)
2. Antecedent–behavior–consequence (A-B-C assessments (Bijou et al., 1968; O'Neill et al., 1997)
3. Scatterplot assessments (Touchette, MacDonald, & Langer, 1985)
4. Descriptive assessment (Lalli, Browder, Mace, & Brown, 1993; Mace & Lalli, 1991)

In the following subsections, we provide brief descriptions of each of these procedures.

Anecdotal Record Keeping

Anecdotal record keeping involves observing the individual within natural settings and writing down specific behaviors and relevant associated variables. This type of recording tends to be narrative in nature and can be quite informative if followed up with an interview and/or with an analysis of the information using a behavioral stream procedure or an A-B-C procedure.

A-B-C Assessment

Examples of standard and extended A-B-C assessments are shown in Figure 4.2. With the extended version, the evaluator observes and records the interfering behavior and related variables (i.e., date; time of day; variables occurring prior to the interfering behavior; the interfering behavior; variables that occurred following the interfering behavior; the resulting change in the frequency, duration, or intensity of the interfering behavior).

Scatterplot Assessments

The most basic type of scatterplot assessment involves recording the time of day at which problem behavior occurred across several days. With this type of assessment, visual inspection of the data sheets allows one to identify possible associations between the interfering behavior, time of day, and related tasks and/or activities. By correlating the target behavior with the time of day, tasks, activities, staff, and other variables, one is able to iden-

A: Antecedent	B: Behavior	C: Consequence

Date/Time	Setting	Antecedent	Behavior	Consequence	Effect
When did the interfering behavior occur?	**Where** did the interfering occur?	What happened immediately **prior** (i.e., triggered) to the interfering behavior?	Describe the interfering **behavior.**	What did you do or what happened **after** the interfering behavior occurred?	What **effect** did the consequence have on the frequency, duration, and/or intensity of the interfering behavior?

FIGURE 4.2. Examples of A-B-C and extended A-B-C assessment procedures.

tify those variables associated with the occurrence of interfering behavior and to form hypotheses regarding the possible cause–effect relationships.

Descriptive Assessments

Descriptive assessments involve the real-time recording of variables that trigger interfering behavior, the interfering behavior, and consequent variables. Descriptive FBA is conducted by directly observing the referred student within natural settings. By recording the target behavior and related antecedent and consequence variables, one can compute conditional probabilities of behavior in relationship to these variables. For example, if a student calls out in the middle of the teacher's lecture 20 times during an observation session and the teacher verbally reprimands the student following 15 of those instances, the probability that her calling out behavior will result in some form of teacher attention is .75. Conversely, the student raised her hand to speak 10 times and was only acknowledged once by the teacher. Thus, the probability of gaining teacher attention for a more appropriate behavior is only .10. Relative to the interfering behavior, the student is engaging in a behavior that is very effective for her, at least in terms of gaining teacher attention.

These probabilities, like the information derived from other methods of direct observation, are used to generate hypotheses that appear to trigger and reinforce interfering behavior. The primary purpose of direct functional behavioral assessment procedures is to identify those variables that are associated with the target behavior(s). Although valuable in identifying these relationships, information gathered without systematically isolating and manipulating environmental variables is only *suggestive* of functional relationships (McComas & Mace, 2000).

Functional Behavioral Analysis

Functional behavioral analysis refers to the process of gathering information to determine relations between variables, particularly functional relations (Shriver, Anderson, & Proctor, 2001). Within the field of applied behavior analysis, a *functional relationship* exists when a cause–effect relationship between variables has been experimentally demonstrated. When we are evaluating the accuracy of FBA procedures, an experimental functional analysis of behavior is considered the most accurate measure of a functional relation and is considered the best "proof" of the accuracy of hypothesized functional relationships (Shriver et al., 2001). Remember, with indirect FBA and direct descriptive FBA procedures, antecedent and reinforcing consequences are identified; functional relationships are hypothesized. That is, there is a high degree of likelihood of cause–effect relationships, but we haven't *proven* these functional relationships. The purpose of functional behavioral analysis is to prove that the hypothesized relationships are in fact causal and not simply "correlational."

Functional behavioral analysis may involve two general approaches: (1) structural analysis and (2) consequence analysis.

Structural Analysis

Structural analysis involves arranging *antecedent* conditions and observing and/or recording the occurrence of interfering behavior within that specific context. This assessment is typically conducted in order to test hypotheses about variables that trigger the onset of interfering behaviors (O'Neill et al., 1997). Here is an example:

Based on interviews and observations, it was hypothesized that a third-grade student's yelling behavior occurred within the context of difficult tasks (in particular, math worksheets). The school psychologist met with the classroom teacher and arranged to present the student with six sets of math worksheets (three easy worksheets and three worksheets that were considered difficult but represented the type of work typically expected of the student). The school psychologist observed and recorded the occurrence of yelling behavior across the presentation and completion of the six math worksheets. The results of this analysis showed that yelling behavior occurred at much higher rates during the presentation and completion of the difficult math worksheets and at very low rates to no occurrence of yelling behavior when the student was presented with easy math worksheets. These data were consistent with the results of interviews and observations and confirmed the hypothesis that yelling behavior occurred in the context of difficult tasks. The school psychologist hypothesized that yelling behavior was motivated by negative reinforcement (i.e., escape from and/or

---

OHHH, A QUICK NOTE

It is far beyond the scope of this book to train practitioners to conduct either brief or extended functional behavioral analyses. These methodologies require training that includes both didactic (i.e., course work and/or workshops) and supervised implementation of functional behavioral analysis procedures. We offered a description of these procedures to guide advanced practitioners and to familiarize less-experienced practitioners to help them understand the need for referral.

---

avoidance of tasks' demands). Subsequent curriculum-based assessments indicated that the math curriculum was "too advanced" for this student. When she was presented with additional instructional supports and modifications in assignments, yelling behavior was eliminated and on-task behavior, task completion, and task accuracy increased markedly.

Consequence Analysis

Consequence analysis involves arranging situations and providing specific consequences contingent on the occurrence of specific interfering behaviors. This assessment is typically conducted in order to test hypotheses about variables that maintain interfering behaviors (O'Neill et al., 1997). An example follows:

> The fifth-grade classroom teacher had been keeping an anecdotal log of a student's "angry" behavior. Harley's anger had been defined as pushing desks and chairs, throwing books on the floor, looking mean at the teacher, telling others to shut up, and other similar behaviors. The school psychologist was asked by the principal to consult

---

OHHH, YEAH, ANOTHER THING ABOUT
FUNCTIONAL BEHAVIORAL ANALYSIS OF INTERFERING BEHAVIOR

It is our experience that a combination of indirect FBA and direct descriptive FBA procedures adequately address the vast majority of referral issues faced by practitioners within school settings. This book is meant to address these types of situations. However, there are times when indirect and direct descriptive FBAs do not yield conclusive findings. In such cases, practitioners may want to:

- Examine existing data and/or revisit the indirect FBA and direct descriptive FBA process OR
- Conduct an experimental analysis of behavior OR
- Refer the student to a colleague or another team with competencies in functional behavioral analysis

---

with the teacher prior to her making a referral to the teacher support team. In examining the anecdotal log, the school psychologist noted that the teacher indicated one of two general things occurred when Harley became angry: she either let him take a 5-minute cooldown period, or she talked with him about the negative effects associated with his behavior. Thus, the school psychologist was unsure if *escape*, from the cooldown period, or if *attention*, from the teacher talking with him, or *both*, were maintaining the angry behavior. Prior to the next two observations of 30 minutes each, the school psychologist arranged with the teacher for her to systematically provide either attention or escape contingent upon angry behavior to determine which was functionally related to the target behaviors. The data indicated that, although angry behavior occurred when the teacher provided access to a cooldown period, angry behavior occurred three times as much when the teacher interacted with Harley contingent upon his angry behavior. Therefore, it appeared that teacher attention was functionally related to the exhibition of angry behavior by Harley.

TREATMENT VALIDITY OF FUNCTIONAL BEHAVIORAL ASSESSMENT

It is important to note that ultimately the utility of FBA is the degree with which the results of assessment are used to design effective interventions. The treatment validity of FBA refers to whether the assessment results contribute to effective intervention. In other words, even if an FBA may have yielded reliable and accurate assessment results, if the data do not contribute to the development of effective interventions then the assessment method is not considered useful (Shriver et al., 2001). This is an extremely important point. FBAs should be conducted not only to understand and predict behavior but to lead to the development of effective interventions. FBAs that result in the writing of a comprehensive report that, after being shared with team members, is simply filed away does not meet the standard of treatment validity. The ultimate value of the FBA is subsequent interventions that result in meaningful and lasting behavior change. Clearly, many factors influence the efficacy of interventions (e.g., resources, treatment integrity, trained staff) as well as inaccurate FBAs. It is critical, then, that in addition to conducting sound assessments, practitioners need to systematically evaluate the effectiveness of the interventions that were based on the assessment results. Only by formally evaluating interventions can we demonstrate the treatment validity of the assessment results (see the accompanying box on page 49).

SUMMARY

It is probably safe to say that many school practitioners subscribe to the empirical rigors of behavioral assessments that include a *functional behavioral analysis.* The implementation of these procedures within school settings, however, is an arduous process that is impractical in many circumstances. Moreover, although functional behavior analyses may be highly

A NOTE ABOUT FUNCTIONAL ANALYSIS OF INTERVENTIONS

Another model of functional analysis involves the systematic evaluation of the effectiveness of interventions. When we formally evaluate the degree with which an intervention *causes* a change in behavior(s), a functional relationship between the intervention and the resulting behavior change is demonstrated. A functional relationship is established when (1) the target behavior changes when an intervention is implemented while all other variables are held constant and (2) the process is repeated one or more times and the behavior changes each time (Miltenberger, 1997).

The best-practices approach to the evaluation of interventions involves the use of single-case experimental design methodologies. Using single-case experimental designs, we can demonstrate that the intervention was responsible for the observed behavior change and rule out the influence of extraneous variables (confounding or irrelevant variables). Steege, Brown-Chidsey, and Mace (2002) describe single-case experimental design methodology and the best-practices approach of evaluating the effectiveness of interventions.

accurate at the time of assessment, their temporal stability may be in question due to the tendency of behavioral function to change across time, situations, and people. In addition, whereas indirect FBAs are practical and efficient, they often yield inaccurate findings. The same can be said of direct descriptive FBA procedures. What is a practitioner to do?

The Solution: Within this book, we endorse an FBA model that is procedurally rigorous and practical for implementation by school psychologists and related professionals. We propose a hypothesis-testing approach that incorporates a combination of interviews and direct observation procedures that are used at a minimum to:

- Identify and describe interfering behaviors
- Document the relative occurrence of interfering behaviors
- Identify variables associated with the occurrence of interfering behaviors
- Identify hypotheses regarding the function of these behaviors
- Design and evaluate the effectiveness of interventions

It is important to recognize that in most cases comprehensive indirect FBA and direct descriptive FBA procedures will yield accurate data that are useful in designing and evaluating socially valid and effective positive behavioral support interventions. In some cases, however, practitioners may find that these procedures are insufficient. In such cases, practitioners may need to reevaluate the accuracy of their assessments and conduct more in-depth assessments (e.g., extended or brief FBAs). It is our expectation that this volume will be useful for addressing a wide range of target behaviors and referral questions faced by practitioners within school settings. Our experience has shown that the methodologies described in this book have been applicable for assessing a wide range of populations (e.g., students with autism, mental retardation, attentional deficits, behavioral disabilities, specific learning disabilities, and typically developing students) and behaviors (e.g., aggression, self-injury, oppositional–defiant behavior, tantrums, disruption, and habits), as well as in a variety of settings (e.g., special education classrooms, regular education classrooms, private homes, clinics, hospitals, in-patient facilities, and group homes).

It is also our experience that many factors contribute to the accuracy of the FBA and the effectiveness of subsequent interventions (e.g., knowledge and experience of teachers, school resources, administrative supports). Although the practitioner may not be able to control all of these variables, he/she is in a position to conduct a best-practices FBA. The practitioner has a professional responsibility and an ethical obligation to conduct an FBA that is technically sound and sufficiently comprehensive to result in an understanding of the variables that contribute to the occurrence of problem behavior and that lead to interventions that result in socially meaningful behavior change.

5

Observing and Recording Behavior

> Behavior is a difficult subject matter, not because it is inaccessible, but because it is extremely complex. Since it is a process, rather than a thing, it cannot be held still for observation. It is changing, fluid, evanescent, and for this reason it makes great technical demands upon the ingenuity and energy of the scientist. But there is nothing essentially insoluble about the problems which arise from this fact.
>
> —B. F. SKINNER (1953, p. 15)

Conducting a complete FBA is a process that involves several interrelated stages. This process is usually initiated by a referral for assessment and intervention and begins by defining and recording behaviors.

DEFINING AND RECORDING BEHAVIOR

The initial step in conducting an FBA involves identifying and describing target behaviors. In most cases, this involves a two-stage process of interviews and direct observations for the purpose of clarifying and describing target behaviors. This is a critical step because the accuracy of the FBA is dependent upon precise definitions of behaviors. When behaviors are precisely defined, we say that they have been "operationally" defined or defined in "concrete, observable terms."

Consider the case in which a classroom teacher referred a student with concerns regarding what was labeled as "aggressive behavior." Based solely on this information, the school psychologist conducted an observation within the classroom setting. The school psychologist used a frequency-recording procedure to measure the occurrences of aggressive behavior. After 45 minutes of careful observations, she had recorded no occurrences of aggressive behavior. She did note, however, that the student on several occasions engaged in a behavior that she labeled "inappropriate verbal behaviors directed towards classmates." Following the observation session, the school psychologist and classroom teacher met and reviewed the observation results. The classroom teacher was amazed when the school psychologist reported that she had not observed any occurrences of "aggressive behavior." Only after several minutes of discussion did they realize that they had not been talking a common language. Although both had indeed been observing the same behaviors (i.e., swearing at classmates, derogatory remarks directed to classmates, etc.), the teacher labeled them "aggressive" while the school psychologist labeled them "inappropriate verbalizations." Based on their discussion of the characteristics of the behaviors exhibited by the student and by reviewing several examples of the behaviors, they mutually decided to change the description of these verbalizations from "aggressive behavior" to "verbal aggression directed toward classmates."

In short, behaviors need to be described in a way that is understandable to all members of the team. Behavioral definitions need to be unambiguous and concise. Specifically, this means that behaviors should be described in such a way that after reviewing a written description of a target behavior, two observers should be able to observe a student and agree that the target behavior has or has not occurred. As a general rule, a description of behavior should meet three criteria (Kazdin, 2001):

- Objectivity
- Clarity
- Completeness

To be *objective*, the description of behavior should refer to observable features and not to internal characteristics, intentions, meanings, etc. To be *clear*, the definition should be so unambiguous that it can be accurately repeated and paraphrased by others. To be *complete*, the definition must delineate the observable characteristics of the behavior. We recommend a two-stage process of defining behaviors: (1) interviews and (2) observations.

STAGE 1: THE INTERVIEW

The interview should be conducted with persons very familiar with the student referred for evaluation. At this point in the functional behavioral assessment process, the interview should focus on identifying *observable* behavior-relevant characteristics displayed by the referred student. For example, in the previous case of aggressive behavior, the school practitioner would ask the teacher to clearly describe the observable characteristics that constitute aggressive behavior. Specific questions such as the following could be asked during a semistructured interview:

SCHOOL PRACTITIONER: You have indicated that Bob frequently displays aggressive behaviors in the classroom. What do you mean by the word "aggressive"?

CLASSROOM TEACHER: Well, he is often mean spirited. He is aggressive with his classmates.

SCHOOL PRACTITIONER: You said that he is mean spirited and aggressive. Could you give me an example of these behaviors?

CLASSROOM TEACHER: Yes. He says nasty things to classmates as if to provoke them.

SCHOOL PRACTITIONER: Give me some examples of the nasty things he says to classmates.

CLASSROOM TEACHER: Sure. Just yesterday during a group discussion in social studies class, one of the other students, Cindy, asked a question. Bob called Cindy a stupid moron. When I asked him to apologize for his comment, he responded, "Cindy, I'm so sorry that you're such a stupid moron."

SCHOOL PRACTITIONER: In this example, the aggressive behavior exhibited by Bob is a form of verbal aggression. Does Bob display any other forms of aggressive behavior. For example, is he physically aggressive with others (e.g., hits, kicks, pushes, or scratches)?

CLASSROOM TEACHER: Oh, no. He's never been assaultive. Bob's aggressive behavior only involves verbal aggression.

SCHOOL PRACTITIONER: Let's further define what is meant by verbal aggression. Verbal aggression includes statements such as "stupid moron." What other things does Bob do that are verbally aggressive?

CLASSROOM TEACHER: Well, he might also swear at another student or refer to someone in a derogatory way such as "You loser," "You jerk," "What an idiot," "Screw you, asshole."

SCHOOL PRACTITIONER: OK. Aggressive verbal behavior also includes derogatory and inappropriate verbal comments directed to classmates.

CLASSROOM TEACHER: Yes. And toward teachers as well. For example, yesterday in class I had a little difficulty setting up my Power Point presentation. He called me a "technologically challenged idiot."

SCHOOL PRACTITIONER: Ouch. So verbal aggression may also be directed at teachers. How about other school staff?

CLASSROOM TEACHER: Yes, he does it to other staff, including Ms. Adams. She's the principal, you know.

SCHOOL PRACTITIONER: The first step of the functional behavioral assessment process involves clarifying and describing the target behaviors. With Bob, we have identified verbal aggression as the behavior of concern. Let's consider these possible definitions of verbal aggression:

> *Verbal aggression directed to classmates (VBC)*: Bob directing derogatory comments (e.g., "You idiot") and/or inappropriate language (e.g., swearing) to classmates
> *Verbal aggression directed to staff (VBS)*: Bob directing derogatory comments (e.g., "You idiot") and/or inappropriate language (e.g., swearing) to school staff
> Are these clear and unambiguous definitions?

CLASSROOM TEACHER: Yes. I think we've nailed it. This is very clear.

SCHOOL PRACTITIONER: Great! What I am planning to do next is to conduct a classroom observation I will use these definitions to record occurrences of VBC and VBS behaviors. Are there days, times of day, or class sessions that you recommend I conduct the observations where the behaviors are most likely to occur?

In this example, both the school practitioner and the teacher are clear about just what constitutes aggressive behavior. Making sure that the behavior is operationally defined prior to conducting the first observation will probably save the school practitioner time and a bit of frustration. In addition, something else was gleaned from the above interview that has particular relevance for the FBA. Want to take a guess as to what it is? For the answer, see the accompanying box.

To assist both school practitioners and teachers in this first stage of the FBA process, we have included a representative listing of some of the most common referral problems and examples of their corresponding "operational" definitions see the accompanying table. This is by no means a comprehensive list. Rather, it is a set of exemplars to serve as a prompt for writing clear behavioral definitions. The words that are underlined in the "Referral problem" column are "red-flag" words that should immediately be clarified.

Referral problem	Sample operational definition
Carter is <u>off task</u>	When given a written assignment to complete at his desk, Carter looks out the window, walks around the class, or walks over to the free-reading center.
Jeremy shows <u>disrespect</u> toward his teachers	When given a direction or command, Jeremy tells his teachers to shut up, not to tell him what to do, and get off his back. He then refuses to do the work by putting his head down on his desk or leaving the classroom.
Wilson has an <u>attitude</u> problem	When spoken to by an adult, Wilson frowns and turns away and does not do what has been asked or directed.
Nyetha is very <u>sad</u> and <u>depressed</u>	During times when she is working or playing alone, Nyetha often cries quietly.
Craig has a <u>learning disability</u> in math calculations	Craig is able to complete 1 × 1 multiplication problems with 20–30% accuracy.

During the interview, the teacher noted that the verbally aggressive behavior occurs toward both peers and adults in the school environment. That piece of information is especially relevant for FBA because, although the same type of behaviors are occurring, they may have very different functions. For instance, the function of verbal aggression toward classmates may be to attract attention from peers, whereas verbal aggression toward adults may be maintained by escape/avoidance from academic instruction. Given that the functions may be different, the resulting interventions will likely look different as well. In addition to the implications for treatment, realizing that the verbally aggressive behavior may have different functions across targets also allows one to understand that successfully treating verbally aggressive behavior toward peers may not result in reductions in verbally aggressive behavior toward adults.

STAGE 2: THE DIRECT OBSERVATION

Following the interview, the next step in the FBA process typically involves a direct observation of the referred student. Direct observation of behavior is the core of behavioral assessment and is one of the most commonly used behavioral assessment techniques for addressing student's behaviors (C. H. Skinner, Dittmer, & Howell, 2000).

Generally, we recommend that the initial observation take place within naturally occurring settings and circumstances (e.g., with a student in her class while she is engaged in naturally occurring tasks/activities). At the most basic level, the direct observation involves only recording target behaviors. Observers could also conduct more comprehensive observations and record not only the target behaviors but contextual variables associated with the occurrence of target behavior (i.e., antecedents and consequences). Regardless of the FBA procedure used, the same behavior-recording procedures apply.

There are several methods for collecting and recording direct observation data (e.g., frequency recording, duration recording, and interval recording), and no one procedure is necessarily superior to another. The selection of a measurement procedure should be driven by each of the following:

1. The dimensions of behavior (i.e., topography, frequency, duration)
2. The goals of the intervention
3. Pragmatic considerations such as time, resources, and competency of observers

The subsections below include descriptions and examples of data-recording procedures that are commonly used within a functional behavioral assessment. These procedures may be used by the evaluator to record behavior during a planned observation. These procedures are also routinely used by teachers and staff to record behavior both prior to the intervention (i.e., the FBA process) and during the intervention to measure the effectiveness of the treatment strategies. Figures 5.1, 5.2, 5.3, and 5.4, in addition to illustrating typical data-recording procedures, provide examples of clear, unambiguous descriptions of behaviors.

Frequency Recording

Frequency recording involves observing, counting, and recording the number of times a behavior has occurred. This procedure typically is used to record occurrences of discrete, low-rate behaviors (i.e., behaviors that have a definite beginning and end and which do not often occur). Although frequency recording is often a very accurate method for recording discrete behaviors, it tends to provide an underestimate of sustained behaviors (e.g., time on task), an inaccurate record of very-high-rate behaviors, and the potential unreliability of observations when behavior onset and cessation are difficult to discriminate.

Figure 5.1 illustrates the application of a frequency-recording procedure. In this example, verbal aggression directed to classmates (VBC) was recorded using a frequency-recording procedure. The recording of behavior was conducted by an educational technician who was assigned to the special education program in which Bob received services.

Target Behavior:	*Verbal aggression directed toward classmates (VBC)*
Definition:	*Verbal statements directed at classmates that include swearing, insults (e.g., "You're ugly," "I hate your guts") or threats (e.g., "I'm going to hit you"). Note: record as discrete episodes when occurrences of VBC are separated by 15 seconds of no VBC.*
Procedure:	*Using a tallying system, record each occurrence of VBC.*
Rationale:	*VBC behaviors occur singularly (obviously a discrete event) or as a group (a response set, or episode). Recording each VBC statement may be unwieldy.*
VBC:	ᚼᚼ ᚼᚼ II
Frequency:	*12*
Program hours:	*6*
Rate:	*2 occurrences per hour*

FIGURE 5.1. Example of frequency recording procedure.

Twelve (12) occurrences of VBC were recorded. Because the length of observations may vary across days, due to shortened school days or to the unavailability of an observer/recorder, raw data (i.e., 12) were converted to rate per hour of VBC. Thus, the number of occurrences, 12, in a 6-hour school day is converted to a rate of 2 occurrences of VBC per hour.

Duration Recording

This procedure involves observing, timing, and recording the total amount of time a behavior has occurred. It is most applicable for recording continuous behaviors (e.g., sustained behaviors such as on-task activity and stereotypy). Duration recording is typically done through use of a stopwatch and can be expressed as a percentage of time. It is difficult to use in measuring high-rate, short-duration behaviors and multiple behaviors.

Figure 5.2 illustrates the use of a duration-recording procedure. In this example, each tantrum (T) was recorded using both frequency and duration-recording procedures. The recording of behavior was conducted by an educational technician who was assigned to the preschool special education program in which the student received services. The educational technician counted and recorded the number of times that Bob exhibited tantrums. During a 6-hour program day, five occurrences of tantrum behavior were observed and recorded. Why record duration when frequency is so simple? With this type of behavior, frequency is less accurate than duration. There is a big difference between tantrums that last 5 seconds each time compared to one tantrum that lasts 50 minutes. Thus having both frequency and duration data provides a clearer picture of the tantrum behavior than either one alone. In addition to recording the frequency of behavior, the observer also used a stopwatch to record the length of each tantrum. Tantrum behaviors ranged from a low of 3 minutes and 4 seconds to a high of 12 minutes. The cumulative duration of tantrum behaviors (i.e., 36 minutes and 53 seconds) was determined by adding the respective timed

Target Behavior:	*Tantrum behavior*
Definition:	*A response set including two or more of the following behaviors: screaming, crying, throwing objects/materials, flopping to the floor, and/or kicking objects.*
Procedure:	*Using a stopwatch, record the length of time from the onset to the end of the tantrum behavior.*
Rationale:	*By recording the length of each tantrum, the recorder is measuring both the frequency of the tantrums and the duration. Frequency recording alone would be very misleading. For example, one (1) tantrum of 30-second duration is very different from one (1) tantrum of 1 hour.*
Tantrum (T):	*3'4"; 8'10"; 9'00"; 12'00"; 4'39"*
Frequency:	*5*
Program hours:	*6*
Rate:	*0.833 times per hour*
Cumulative duration:	*36 minutes and 53 seconds (i.e., 36'53")*
Average duration:	*6.67 minutes per occurrence*

Percent duration (i.e., percentage of time in which person displayed tantrum behavior):

$$\frac{36'39"}{360 \text{ program minutes}} = 11\% \text{ of the program day}$$

FIGURE 5.2. Example of duration-recording procedure.

lengths of each of the five tantrum behaviors. Similar to the issues discussed with frequency recording, it is often more accurate to convert and report data in terms of rate as opposed to raw numbers. In this case, tantrum behavior could be reported as occurring at a rate of 0.8333 times per hour, an average duration (i.e., the mean duration of tantrums) of 6.661 minutes per occurrence, or a duration of 11% of the program day.

Interval Recording

This procedure involves observing and recording the occurrence and nonoccurrence of behaviors at predetermined units of time (i.e., intervals ranging from several seconds to several minutes or even hours). There are three types of interval-recording procedures, each with its own advantages and disadvantages:

- *Whole interval*—in which a behavior is recorded only if it was observed to occur during the *entire* interval
- *Partial interval*—in which a behavior is recorded if it was observed for *any part* of the interval
- *Momentary time sampling*—in which the observer looks at the student only at predetermined points in time and notes if the target behavior is occurring at the precise moment the observation occurs

The accompanying table gives direction as to which recording procedure to use in a particular circumstance.

If . . .	Then choose this recording procedure
Continuous performance of a behavior is desired (e.g., on-task behavior)	Whole-interval recording
The behavior occurs at a very high frequency and very rapidly (e.g., talking, head banging, hand flapping)	Partial-interval recording
It is difficult to continuously monitor the student	Momentary time sampling or performance-based recording
The teacher desires a low-effort method for collecting data	Momentary time sampling or performance-based recording

Of these three methods, whole-interval recording is recommended when continuous occurrence of the target behavior is expected (e.g., when recording sustained attention to a task). Partial interval recording is preferred for measurement of high-frequency and rapidly occurring (e.g., self-injurious head banging) behaviors. Momentary time sampling is useful when continuous observation of a student is not practical or when an observer is monitoring and measuring target behaviors with several students in one setting. This procedure may underestimate the occurrence of low rate behaviors. Note that interval-recording procedures provide only estimates of rate and duration of occurrence of target behaviors. The results of observations are reported in terms of the number or percentage of intervals in which target behaviors occur. Of the interval-recording procedures, partial-interval recording is the most frequently used.

Figure 5.3 displays a 6-second whole-interval recording procedure that was used to measure the on-task behavior of a student with a history of attentional deficits who had been referred to a behavioral consultant for FBA. The behavioral consultant initially attempted a partial-interval recording procedure, but she found that even a split second of on-task behavior was recorded within each 6-second interval, resulting in an overestimation of on-task behavior. She selected the whole-interval recording procedure because the student would need to exhibit on-task behavior throughout the entire interval to be recorded. Because the goal of the assessment and subsequent positive behavioral support intervention was to increase *sustained behavior*, the whole-interval recording procedure provided a more sensitive and accurate measure of behavior. In this example, on-task behavior was recorded only when it was observed to occur during the entire 6-second interval. The nonoccurrence of on-task behavior was also recorded. Nonoccurrence was recorded when on-task behavior did not occur for the whole interval. This could include either the student not exhibiting the defined behavior or exhibiting an inappropriate behavior (talking out, tossing a pencil, etc.) The behavioral consultant conducted several

Target Behavior:	On-task behavior
Definition	Visual, motor, and/or verbal attention to and/or within tasks and activities.
Procedure:	6-second whole-interval recording procedure. Record a "+" in each 6-second interval if on-task behavior occurred for the entire interval. Record a "0" in each 6-second interval if on-task behavior did not occur during the whole interval (e.g., 0 seconds or 1–5 seconds).

	6	12	18	24	30	36	42	48	54	60
1 minute	+	0	+	0	0	+	+	0	0	+
2 minutes	+	+	0	+	+	0	0	+	+	+
3 minutes	+	0	+	+	+	0	0	0	+	+
4 minutes	0	0	0	+	0	+	+	+	+	0
5 minutes	+	+	+	+	+	+	+	0	0	0

$$\text{Percent occurrence} = \frac{\text{number of "+" intervals}}{\text{total number of intervals}} \times 100$$

Example: $\frac{30}{50} \times 100 = 60\%$ occurrence of on-task behavior

FIGURE 5.3. Example of whole-interval recording procedure.

observations during different classroom settings (e.g., group math instruction, spelling examination, independent reading, completion of math worksheets, and afternoon recess). For purposes of illustration of whole-interval recording, Figure 5.3 shows the data collected during the first 5 minutes of one of the observations. During this observation, on-task behavior was recorded 30 times out of 50 intervals (60%) in which behavior was recorded.

The following case example illustrates the use of a partial-interval recording procedure. The psychologist conducted an FBA of a child with developmental disabilities who exhibited SIB (i.e., hand biting, face slapping, and head banging). Direct descriptive FBA involved direct measures of each of the target behaviors within school (e.g., academic instruction, functional life skills instruction, leisure skills instruction, recess, self-help skills instruction, and vocational skills instruction) and home (e.g., hanging out with siblings, dinner, dinner cleanup) environments. During these observations, antecedent and consequent variables were not manipulated. School personnel and family members were asked to carry on with typical routines and to act natural. Because there were multiple target behaviors and each one could be very brief (e.g., 1–2 seconds), the psychologist decided to use a 6-second partial-interval recording procedure to record each behavior. The psychologist considered only recording SIB when any of the three behaviors occurred. However, anecdotal observations and interviews with school staff and family indicated that these behaviors did not occur as a response set, and that oftentimes only one behavior occurred during a behavioral incident whereas at other times two or three of the behaviors were exhibited. The psychologist also decided to record the occurrence of active participation. Active participation was recorded to (1) identify levels of occurrence of appropriate behavior within each setting/activity and (2) to compare the occurrence of appropriate behavior and interfering behaviors across the various settings/activity.

For ease of recording and to increase the accuracy of data collection, the psychologist developed a behavior-recording data sheet that included each of the behavioral codes within each 6-second interval. Each time that any of the behaviors occurred, the psychologist circled the corresponding code. Figure 5.4 shows a completed partial-interval recording sheet for one observation conducted during an academic leisure task within the school setting. The results of the observation showed that self-injurious hand biting occurred during 48% of the intervals observed, self-injurious face slapping occurred during 22% of the intervals observed, and self-injurious head banging occurred during 12% of the intervals observed. Active participation was recorded for 21% of the intervals observed. Note that in several intervals there was no occurrence of any of the target behaviors.

Permanent Product Recording

Another aspect of a behavior that may be recorded is its product. Permanent product recording is used when a behavior results in specific *tangible* outcomes (Miltenberger, 1997). This procedure involves recording the number of products (e.g., number of homework assignments completed, number of bottles sorted accurately). It is used to record a wide range of products, or outcomes, of behavior. One advantage of this method is that the observer need not be present when the behavior occurs. One possible drawback to this procedure is that practitioners cannot always determine who exhibited the behaviors that led to the product recorded. For example, a teacher cannot determine whether a student completed his/her own homework, whether assistance was provided, or whether someone else completed the assignments.

Performance-Based Behavioral Recordings

These procedures involve observing and rating a behavior according to a predetermined scale as an estimate of occurrence, duration, and/or intensity of behaviors. This procedure is typically used when frequency, duration, partial-interval, or whole-interval procedures are not practical given the professional responsibilities, resources, and experience of the observers. Performance-based interval-recording procedures can be used simultaneously to record multiple behaviors (both adaptive and interfering). A particular advantage of this procedure is the capacity simultaneously to provide direct instructional/behavioral supports and to record data. Although performance-based assessment procedures have been widely used within the field of education to evaluate student academic performance, their use within behavioral assessments is relatively recent. For example, Iwata, Pace, Kissel, Nau, and Farber (1990) used a performance-based assessment procedure to rate the intensity of SIB and Steege, Davin, and Hathaway (2001) developed a performance-based behavioral assessment procedure to record behaviors, including low-rate and sustained behaviors. Steege et al. (2001) first identified and described specific behaviors and then

Procedure: Partial-interval recording procedure

Circle the number corresponding to the behavior in each 6-second interval in which the behavior occurred.

(Note: record even if the behavior occurred only for a split second.)

Target Behaviors	Number of Intervals	Percent Occurrence
(A) Self-injurious hand biting	48	48%
(B) Self-injurious face slapping	22	22%
(C) Self-injurious head banging	12	12%
(D) Active participation	21	21%

	6	12	18	24	30	36	42	48	54	60
1	(A) B / C D	A (B) / C D	A (B) / C D	A (B) / C D	A B / C (D)	A B / C (D)	A B / C (D)	A B / C (D)	A B / C (D)	A B / C (D)
2	A B / (C) D	A B / C (D)	(A) (B) / C D	(A) (B) / C D	(A) (B) / C D	(A) B / C D	(A) B / C D	(A) B / C D	(A) B / C D	(A) B / C D
3	(A) (B) / C D	(A) (B) / C D	(A) (B) / C D	(A) (B) / C D	(A) (B) / C D	(A) B / C D	(A) B / C D	A B / C D	A B / C (D)	A B / (C) D
4	A B / (C) D	A B / (C) D	A B / C D	A B / C D	A B / C D	A B / C (D)	A B / C (D)	A B / C (D)	A B / C (D)	A B / C (D)
5	A B / C D	A B / C D	A B / C D	A B / C (D)	(A) (B) / C D	(A) (B) / C D	(A) (B) / C D	(A) (B) / C D	(A) (B) / C D	(A) B / C D
6	(A) B / C D	(A) B / C D	A B / C (D)	A B / C (D)	A B / C D	A B / C D	A B / (C) D	A B / (C) D	A B / (C) D	A B / (C) D
7	A B / (C) D	A B / C D	(A) B / C D	(A) B / C D	(A) B / C D	(A) B / C D	(A) B / C D	A B / C D	A B / C D	(A) B / C D
8	(A) B / C D	(A) B / C D	(A) B / C D	A B / C D	A B / C D	(A) B / C D	(A) B / C D	(A) B / C D	(A) B / C D	(A) (B) / C D
9	(A) (B) / C D	(A) (B) / C D	(A) (B) / C D	(A) (B) / C D	(A) (B) / C D	A B / C D	A B / C D	(A) B / C D	(A) B / C D	(A) B / C D
10	(A) B / C D	(A) B / C D	A B / C (D)	A B / C (D)	A B / C (D)	A B / C (D)	A B / (C) D	A B / (C) D	A B / (C) D	A B / (C) D

FIGURE 5.4. Example of partial-interval recording procedure.

developed a rating scale that included assigned values corresponding to specific dimensions of behavior. Target behaviors were observed and recorded based on the rating scale. These procedures were demonstrated to have acceptable levels of reliability and validity. However, it should be noted that these methods may yield inaccurate results, especially with novice evaluators. Therefore, the precision of these procedures is maximized when (1) behaviors are defined in explicit and unambiguous terms, (2) rating scales are clearly defined for each behavior, (3) adequate training and support are provided to staff prior to and during the initial phases of implementation, and (4) ongoing follow-up is provided to check on the reliability and accuracy of behavior recordings. Figure 5.5 illustrates a performance-based recording procedure to record appropriate behaviors (e.g., active participation) and interfering behaviors (e.g., stereotypical behaviors of a student with developmental disabilities within a functional life skills program).

The performance-based recording procedure was used to estimate the relative occurrence of both active participation and stereotypy. At the end of each 15-minute interval, the staff person recorded the following:

- Setting
- Specific activity
- Rating of active participation
- Rating of stereotypy
- His/her initials

These data show that both behaviors varied across times of day, settings, and activities.

Interobserver Agreement

An important consideration in measuring student behavior is the reliability of the recording method. Reliability of measurement is usually defined in terms of interobserver agreement. Interobserver agreement refers to common findings by two or more observers or raters on the occurrence and nonoccurrence of target behaviors, the ratings of behaviors, or the ratings of permanent products. There are several methods of determining the degree of interobserver agreement. The most commonly used method involves calculating the ratio of agreements to the total number of recordings of behavior (Steege et al., 2002). For example, suppose that using an event-recording procedure to measure a student's calling out behavior during teacher instructional time, two observers simultaneously and independently observed and recorded target behaviors. The primary observer recorded 15 occurrences of the target behavior, while the secondary observer recorded 14 occurrences of the behavior. The total number of recordings of behavior was 15. The number of agreements was 14, resulting in the following ratio:

14/15, or 93% interobserver agreement

Generally speaking, an interobserver agreement percentage at or above 80% is considered the standard for concluding that the measurement of student behavior is reliable and

Target Behaviors

Active Participation (AP): visual, verbal, motor, on-task responding; engaged in the task activity

Stereotypy (S): waving hands in face, repetitive rocking, and/or repeated spinning/twirling tapping of objects

Recording Procedure: Performance-Based Recording

0 = NO AP or S
1 = 1″ to 2′59″ of AP or S
2 = 3′ to 5′59″ of AP or S
3 = 6′ to 8′59″ of AP or S
4 = 9′ to 11′59″ of AP or S
5 = 12′ to 15′ of AP or S

Time	Setting	Activity	Active Participation	Stereotypy	Staff Person
8:00 a.m. to 8:15	hallway, classroom	transition to class, hanging coat, backpack	4	1	MWS
8:15 to 8:30	special education classroom	morning circle time	2	2	MWS
8:30 to 8:45	special education classroom	morning circle time	1	3	MWS
8:45 to 9:00	second-grade classroom	reading group	1	4	MWS
9:00 to 9:15	second-grade classroom	reading group	2	3	MWS
9:15 to 9:30	second-grade classroom	snack	5	0	MWS

FIGURE 5.5. Example of performance-based recording procedure.

valid (Miltenberger, 2001). Within research circles, it is recommended that interobserver agreement data be conducted for 25–30% of the sessions/samples (Steege et al., 2002). Within applied settings, when research outcomes are not expected, it is a good idea to intermittently use a second observer/recorder to measure interobserver agreement. How much is enough is highly dependent on the results of the observations. For example, if there is a high level of agreement between or among observers, fewer paired observations/ recordings are necessary. On the other hand, if the level of agreement falls below 80%, then additional training, supervision, and monitoring needs to be offered. In situations in which a second observer/rater is unavailable, videotaping a sampling of sessions may be conducted. The videotape can then be viewed and behaviors recorded with a second observer.

SUMMARY

Remember the old adage, "Give a boy a hammer and he looks for a nail to pound"? Similarly, give a school practitioner a data-recording procedure and he/she looks for a behavior to record. If only it were that simple. Unfortunately, not every data recording procedure fits every behavior: when a data-recording procedure is well matched to the characteristics of the behavior, it results in accurate and meaningful measurement; when there is a poor match between recording procedure and the behavior, the resulting measurement is often meaningless. One needs to be selective about the data-recording procedure that is chosen in a particular situation. The recording procedure should be matched to the dimensions of the behavior after the behavior has been operationally defined. Doing so will allow you to make accurate estimates of behavior and meaningful decisions throughout the FBA process.

6

Indirect Functional Behavioral Assessment

Once you eliminate the impossible, whatever remains,
no matter how improbable, must be the truth.

—SHERLOCK HOLMES (by Sir Arthur Conan Doyle)

THE NEED FOR A GAME PLAN

Conducting an FBA is quite often a complex task, involving a wide range of variables to consider. As we initiate an FBA, it is important to recognize that it is really both a sequential and a simultaneous process. It is a sequential process in that we tend to assess behavior by marching through a set of preestablished investigative procedures. It is a simultaneous process in that we are continuously considering a host of variables that could be contributing to the occurrence of interfering behaviors. Consider the visual image depicted in Figure 6.1.

Here, as the school practitioner begins the FBA process, she is trying to remember to be sure to address each of the issues/variables one needs to consider when conducting a comprehensive FBA. She's finding this to be a daunting task that requires a tremendous amount of focus and organization. We've been there. In fact, in the old days, we often initiated an FBA armed only with a clipboard, graph paper, a pencil, and our own ingenuity. We invariably neglected to ask specific questions and missed potentially contributory variables. You've probably done that too. For example, 30 minutes after the initial interview with the classroom teacher and while you are driving to a student assistance team (SAT) at another school you think, "Hey! I forgot to ask about specific setting events" and "It sounds as if disruptive behaviors are motivated by teacher attention.—But wait a minute, I forgot to ask how other students in the class respond when Jerry engages in disruptive

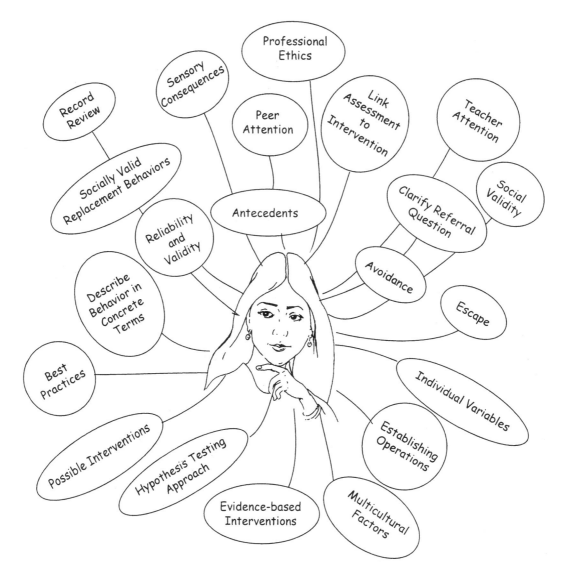

FIGURE 6.1. All things considered . . . in the professional life of a school-based practitioner.

behavior," and (45 seconds later after you regained your composure after nearly running a red light because you were not concentrating on your driving behavior) "Holy cow! What about the difficulty of the tasks? Perhaps disruptive behavior is motivated by escape/avoidance of specific tasks due to an underlying specific learning disability?"

In our experience in conducting hundreds of FBAs over the past 17 years, we have found that the accuracy of the FBA process is increased when we follow a collaborative problem-solving process that is based on a game plan that includes (1) a conceptual framework that is rooted in the principles of applied behavior analysis and (2) the necessary tools to conduct the assessment.

GUIDING CONCEPTUAL FRAMEWORK

We view the FBA process as an investigative journey that is based on the principles of applied behavior analysis. Essentially, from the initial record review or interview until the final evaluations of the effectiveness of the intervention, we are continuously assessing and reassessing behaviors against a backdrop of the A-I-B-C model. The basic premise used throughout the FBA process is that interfering behaviors are the result of an interaction among the following variables: (1) antecedent, (2) individual, and (3) consequence. We must also keep in mind that all behaviors are motivated by: (1) positive reinforcement, (2) negative reinforcement, and (3) automatic reinforcement.

We use the decision tree (see Figure 4.1) in a linear fashion to consider the possible functions of behavior. It is important to refer to this model, or a similar model, and/or to keep in mind all the various functions of behavior as you begin the FBA process. You need to keep an open mind and consider the full range of variables that influence behavior. We have found that the decision tree helps us to both "rule in" and "rule out" the behavioral function(s) associated with referral behaviors.

Another important aspect of the game plan is having adequate resources, or tools to conduct the FBA. I (Steege) am reminded of one of the first school psychologists I met during the early stages of my career. Her name was Rosemary. My oh my, how she had resources! Because she traveled from school to school in rural Iowa, she bought a postal Jeep that only had the driver's seat; she built custom-fitted shelves and cabinets in the remaining cavity of the Jeep, and she crammed it full of test equipment, protocols, materials, readings/handouts, supplies, and miscellaneous school psychology paraphernalia. As I said, she had resources. Rosemary had whatever she needed, and then some, to address any referral question, testing situation, intervention plan, or school psychology crisis situation. She had it all. Well, I have never replicated Rosemary's traveling School Psychology Extravaganza. In my case, things like car seats, baseball equipment, basketball gear, golf clubs, sailing stuff, not to mention my wife and sons, took precedent. However, I have never forgotten the lessons I leaned from Rosemary: *Be prepared. Make sure you have the equipment and resources you need to get the job done efficiently and effectively.*

Just like with Rosemary's Jeep, we have crammed a lot of assessment protocols into this and the following chapters. These protocols are the tools that we use in conducting the FBA. Not every procedure is applicable to every case you encounter. Just as one needs to match the data-recording procedure to the dimensions of the behavior and the resources of the observers/recorders, one needs to be selective about the choice of FBA procedures. This is not a one-size-fits-all process. You need to carefully consider the referral behaviors and all available resources and develop a game plan that will allow you to conduct an efficient and effective FBA.

In this chapter and Chapter 7 we offer several indirect FBA and direct descriptive FBA procedures that will give you, the practitioner, the tools necessary to conduct reliable and accurate assessments. It has been our experience that using the procedures described in the following sections will allow you to get the job done efficiently and effectively. This chapter includes examples and brief descriptions of several procedures that we use when conducting an indirect FBA. Chapter 7 includes examples and brief descriptions of several procedures that we use when conducting a direct descriptive FBA.

INDIRECT FUNCTIONAL BEHAVIORAL ASSESSMENT

Indirect assessment is so named because information regarding antecedents and consequences and other critical variables are gathered *indirectly* via interviews, rating scales, screening forms, etc. The data obtained from these measures is generally not as reliable as those obtained from more direct procedures and are considered to be a useful *adjunct* to more direct measures. Indirect measures may be some of the first procedures used in an FBA because they allow one to construct more meaningful observations and to begin developing hypotheses about the function of behavior. This chapter describes some of the most common methods of indirect functional behavioral assessment that we use and how they are related to the overall FBA process. All of these forms and the categories within them are merely examples. They may be used "as is" or may be modified to meet the demands of a particular assessment or situation. As explained previously, the reason for using the forms is that they "force" one to consider specific categories of variables, whereas an open-ended question such as "What are the triggers?" or "What are the consequences that reinforce the behavior?" often results in vague answers such as "I just don't know" or "We're not sure. The behavior just seems to happen out of the blue." We have found that the indirect FBA procedures described in the following subsections to be very useful in:

- Identifying and describing behaviors
- Identifying and describing antecedent, individual, and consequence variables
- Identifying hypotheses regarding the function(s) of behaviors

We typically use the indirect FBA during the first stage of the FBA, with the results of the assessment used to inform and guide the next stage of the process, namely, direct descriptive FBAs.

Considerations for Evaluators Conducting Indirect FBAs

The entire FBA process is a hypothesis-testing approach. It is an investigative process in which one is collecting information, identifying potential relationships, collecting more data, analyzing the influences of variables, and confirming or disconfirming hypotheses. Remember, hypotheses are not etched in stone. Many times they are more like drawings in the sand—with the next wave of data washing them away. We need to always keep in mind that indirect FBA procedures are based on information that is gathered from other sources. When conducting interviews, we need to exercise sound critical thinking skills. We need to actively listen to the interviewee and be acutely aware that any opinion, "fact," or "conclusion" offered by the interviewee may be inaccurate or biased. In short, information from interviewees needs to be considered with "a grain of salt"—and sometimes with a whole shaker full! On the other hand, there are many instances in which the interviewee offers information that is "right on." So, don't prematurely throw out any ideas, suggestions, or opinions. Instead, consider *all the data* as you formalize your hypotheses.

Perhaps the easiest part of the FBA process is the identification of interfering behaviors. After all, interfering behavior is what prompted the FBA. Also parents, teachers, staff, and significant others are usually quite good at *identifying* behaviors that are problematic or just downright annoying. However, these informants often experience considerable difficulty in *describing* interfering behavior in concrete terms. The description of interfering behaviors is usually a fairly straightforward proposition. As previously discussed, it involves describing the behavior in behavioral terms. When informants are having difficulty verbally describing behavior, we sometimes ask them to model or "act out" the behavior. This provides us with a visual image of the behavior and often assists with the written description of the target behavior. A word of caution is needed here. We want to emphasize that we do not always ask the informant to act out the behavior in question. Some behaviors are either very difficult to replicate or—and probably most importantly—you would not want to have performed. Why, you ask? Well, some behaviors may be dangerous to self or others (e.g., aggression, property destruction), may be inappropriate to model (e.g., sexual behaviors), or very difficult to replicate (e.g., manipulative soiling, ruminative vomiting). The key issue here is that it is critical to the accuracy of the entire FBA process that interfering behaviors are described in behavioral terms and that all members of the team agree that the definition of the interfering behavior reflects the actual behavior(s) of concern exhibited by the individual.

Following are descriptions of five structured indirect FBA procedures that we have developed, piloted, and recommend in conducting indirect FBAs:

- The Functional Behavioral Assessment Screening Form (FBASF)
- The Behavioral Stream Interview (BSI)
- The Antecedent Variables Assessment Form (AVAF)
- The Individual Variables Assessment Form (IVAF)
- The Consequence Variables Assessment Form (CVAF)

It is extremely important to remember that any FBA, whether indirect or direct descriptive, almost always involves a record review in the early stages of the process. The accompanying table can serve as a guide for information that is typically contained in a student's cumulative record and how that information may be pertinent to the FBA process.

Category	What to look for	Why important for FBA
Attendance history	Patterns of absences and total number of absences	May give clues about antecedents for problem behavior and possible skill deficits from lack of opportunity to receive instruction

Category	What to look for	Why important for FBA
Standardized test scores	Current and historical results of state standardized testing	May indicate academic subjects and activities that are most difficult for the student (skill deficits) and may be helpful for identifying at what age/grade the deficits became more pronounced (useful for planning curriculum-based measurements)
Medical history	Vision and hearing problems as well as other problems that may be related to school performance (e.g., motor difficulties, head traumas, long-term illnesses, enuresis) and current medication use	Helpful for identifying conditions that may exacerbate existing problematic behavior or increase the likelihood of other problematic use behaviors (see Chapter 10 for more on setting events and establishing operations)
Social history	Frequent changes in address, foster home placement, recent occurrence of stressful events (e.g., divorce, remarriage of parent, death, number of schools attended)	Points to possible establishing operations or setting events that may be impacting school behavior
Disciplinary history	Types of problematic behaviors, times and locations in which they occurred, disciplinary penalty imposed, and increase/decrease in frequency/intensity of problem behavior	Helps to identify patterns of behavior (antecedents), effective and ineffective disciplinary strategies, and possible maintaining consequences, and helps chart the progression of problematic behavior
Previous FBA or related assessment results	Other assessments that have been conducted that focus on academic skills, behavioral functioning, language skills, etc.	Possible changes in function of behavior, previous antecedents, history of behavior and interventions, and programming decisions
Previous interventions	Formal and informal interventions that are documented in some way	Identify interventions that have been successful or unsuccessful and why they were or were not successful: if successful, why are they not currently being used; likewise, why are unsuccessful interventions continuing to be applied?

Category	What to look for	Why important for FBA
IEP	Instructional goals and objectives, how/if they are being taught, how/if they are being monitored, and other data supporting student performance	Provides information on the degree to which the behaviors of concern are being addressed in the classroom and on the extent to which the teacher collects and records behavioral data

General Directions for Evaluators Using Indirect FBA Procedures

Other than the BSI, the remaining procedures include an assessment protocol (or form) that is designed to provide structure to the assessment process. There are two ways in which the evaluator can use these protocols. The first and most frequently used method involves employing the protocols within a semistructured interview. Providing the interviewee with a copy of the protocol during the interview often increases the fluency and accuracy of the interview. The second method involves providing the informant with copies of the forms and asking him/her to complete them. This latter method is only recommended in those cases in which the informant is well grounded in FBA principles and methodologies.

The Functional Behavioral Assessment Screening Form

Description

The FBASF is an FBA recording form that is used in the initial stages of the FBA process. The FBASF is used to record the following:

- Behavioral strengths (i.e., adaptive behaviors, skills, and characteristics that are functional and appropriate)
- Interfering behaviors (i.e., priority problem behaviors)
- Reinforcers (i.e., events, activities, objects, people, foods, situations, or stimuli that appear to be preferred by this person)
- Communication skills (i.e., verbal skills, signs, gestures, symbol, and/or electronic devices)

Because the focus of the FBA is on interfering behaviors, we have found that in the initial stages of the FBA process it is helpful to get a more balanced view of the individual. Identifying behavioral strengths, reinforcers, and communication skills provides us with valuable information that can be used in building behavioral support plans. Interviewees sometimes find it difficult to identify behavioral strengths. Behavioral strengths include both *interindividual* strengths (i.e. relative strengths compared to other people of the same age) and *intraindividual* strengths (i.e. behaviors that are personal strengths for the individual). A behavioral strength may be a mastered skill (e.g., above-grade-level reading skills), an emerging behavior (e.g., acquiring cooperative play skills), or a personal characteristic (e.g., a good sense of humor). Interviewees often report that the identification of potent and/or consistent reinforcers is difficult. In these cases a more formal assessment of reinforcer preferences may be indicated.

Example of the Use of the FBASF

Figure 6.2 is a copy of a blank FBASF, and Figure 6.3 includes an example of a completed FBASF. The FBASF was completed during an interview with the parents of a student with developmental disabilities who exhibited several interfering behaviors. Behavioral strengths were identified through both the interview and through review of recently completed adaptive behavior assessments. Three interfering behaviors were identified and described, several reinforcers were identified, and the methods of communication were identified and briefly described. The information gathered concerning interfering behaviors using the FBASF was used to guide the evaluator throughout the rest of the FBA process. Moreover, the information regarding behavioral strengths, reinforcers, and communication skills was useful in designing positive behavioral support interventions.

The Behavioral Stream Interview

Another form of interview involves identifying contextual variables associated with interfering behaviors. We refer to this type of interview as the Behavioral Stream Interview (BSI). This type of interview is based on the notion that there are many variables, among them antecedent, individual, and consequence variables, in the student's environment that impact challenging behavior and that these variables interact in some predictable manner. Moreover, these variables are not stagnant. The ongoing flow of behavior and related stimuli are comparable to a river—sometimes a stream that gently meanders through a meadow, and at other times a raging torrent rushing through mountainous canyons. The behavioral stream interview helps to identify these patterns by determining the sequence in which the variables occur. Unlike a *photograph* in which we take a snapshot of a singular antecedent–behavior–consequence interaction (A-B-C), the behavioral stream interview is similar to a *video* in which the entire sequence of events is captured.

Consider the image of a single photograph of a canoeist paddling through a Class III rapids versus a 5-minute video of the same situation and you will understand the difference between a simple A-B-C analysis and a behavioral stream interview.

FUNCTIONAL BEHAVIORAL ASSESSMENT SCREENING FORM (FBASF)

Name _____ Date of Birth _____ Grade _____

School/Program _____ Date form completed _____

Person(s) completing this form _____

Behavioral Strengths: Identify and briefly describe adaptive behaviors, skills, and characteristics that are functional and appropriate.

1. _____
2. _____
3. _____
4. _____
5. _____

Interfering Behaviors: Identify and describe priority problem behaviors.

1. _____
2. _____
3. _____
4. _____
5. _____

Survey of Reinforcers: Describe events, activities, objects, people, foods, situations, or stimuli that appear to be preferred by this person.

1. _____
2. _____
3. _____
4. _____
5. _____

Communication Skills: Describe the primary methods the person uses to communicate (e.g., speech, signs, gestures, symbols, electronic devices).

_____

_____

_____

_____

_____

FIGURE 6.2. Blank Functional Behavioral Assessment Screening Form (FBASF). Reprinted with permission from John F. Murphy Homes, Inc. From T. Steuart Watson and Mark W. Steege (2003). Copyright by The Guilford Press. Permission to photocopy this figure is granted to purchasers of this book for personal use only. See copyright page for details.

FUNCTIONAL BEHAVIORAL ASSESSMENT SCREENING FORM (FBASF)

Name _Sandy_ _____ Date of Birth _5-15-1986_ Grade _10_

School/Program _Sabre Island_ _____ Date form completed _5-15-02_

Person(s) completing this form _John Halyard, School Psychologist_ _____

Behavioral Strengths: Identify and briefly describe adaptive behaviors, skills, and characteristics that are functional and appropriate.

1. _initiaes social interactions with classmates_
2. _independent in all aspects of personal care_
3. _good sense of humor_
4. _math skills_
5. _peer relationships_

Interfering Behaviors: Identify and describe priority problem behaviors.

1. _verbal aggression (i.e., swears, screams, argues with teachers)_
2. _opposition (i.e., verbal refusal to complete tasks/assignments)_
3. _withdrawal (i.e., avoiding eye contact, refusing to respond, "sulking")_
4. _____
5. _____

Survey of Reinforcers: Describe events, activities, objects, people, foods, situations, or stimuli that appear to be preferred by this person.

1. _food (e.g., snacks, soda, gum)_
2. _sports (e.g., gym class, Special Olympics)_
3. _activities (e.g., movies, computer games, math games)_
4. _social interactions with classmates_
5. _____

Communication Skills: Describe the primary methods the person uses to communicate (e.g., speech, signs, gestures, symbols, electronic devices).

Sandy communicates with verbal speech. His receptive language skills appear to be much stronger than his

expressive language skills.

_____

_____

_____

_____

FIGURE 6.3. Example of completed FBASF.

Case Example of a Behavioral Stream Interview

In this case example of a BSI, the psychologist has worked with Bob for a number of years and is very familiar with his history, medical status, and the programming offered within the residential program.

PSYCHOLOGIST: Thanks for taking time out of your busy schedules to meet to discuss Bob. I understand that recently Bob has been displaying an increase in the frequency, intensity, and duration of aggressive behaviors. I've known Bob for several years, and it appears that there has been a marked increase in aggressive behaviors over the past few weeks. Could you briefly describe these behaviors?

ADMINISTRATOR: Sure . . . he has exhibited several occurrences of aggressive behavior.

PSYCHOLOGIST: Could you give me an example of what you mean by "aggressive behavior"?

ADMINISTRATOR: Well . . . his aggressive behavior involves the following: striking others with his fist, pushing others, and striking others with his forearm.

PSYCHOLOGIST: Are there any other forms of aggressive behavior?

ADMINISTRATOR: No . . . that's pretty much it.

PSYCHOLOGIST: I would like to review two to three recent examples of aggressive behavior with you and your staff. It will be helpful to interview the folks who have been working directly with Bob when these incidents occurred. The purpose of this interview is to gather as much information about not only the aggressive behavior but the variables that trigger and reinforce the behavior. My goal here is to evaluate Bob, not to evaluate the staff. But we all know that Bob's behavior is influenced by the environment in which he lives so we need to look at the larger picture. As part of that assessment, one of the things I have found to be very useful is to conduct an interview called a Behavioral Stream Interview. I will be using this form [a copy of the form is then provided to each member of the team] to write down the critical variables that occurred during these incidents of aggressive behavior. This information will be very useful for us in determining why Bob has been displaying such high rates of severe aggression over the past few weeks. Does anyone have any questions before we begin?

ADMINISTRATOR: No . . . let's get started . . . This looks like an interesting process that will lead to more effective interventions and supports for Bob.

PSYCHOLOGIST: That's the plan . . . Let's start with a recent incidence of aggressive behavior . . . Tell me what happened.

ADMINISTRATOR: Well, it happened out of the blue. Bob was having a really great day . . . and just before dinner . . . around 5:45 P.M. he hit Jeff [a staff member] on the back. This resulted in a 48-minute, three-person restraint.

PSYCHOLOGIST: Let's back up . . . What was going on before the incidence of aggression? . . . What were the activities and interactions that occurred prior to the aggressive incident?

JEFF: Bob and I were outside playing pass with a football. He really likes to throw the ball around . . . Sandy [another staff person] came to the backdoor and yelled, "It's time for dinner." I told Bob that we needed to go inside and wash our hands before dinner. That's when he hit me.

PSYCHOLOGIST: Did anything else happen before he hit you. Think back to that situation . . . After you prompted Bob to go inside to wash hands before dinner, did anything else happen?

JEFF: Yes, now that I think of it . . . yeah . . . I told Bob that we needed to stop playing pass with the football . . . He threw the ball over the fence into the neighbor's yard. I said, "We will have to get the ball after supper" and I put my arm on his shoulder and said "It's time for dinner. We need to go in and wash our hands." That's when he hit me.

PSYCHOLOGIST: Describe how he hit you.

JEFF: He screamed "AHHHH" and using a closed fist he used a chopping motion to hit me two to three times on the arm and chest areas. It wasn't very hard, but it met the criteria of aggressive behavior.

PSYCHOLOGIST: What did you do next?

JEFF: I followed the behavioral support protocol and first delivered a verbal reprimand— "Bob, no hitting"—and that's when he hit me again . . . This time three to four times and much harder. That's when I began to use protective emergency restraints . . . Within less than a minute Sandy and Jorge arrived and the three of us used the emergency restraint procedure. The entire restraint lasted 48 minutes.

In this example, it is clear that the aggressive behavior did not occur "out of the blue." In fact, behavior never occurs out of the blue, or randomly. It is caused by an interaction of antecedent–individual–consequence variables. We could hypothesize that the functions of Bob's aggressive behaviors were as follows:

- Positive reinforcement (i.e., Bob's interest in continuing to play with the football)
- Negative reinforcement (i.e., Bob's avoidance of washing his hands)
- Negative reinforcement (i.e., withdrawal from tactile contact and/or social disapproval)

When one is conducting an FBA, it is important not only to consider each of these variables but also to take into account the *stream* of antecedent, individual, and consequence variables that constitute a "behavioral incident." For example, with a typical A-B-C assessment, upon the occurrence of interfering behavior the observer is expected to record the interfering behavior and the relevant immediate antecedent and consequence variables. Oftentimes, observers identify the one immediate antecedent and the one immediate consequence that occurred within a behavioral incident. Consider the following example in which a high school student displayed aggressive behavior toward a teacher within a classroom setting. The observer used an A-B-C interview procedure to record the following:

Antecedent	Behavior	Consequence
Teacher requested John to sit down and to be quiet.	John shoved the teacher.	Verbal reprimand; John was directed to the principal's office.

In this case, a singular A-B-C recording did not fully capture all of the relevant variables associated with this behavioral incident. In fact, there were several additional incidents that preceded this recording. When a series of behavioral incidents occur, it is our experience that observers often verbally report and/or record the final incident. In these cases, the observer is reporting only a small section of what we refer to as the "behavioral stream." A behavioral stream involves the occurrence of a series of behavioral incidents—the unfolding of interrelated variables that constitute the continuous flow of antecedents, individual, interfering, and consequence variables. Indeed, when we consider a single A-B-C analysis, the behavioral incident appears to have a discrete beginning and end. However, the analysis of the flow of behavior and contextual variables provides a much richer and more comprehensive understanding of behavior. One also needs to consider that, when analyzing the stream of behavior, a variable that operates as a consequence for one behavior is an antecedent for a subsequent behavior. For example, consider the case in which a child exhibits interfering behavior within the home setting. In this example, the consequence of social attention (i.e., a verbal reprimand) delivered by the parent also served as the antecedent for a subsequent behavior (i.e., verbal opposition). Although one strategy might involve teaching observers and recorders to record each occurrence of interfering behavior and the relevant antecedent and consequence variables (i.e., a simple A-B-C), we have found it to be more informative and easier for the observers to record behavior using the following behavioral stream format.

Case Example of Behavioral Stream Recording

This example involves an elementary student diagnosed with emotional/behavioral disorders who displays a set of behaviors referred to as tantrum behavior. Tantrum behavior is defined as a response set including two or more of the following: verbal opposition, swearing, screaming, and throwing or damaging materials. An incident of tantrum behavior was recorded using an A-B-C analysis as follows:

Antecedent	Behavior	Consequence
Teacher prompted Seth to participate in assigned task.	Seth exhibited tantrum behavior.	Seth was sent to time-out area for 5 minutes.

The behavioral stream recording of the same incident looked like this:

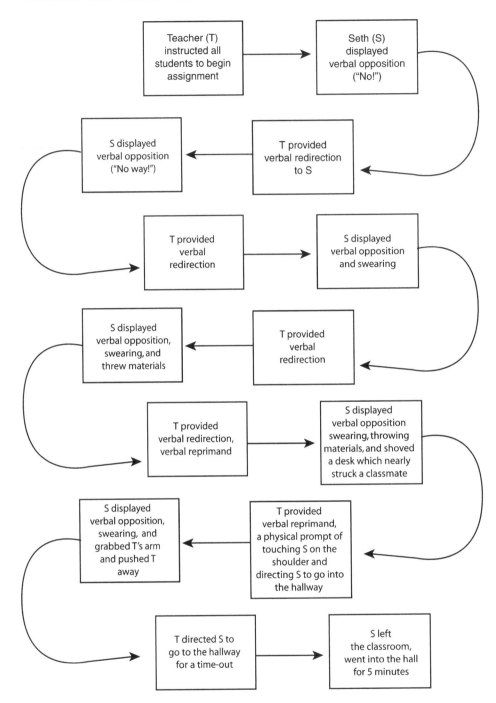

When one is conducting behavioral stream recording, it is not necessary to label stimuli or variables as antecedents or consequences while completing the recording. Instead, the focus is on describing the sequence of behaviors as the behavioral incident unfolds. It really is a matter of recording from a "he said/he did"—"she said/she did" perspective. Review and analysis of the behavioral stream recordings involves the identification of relevant triggers for problem behavior and the maintaining consequences. In the previous example, the A-B-C recording provided only a snapshot of what was otherwise a much more complicated scenario. The BSI captured the larger picture and provided details that allow for a more comprehensive understanding of the behavioral incident.

An additional advantage of using BSI is that they are easily incorporated into the assessment report. Using the format in the written report and when describing the results of the observation allows others to see the complex relationships among a host of variables. As a result, more effective and efficient interventions can be designed.

Considerations When Evaluators Are Using the AVAF, IVAF, and CVAF Procedures

The AVAF, IVAF, and CVAF procedures include a wide range of variables that have been found to trigger and reinforce interfering behaviors. Unlike a checklist where relevant variables are only identified, these procedures are designed to both *identify* relevant variables and *describe* how those events serve to trigger or reinforce the interfering behaviors. When one is using these forms regarding the behavior of a specific individual, it is unlikely that all of the variables listed on the forms will be identified as contributing to the occurrence of interfering behaviors. In many cases, only a few variables will be identified. In cases where multiple interfering behaviors have been identified with one person, sequential review of potentially relevant antecedents on a "behavior-by behavior" basis is recommended. In other words, we recommend using a new form for the assessment of each interfering behavior. For example, with an individual who displays aggressive, oppositional, and tantrum behaviors, we would recommend using a separate AVAF, IVAF, and CVAF recording sheet for the assessment of each behavior.

The Antecedent Variables Assessment Form

The AVAF is a recording form that is used in the initial stages of the FBA process. The AVAF is used to identify and describe the variables that set the occasion for, or trigger, interfering behavior. The AVAF contains items across four variables that are typically related to interfering behavior in schools as well as one item prompting the evaluator to identify possible response chains. The four variables included on the AVAF are:

- Environmental
- Instructional
- Social
- Transition

Although there are other antecedent variables that may be related to interfering behavior, these are the ones most typically found in a school-based setting. Figure 6.4 is a copy of a blank AVAF, and Figure 6.5 includes an example of a completed AVAF.

ANTECEDENT VARIABLES ASSESSMENT FORM (AVAF)

Name _____ Date of Birth _____ Grade _____

School/Program _____ Date form completed _____

Person(s) completing this form _____

Interfering Behavior: _____

Environmental Variables: Briefly describe how the following variables trigger the occurrence of the interfering behavior.

Auditory stimulation (i.e., noise level) _____

_____

Visual stimulation _____

_____

Room arrangement _____

_____

Specific settings _____

_____

Time of day _____

_____

Instructional Variables: Briefly describe how the following variables trigger the occurrence of the interfering behavior.

Specific tasks/activities _____

_____

Task difficulty _____

_____

Errors or mistakes in responding _____

_____

Insufficient or inconsistent reinforcement _____

_____

Tasks not meaningful _____

_____

Pace of instruction (too fast or too slow) _____

_____

Lack of choice in tasks or activities _____

_____

Large-group instruction _____

_____

Independent seat work _____

_____

Cooperative learning or small-group tasks _____

_____

(continued

FIGURE 6.4. Blank AVAF. Reprinted with permission from John F. Murphy Homes, Inc. From T. Steuart Watson and Mark W. Steege (2003). Copyright by The Guilford Press. Permission to photocopy this figure is granted to purchasers of this book for personal use only. See copyright page for details.

ANTECEDENT VARIABLES ASSESSMENT FORM (AVAF)

(page 2 of 2)

Sequence of tasks/activities _____

_____

Correction or instruction following mistake(s)/error(s) _____

_____

Social Variables: Briefly describe how the following variables trigger the occurrence of the interfering behavior.

Specific people present _____

_____

Number of people present _____

_____

Proximity of others _____

_____

Interfering behavior of others _____

_____

Transition Variables: Briefly describe how the following variables trigger the occurrence of the interfering behavior.

Transitions to tasks/activities _____

_____

Transitions from tasks/activities _____

_____

Change in routine/schedule _____

_____

Change of staff/caregivers _____

_____

Transportation to or from school (e.g., bus, walking, car with friends) _____

_____

Interfering bahaviors often occur in a cluster or as part of a response chain. List and briefly describe those interfering behaviors that occur prior to and simultaneous with the priority interfering behavior.

Prior to _____

_____

Simultaneous with _____

_____

ANTECEDENT VARIABLES ASSESSMENT FORM (AVAF)

Name _Robert_   Date of Birth _11-15-86_   Grade _10_

School/Program _Oceanview High School_   Date form completed _11-17-02_

Person(s) completing this form _Pam Seacraft (School Psychologist)_

Interfering Behavior: _Inappropriate Verbal Behavior_

Environmental Variables: Briefly describe how the following variables trigger the occurrence of the interfering behavior.

Auditory stimulation (i.e., noise level) _N/A_

Visual stimulation _N/A_

Room arrangement _N/A_

Specific settings _English & Geometry Classes_

Time of day _9:50 am (English)   1 pm (Geometry)_

Instructional Variables: Briefly describe how the following variables trigger the occurrence of the interfering behavior.

Specific tasks/activities _N/A_

Task difficulty _N/A_

Errors or mistakes in responding _N/A_

Insufficient or inconsistent reinforcement _N/A_

Tasks not meaningful _N/A_

Pace of instruction (too fast or too slow) _N/A_

Lack of choice in tasks or activities _N/A_

Large-group instruction _Yes, especially if this involves interactions or cooperative work with classmates._

Independent seat work _N/A_

Cooperative learning or small-group tasks _Yes! inappropriate verbal behaviors with peers._

(continued)

FIGURE 6.5. Example of completed AVAF.

Sequence of tasks/activities _N/A_

Correction or instruction following mistake(s)/error(s) _N/A_

Social Variables: Briefly describe how the following variables trigger the occurrence of the interfering behavior.

Specific people present _specific classmates (i.e., Tom B., Pedro M., Drew P., Manny R., and Nomar G.)_

Number of people present _yes, especially when in a crowd, or unstructured situation_

Proximity of others _yes, when in a crowd and others are very close to Robert_

Interfering behavior of others _yes, if other students shout or swear at Robert_

Transition Variables: Briefly describe how the following variables trigger the occurrence of the interfering behavior.

Transitions to tasks/activities _yes. hallways; entering classes; between structured tasks or activities in class_

Transitions from tasks/activities _yes. hallways; leaving classes_

Change in routine/schedule _N/A_

Change of staff/caregivers _N/A_

Transportation to or from school (e.g., bus, walking, car with friends) _not reported_

Interfering bahaviors often occur in a cluster or as part of a response chain. List and briefly describe those interfering behaviors that occur prior to and simultaneous with the priority interfering behavior.

Prior to _Robert often first exhibits facial tensing and agitated movements prior to engaging in inappropriate verbal behaviors_

Simultaneous with _waving arms, stomping feet_

The Individual Variables Assessment Form

The IVAF is a recording form that is used during the initial phase of the FBA process. The IVAF is used to identify and describe those individual variables that are associated with the occurrence of interfering behavior. Like the AVAF, the IVAF contains those individual variables that are most typically associated with interfering behavior. Therefore, there are undoubtedly other individual variables not accounted for by this form. Figure 6.6 is a copy of a blank IVAF, and Figure 6.7 is an example of a completed IVAF.

The Consequence Variables Assessment Form

The CVAF is also a recording form that is used during the initial stages of the FBA process. The CVAF is used to identify and describe those variables that typically follow the occurrence of interfering behaviors. The CVAF includes a set of supplementary questions that may be used to further clarify relationships between specific consequences and interfering behaviors. Figure 6.8 is a copy of a blank CAVF, and Figure 6.9 is an example of a completed CAVF.

Examples of the Use of the AVAF, IVAF, and CVAF

Figures 6.5, 6.7, and 6.9 illustrate the application of the AVAF, IVAF, and CVAF during the FBA of a single interfering behavior. The student was a sophomore in high school who was referred for psychological evaluation, including an FBA, to address disruptive behaviors occurring within the school setting. This was the first time that this student had been brought to the attention of the SAT. The priority interfering behavior was "inappropriate verbal behavior." The behavior was defined as: swearing (e.g., "F   you," "Go to hell") and/or name calling (e.g., "idiot," "bitch," "moron"). Because the classroom teacher was not experienced in conducting FBAs and was unfamiliar with these assessment forms, the school practitioner decided to use the AVAF, IVAF, and CVAF procedures as part of her semistructured interview. Because this behavior was reported to occur at the highest rates during English and geometry classes, the school practitioner arranged an interview simultaneously with both teachers. To assist with both interviewees' comprehension of the assessment items, blank copies of the forms were given to the teachers during the interviews. Review of the completed forms indicated that only a few relevant antecedent, individual, and consequence variables were identified. Based on the results of these assessments, it was hypothesized that inappropriate verbal behavior typically occurred during unstructured classroom situations, was related to the student's delays in social and self-control skills, and was maintained by social attention (i.e., reactions of classmates and the classroom teacher) from classmates and from the reactions of the classroom teacher. These results suggested that the interfering behaviors were motivated by positive reinforcement (i.e., social attention from classmates and teachers). To further evaluate inappropriate verbal behavior, the school practitioner scheduled direct observations within each of classes and instructed the two teachers in the use of the Functional Behavioral Assessment Observation Form (see Chapter 7).

INDIVIDUAL VARIABLES ASSESSMENT FORM (IVAF)

Name _____ Date of Birth _____ Grade _____

School/Program _____ Date form completed _____

Person(s) completing this form _____

Interfering Behavior: _____

Individual Variables: Briefly describe how the following variables appear to be related to the occurrence of the interfering behavior.

Receptive communication skills _____
_____

Expressive communication skills _____
_____

Academic skills _____
_____

Social skills _____
_____

Health issues (e.g., hearing, headache, bowel regularity) _____
_____

Sleep issues _____
_____

Perscribed medications _____
_____

Substance use/abuse _____
_____

Dietary issues _____
_____

Emotional states (e.g., anxiety, depression, anger) _____
_____

Cognitive skills _____
_____

Cognitive state (e.g., "thought disorders," "irrational thinking") _____
_____

Coping skills/strategies _____
_____

Other Individual variables: _____
_____

FIGURE 6.6. Blank IVAF. Reprinted with permission from John F. Murphy Homes, Inc. From T. Steuart Watson and Mark W. Steege (2003). Copyright by The Guilford Press. Permission to photocopy this figure is granted to purchasers of this book for personal use only. See copyright page for details.

INDIVIDUAL VARIABLES ASSESSMENT FORM (IVAF)

Name Robert   Date of Birth 11-15-86   Grade 10

School/Program Oceanview High School   Date form completed 11-17-02

Person(s) completing this form Pam Seacraft (School Psychologist)

Interfering Behavior: Inappropriate Verbal Behavior

Individual Variables: Briefly describe how the following variables appear to be related to the occurrence of the interfering behavior.

Receptive communication skills N/A

Expressive communication skills Robert has a mild speech dysfluency and a mild articulation disorder

Academic skills N/A

Social skills Robert has significant social skills delays, few friends, socially withdrawn

Health issues (e.g., hearing, headache, bowel regularity) N/A

Sleep issues N/A

Perscribed medications N/A

Substance use/abuse N/A

Dietary issues N/A

Emotional states (e.g., anxiety, depression, anger) Robert appears to be anxious when in large crowds and unstructured social situations

Cognitive skills N/A

Cognitive state (e.g., "thought disorders," "irrational thinking") N/A

Coping skills/strategies socially awkward; he appears to have great difficulty in initiating social interaction

Other Individual variables: he seems to be interested in interacting with classmates and teachers, but lacks solid social skills; poor self-control

FIGURE 6.7. Example of completed IVAF.

CONSEQUENCE VARIABLES ASSESSMENT FORM (CVAF)

Name _____ Date of Birth _____ Grade _____

School/Program _____ Date form completed _____

Person(s) completing this form _____

Interfering Behavior: _____

The Consequence Variables Assessment Form (CVAF) is designed to identify variables that reinforce interfering behaviors.

Briefly describe situations in which interfering behavior results in:

    A. Social attention from teachers/staff: _____

    B. Social attention from classmates/peers: _____

    C. The individual obtaining objects: _____

    D. The individual obtaining activities: _____

Briefly describe situations in which interfering behavior results in the cessation of, withdrawal from, and/or avoidance of:

    A. Tasks or assignments: _____

    B. Activities: _____

    C. Settings: _____

    D. Social Interactions (Teachers/Staff): _____

    E. Social Interactions (Classmates/Peers): _____

Briefly describe those behaviors that appear to result in sensory consequences:

    A. Arousal induction (i.e., increases sensory stimulation): _____

        _____

    B. Arousal reduction (i.e., decreases sensory stimulation): _____

        _____

(continued)

FIGURE 6.8. Blank CVAF. Reprinted with permission from John F. Murphy Homes, Inc. From T. Steuart Watson and Mark W. Steege (2003). Copyright by The Guilford Press. Permission to photocopy this figure is granted to purchasers of this book for personal use only. See copyright page for details.

CONSEQUENCE VARIABLES ASSESSMENT FORM
(SUPPLEMENTAL QUESTIONS)
(page 2 of 3)

The Consequence Variables Assessment Form (CVAF) is designed to identify variables that reinforce interfering behaviors. The following questions may be used during an interview to elicit information regarding the motivating functions of interfering behaviors. This is especially helpful when one is attempting to "tease out" the variables that are reinforcing the problem behavior. Following is a list of questions that are matched to possible functions of interfering behaviors.

Positive Reinforcement Function

Positive Reinforcement: Social Attention (Teachers/Staff)

When the interfering behavior occurs, do teachers/staff give verbal or visual feedback, or respond in some way?

Does interfering behavior occur when the individual is not receiving attention from teachers/staff but a classmate/peer (or classmates/peers) is receiving attention?

When the interfering behavior occurs, do teachers/staff provide immediate attention to the individual?

Positive Reinforcement: Social Attention (Classmates/Peers)

When the interfering behavior occurs, do classmates/peers give verbal or visual feedback, or respond in some way?

Does interfering behavior occur when the individual is not receiving attention from classmates/peers but another classmate/peer (or classmates/peers) is receiving attention?

When the interfering behavior occurs, do classmates/peers provide immediate attention to the individual?

Positive Reinforcement (Objects):

Is the interfering likely to occur when the individual is told that he/she cannot have access to a preferred item?

Does the occurrence of interfering behavior result in the individual obtaining a preferred object?

Positive Reinforcement (Activity):

Is the interfering more likely to occur when the individual is told that he/she cannot participate in a preferred activity?

Does the interfering behavior occur when the individual is told that a preferred activity is nearing completion or is finished?

Does the occurrence of interfering behavior result in the individual participating in a preferred activity?

Negative Reinforcement Function

Negative Reinforcement (Tasks/Assignments):

Does the interfering behavior occur when you request the individual to participate in a task/assignment that he/she has opposed (e.g., nonpreferred or difficult task/assignment)?

(continued)

Does the interfering behavior occur when the individual is told that a nonpreferred or difficult instructional task/assignment will continue?

Negative Reinforcement (Activity):

Does the interfering behavior occur when you request the individual to participate in an activity that he/she has opposed (e.g., nonpreferred activity)?

Does the interfering behavior occur when the individual is told that a nonpreferred activity will continue?

Negative Reinforcement (Setting):

Does the interfering behavior result in the individual leaving (asking or being asked to leave) a setting that the individual finds uncomfortable (e.g., too loud, hot/cold, excess stimuli)?

When the interfering behavior occurs, do teachers/staff/classmates/peers attempt to modify the environment (i.e., reduce environmental stimulation)?

Negative Reinforcement (Social: Teachers/Staff)

Does the behavior result in the avoidance or termination of social interactions with teachers/staff?

When the interfering behavior occurs, do teachers/staff stop providing attention to the individual?

Negative Reinforcement (Social: Classmates/Peers)

Does the behavior result in the avoidance or termination of social interactions with classmates/peers?

When the interfering behavior occurs, do classmates/peers stop providing attention to the individual?

<u>**Automatic Reinforcement**</u>

Arousal Induction

Does the interfering behavior appear to result in sensory input that the individual enjoys?

When the interfering behavior occurs, does the behavior appear to result in sensory consequences (e.g., visual, auditory, tactile) that are "self-stimulating"?

Arousal Reduction

Does the interfering behavior appear to result in the reduction of internal states of arousal (e.g., "venting")?

When the interfering behavior occurs does the individual appear to be agitated/frustrated?

When the interfering behavior occurs, does the behavior appear to result in sensory consequences that result in the release of "tension," "anxiety," and/or "frustration"?

CONSEQUENCE VARIABLES ASSESSMENT FORM (CVAF)

Name _Robert_ Date of Birth _11-15-86_ Grade _10_

School/Program _Oceanview High School_ Date form completed _11-17-02_

Person(s) completing this form _Pam Seacraft (School Psychologist)_

Interfering Behavior: _Inappropriate Verbal Behavior_

The Consequence Variables Assessment Form (CVAF) is designed to identify variables that reinforce interfering behaviors.

Briefly describe situations in which interfering behavior results in:
  A. Social attention from teachers/staff: _teacher verbal reprimands_
  B. Social attention from classmates/peers: _laughs, argues, stares_
  C. The individual obtaining objects: _N/A_
  D. The individual obtaining activities: _N/A_

Briefly describe situations in which interfering behavior results in the cessation of, withdrawal from, and/ or avoidance of:
  A. Tasks or assignments: _N/A_
  B. Activities: _N/A_
  C. Settings: _N/A_
  D. Social Interactions (Teachers/Staff): _N/A_
  E. Social Interactions (Classmates/Peers): _N/A_

Briefly describe those behaviors that appear to result in sensory consequences:
  A. Arousal induction (i.e., increases sensory stimulation): _N/A_

  B. Arousal reduction (i.e., decreases sensory stimulation): _N/A_

FIGURE 6.9. Example of completed CVAF.

The Functional Assessment Informant Record for Teachers

The FAIR-T (Edwards, 2002) is a teacher-completed record form that is designed for assessing interfering behaviors for the purpose of developing hypotheses about functional relationships between interfering behaviors displayed by students within general education classrooms and environmental events occurring in those settings. The FAIR-T allows educators to gather information about problem behavior, antecedents, maintaining functions, and previously implemented interventions.

The FAIR-T consists of four sections:

- General Referral Information
- Problem Behaviors

- Antecedents
- Consequences

In describing the uses of the FAIR-T, Edwards (2002) stressed that the FAIR-T, by itself, is not intended to generate sufficient information to develop hypotheses about the function of interfering behaviors and stresses that a follow-up interview is the key to the successful use of the FAIR-T. For example, if academic delays are identified, additional assessments (e.g., curriculum-based measures) are indicated. If interfering behavior is identified within the context of specific settings, then follow-up interviews need to explore the specific variables within those settings that trigger interfering behaviors. Edwards (2002) also recommends that hypotheses regarding the function of interfering behaviors generated from the information provided by the FAIR-T could be further evaluated through direct observation. A copy of the FAIR-T is reproduced in Figure 6.10.

SUMMARY

The temptation to rely solely on indirect FBA procedures is alluring. After all, indirect FBA procedures are relatively efficient and cost-effective methods of conducting an FBA. One needs to keep in mind, however, that simply filling out a form that is titled "functional behavioral assessment" does not necessarily constitute an adequate FBA and in many cases is not a best-practices assessment approach. A poorly designed indirect FBA form and/or a loosely conducted interview will very likely result in inaccurate assessment results, faulty hypotheses, and ineffective interventions.

In this chapter we described several formal indirect FBA procedures. It has also been our experience that there are some cases in which the results of indirect FBA are in and of themselves sufficient for assessing and understanding behavioral function. In these cases, practitioners could consider first conducting a formal indirect FBA as described in this chapter. If the results of the indirect FBA are consistent and make sense, then additional assessments may not be indicated. The assessment results are then used in designing functional-based interventions. The intervention is implemented and evaluated, and if the intervention proves to be successful, then the assessment process has been validated. More importantly, the intervention has been successful! On a practical level, a successful intervention is more important than a valid assessment! If, on the other hand, the results of the indirect FBA are suspect or inconsistent across assessment tools, then additional assessments are recommended. The following chapters provide descriptions of direct observation procedures that are used to further assess interfering behaviors.

FUNCTIONAL ASSESSMENT INFORMANT RECORD FOR TEACHERS

If information is being provided by both the teacher and the classroom aide, indicate both respondents' names. In addition, in instances where divergent information is provided, note the sources of specific information.

Student: _____ Respondent(s): _____

School: _____ Age: _____ Sex: M F Date: _____

1. Describe the referred student. What is he/she like in the classroom? (Write down what you believe is the most important information about the referred student.)

   _____
   _____
   _____
   _____

2. Pick a second student of the same sex who is also difficult to teach. What makes the referred student more difficult than the second student?

   _____
   _____
   _____
   _____

3. a. On what grade level is the student reading?   _____
   b. On what grade level is an average student in the class reading?   _____
4. a. On what grade level is the student performing in math?   _____
   b. On what grade level is an average student in the class performing in math?   _____
5. a. What is the student's classwork completion percentage (0–100%)?   _____
   b. What is the student's classwork accuracy percentage (0–100%)?   _____

6. Is the student taking any medications that might affect the student's behavior?

   _____ Yes   _____ No   If yes, briefly explain:

   _____
   _____

7. Do you have any specific health concerns regarding this student?

   _____ Yes   _____ No   If yes, briefly explain:

   _____
   _____

8. What procedures have you tried in the past to deal with this student's problem behavior?

   _____
   _____

(continued)

FIGURE 6.10. Functional Assessment Informant Record for Teachers (FAIR-T). From Edwards (2002). Copyright 2000 by Sopris West, Inc. Reprinted by permission.

9. Briefly list below the student's typical daily schedule of activities.

Time	Activity	Time	Activity
____	_____	____	_____
____	_____	____	_____
____	_____	____	_____
____	_____	____	_____
____	_____	____	_____
____	_____	____	_____
____	_____	____	_____
____	_____	____	_____
____	_____	____	_____
____	_____	____	_____

10. When during the day (two academic *activities* and *times*) does the student's problem behavior(s) typically occur?

Academic Activity #1 _____ Time _____

Academic Activity #2 _____ Time _____

11. Please indicate *good days* and *times* to observe. (At least two observations are needed.)

Observation #1	Observation #2	Observation #3 (Backup)
Date _____	Date _____	Date _____
Time _____	Time _____	Time _____

Problem Behaviors

Please list one to three problem behaviors in order of severity. Do not use a general description such as "disruptive" but give the actual behavior such as "doesn't stay in his/her seat" or "talks out without permission."

1. _____

_____

2. _____

_____

3. _____

_____

1. Rate how *manageable* the behavior is:

a. Problem Behavior 1   1   2   3   4   5
        Unmanageable   Manageable

b. Problem Behavior 2   1   2   3   4   5
        Unmanageable   Manageable

c. Problem Behavior 3   1   2   3   4   5
        Unmanageable   Manageable

2. Rate how *disruptive* the behavior is:

a. Problem Behavior 1   1   2   3   4   5
        Mildly   Very

b. Problem Behavior 2   1   2   3   4   5
        Mildly   Very

c. Problem Behavior 3   1   2   3   4   5
        Mildly   Very

(continued)

3. How often does the behavior occur *per day* (please circle)?

   a. Problem Behavior 1   <1–3   4–6   7–9   10–12   ≥13

   b. Problem Behavior 2   <1–3   4–6   7–9   10–12   ≥13

   c. Problem Behavior 3   <1–3   4–6   7–9   10–12   ≥13

4. How many *months* has the behavior been present?

   a. Problem Behavior 1   < 1   2   3   4   entire school year

   b. Problem Behavior 2   < 1   2   3   4   entire school year

   c. Problem Behavior 3   < 1   2   3   4   entire school year

Antecedents: Problem Behavior #_____:_____   Yes   No

1. Does the behavior occur more often during a certain *type* of task?   _____   _____
2. Does the behavior occur more often during *easy* tasks?   _____   _____
3. Does the behavior occur more often during *difficult* tasks?   _____   _____
4. Does the behavior occur more often during *certain subject areas?*   _____   _____
5. Does the behavior occur more often during *new* subject material?   _____   _____
6. Does the behavior occur more often when a request is made to *stop* an activity?   _____   _____
7. Does the behavior occur more often when a request is made to *begin a new activity?*   _____   _____
8. Does the behavior occur more often during *transition* periods?   _____   _____
9. Does the behavior occur more often when a *disruption* occurs in the student's normal routine?   _____   _____
10. Does the behavior occur more often when the student's *request has been denied?*   _____   _____
11. Does the behavior occur more often when a *specific person is in the room?*   _____   _____
12. Does the behavior occur more often when a *specific person is absent from the room?*   _____   _____
13. Are there any other behaviors that usually *precede* the problem behavior?   _____   _____
14. Is there anything you could do that would *ensure* the occurrence of the behavior?   _____   _____
15. Are there any events occurring in the child's *home* that seem to precede occurrence of the behavior at school?   _____   _____
16. Does the behavior occur more often in *certain settings*? (circle all that apply)   _____   _____

   large group   small group   independent work   one-to-one interaction

   bathroom   recess   cafeteria   bus

   other: _____

(continued)

Consequences: Problem Behavior #_____:_____

1. Please indicate whether the following consequences occur after the behavior is exhibited.

Consequence	Yes	No
Access to preferred activity	_____	_____
Termination of task	_____	_____
Rewards	_____	_____
Peer attention	_____	_____
Teacher attention	_____	_____
Praise	_____	_____
Ignore	_____	_____
Redirection	_____	_____
Interrupt	_____	_____
Reprimand	_____	_____

2. Is there any task you have stopped presenting to the student as a result of the problem behavior?

_____ Yes   _____ No   If yes, describe:

_____

_____

3. Are there other problem behaviors that often occur after the behavior is exhibited?

_____ Yes   _____ No   If yes, describe:

_____

_____

4. Does the student typically receive praise or any positive consequence when behavior occurs that you would like to see instead of the problem behavior?

_____ Yes   _____ No

Comments: _____

7

Direct Descriptive
Functional Behavioral Assessment

All science is concerned with the relationship of cause and effect. Each scientific discovery increases man's ability to predict the consequences of his actions and thus his ability to control future events.

—Laurence J. Peter

Direct descriptive functional behavioral assessment is perhaps one of the most powerful tools in school-based FBAs. It is powerful because each of the procedures is based on direct observations of behavior in the setting and/or situations in which the target behaviors occur. Thus, hypotheses regarding function and triggers are based on systematic observations and not merely on conjecture or solely on indirect information. Contained in this chapter are the actual forms that we use when conducting observations and a description of their use.

Direct descriptive FBA procedures involve the observation and recording of behaviors. The behavior-recording procedures described in Chapter 5 are used when the evaluator is conducting direct descriptive FBAs. It is important to keep in mind that the evaluator is attempting to observe and record behavior within the context of naturally occurring situations when he/she is conducting direct descriptive FBAs. The evaluator needs to be as unobtrusive as possible. Equally important is the selection of the data-recording procedure. The evaluator needs to make sure that the behavior-recording procedure is matched to (1) the dimensions of the behavior and (2) the resources and skills of the observer.

In many cases, observation and recording of behavior are conducted by the evaluator. However, there are situations in which this is impractical. For example, the behavior may be of a very low frequency and consequently the probability of observing the behavior during a scheduled observation is slim to none; or the presence of the observer may cause the target student to change his/her behavior in such a way that the observation session in no way represents typically occurring behavior. In these instances, the observation and recording of behavior by teachers, parents, educational technicians, etc. is recommended. In fact, there may be some cases in which self-recording by the referred student is recommended.

We have found that the direct descriptive FBA procedures described in the following sections are applicable within applied settings. With these procedures, teachers and staff typically conduct observations and recordings.

TASK DIFFICULTY ANTECEDENT ANALYSIS FORM

This form is particularly useful in those circumstances where other information, from interviews, observations, or one of the assessment forms in the previous chapter for instance, has indicated that the presentation of difficult tasks may be an antecedent (trigger) for the target behavior. The top portion allows the observer to note the setting in which the analysis occurs, the target behavior, and a description of the task. It is important to describe all relevant features of the task (in math, for example, if the student is performing calculations or working word problems) so that other variables can be further analyzed if necessary. It is important to mention that this type of analysis may need to be done for each subject (reading, math, science, etc.) or type of task (written, oral reading in a group, etc.).

Before beginning the observation, you must coordinate with the teacher to identify tasks that are easy (greater than 90% accuracy), medium (70–80% accuracy), or difficult (less than 70% accuracy). You may select tasks that fit each of these categories via examination of work samples and/or curriculum-based measurement (CBM) probes. Once the tasks that fit each category are identified, the teacher should present one of the tasks to the student during the appropriate classroom time. Ideally, one should make repeated observations of the student while counterbalancing the order of presentation of the tasks. Realizing that this is probably unrealistic for most practitioners, randomly select which category will be presented and for how long (a minimum is 5; a maximum might be 10 minutes or so). As soon as the task is presented, begin the 10-second interval recording. If the target behavior occurs, place some type of mark in the box (usually an × or a √) that corresponds to the type of task and interval number. If the target behavior does not occur, place a 0 in the corresponding box. Repeat this procedure for each of the three types of tasks. A blank Task Difficulty Antecedent Analysis Form is included in Figure 7.1. An example of a completed Task Difficulty Antecedent Analysis Form is illustrated in Figure 7.2, along with a brief description of the results.

The data in Figure 7.2 indicate that Jason was disruptive during 13% (4/30) of the intervals while reading easy passages, 23% (7/30) of the intervals while reading passages of medium difficulty, and 57% (17/30) of the intervals while reading difficult passages. If time permits, this type of observation should be conducted another time or two on a different day to determine whether these results are consistent. If similar findings emerge from another task difficulty antecedent analysis, then one might reasonably hypothesize that difficult tasks are an antecedent for Jason's disruptive behavior. Intervention, then, would focus on presenting easier tasks while simultaneously remediating reading skills. Presenting relatively easier tasks during reading also allows for the opportunity to reinforce behaviors that are alternative or incompatible with disruption. As reading skills improve, the difficulty of the tasks might gradually be increased while continuing to reinforce behaviors other than disruption.

TASK DIFFICULTY ANTECEDENT ANALYSIS FORM

Student's Name: _____   School/Grade: _____

Setting: _____   Date: _____

Observer: _____   Time: _____

Target Behavior: _____

_____

Task Description: _____

_____

_____

_____

10-SECOND INTERVALS

	1	2	3	4	5	6	7	8	9	10	11	12	13	14	15	16	17	18	19	20
Easy (90%)																				
Medium (70–80%)																				
Difficult (<70%)																				

	1	2	3	4	5	6	7	8	9	10	11	12	13	14	15	16	17	18	19	20
Easy (90%)																				
Medium (70–80%)																				
Difficult (<70%)																				

FIGURE 7.1. Task Difficulty Antecedent Analysis Form. From T. Steuart Watson and Mark W. Steege (2003). Copyright by The Guilford Press. Permission to photocopy this figure is granted to purchasers of this book for personal use only. See copyright page for details.

TASK DIFFICULTY ANTECEDENT ANALYSIS FORM

Student's Name: _Jason Adams_ School/Grade: _Titusville/2nd_

Setting: _Reading Class_ Date: _September 19, 2000_

Observer: _Steuart Watson_ Time: _8:30–9:00_

Target Behavior: _During reading class, Jason has been disruptive by calling other students names, running in the classroom, and refusing to do his work._

Task Description: _Based on CBM probes, easy, medium, and difficult reading passages from his reading material have been identified. During independent reading time, Jason's teacher will present him with a medium passage followed by an easy and a difficult passage. Each passage will be presented for 5 minutes._

10-SECOND INTERVALS

	1	2	3	4	5	6	7	8	9	10	11	12	13	14	15	16	17	18	19	20
Easy (90%)	o	o	o	o	o	o	o	x	X	o	o	o	o	o	o	o	x	o	o	o
Medium (70–80%)	o	o	o	x	x	o	o	o	O	o	o	x	o	o	x	x	x	o	o	o
Difficult (<70%)	o	x	x	x	o	o	x	o	X	x	o	o	x	x	o	o	x	o	o	x

	1	2	3	4	5	6	7	8	9	10	11	12	13	14	15	16	17	18	19	20
Easy (90%)	o	o	o	o	o	o	x	o	O	o										
Medium (70–80%)	x	o	o	o	x	x	o	o	o	o										
Difficult (<70%)	x	x	x	o	o	o	x	x	x	x										

FIGURE 7.2. Example of a completed Task Difficulty Antecedent Analysis Form.

THE CONDITIONAL PROBABILITY RECORD

The CPR is a form that allows the observer to simultaneously observe and record the antecedents and consequences of behavior. The advantage of doing so allows for the analysis of the likelihood (probability) of a behavior given a particular antecedent and the likelihood of a particular consequence following a behavior. Figure 7.3 is a blank CPR. Figure 7.4 presents an example of a completed CPR, along with an explanation of the results.

The 5-minute excerpt in Figure 7.4, taken from the 15-minute observation period, indicates that Mitch was lying and/or rolling on the floor during 60% of the intervals. Furthermore, of the intervals in which Mitch was lying/rolling on the floor, 41% of those resulted in a verbal reprimand by the teacher and 33% resulted in the teacher physically guiding Mitch back into his seat. Thus, Mitch's on-floor behavior resulted in some form of teacher attention in 74% of the intervals. Likewise, working on the assigned task resulted in no verbal or physical attention from the teacher. In only 33% of the intervals in which Mitch was working was the teacher in physical proximity to him. Thus, one hypothesis is that Mitch's on-floor behavior is maintained by teacher attention because doing so is at least twice as likely to result in some form of teacher attention than working. There may be some peer influence in the form of looking at Mitch (25% of the intervals) or laughing at him (16%), but these consequences are not as probable as teacher attention. There may also be a negative reinforcement component because Mitch is able to escape the task by lying and rolling on the floor. Given the short duration of the observation and the continuous nature of the task, analysis of the antecedents did not yield particularly helpful information in this case. Or did it? If you carefully examine the CPR, you will notice that the on-floor behavior did not initially begin until the teacher sat down at her desk after walking around the classroom. In addition, physical proximity of the teacher was an antecedent during 50% of the intervals in which on-floor behavior occurred. Each of the antecedent and consequent possibilities are easily verified through further observation and analysis.

THE FUNCTIONAL BEHAVIORAL ASSESSMENT OBSERVATION FORM

The FBAOF is an assessment procedure that involves directly observing and recording interfering behavior(s) and associated contextual variables. The FBAOF is typically used to record "behavioral episodes" or "behavioral incidents" involving a single interfering behavior. Each time that an interfering behavior occurs, the observer uses the FBAOF to record the following:

1. Date and time of day
2. Setting events (i.e., tasks, activities, locations, etc.)
3. Antecedents (i.e., specific environmental, social, instructional, or transitional events that appear to trigger the behavior)

CONDITIONAL PROBABILITY RECORD (CPR)

Student: _____

Date of Observation: _____ Observer: _____

Setting: _____ Time of Day: _____

Behavior 1: _____ Behavior 2: _____

	Antecedents			Target Behaviors		Consequences		
	Academic	Task	Teacher	Behavior 1	Behavior 2	Teacher	Peers	Academic
0:15								
0:30								
0:45								
1:00								
1:15								
1:30								
1:45								
2:00								
2:15								
2:30								
2:45								
3:00								
3:15								
3:30								
3:45								
4:00								
4:15								
4:30								
4:45								
5:00								

Any of the categories may be coded according to the observer's preferences or the data that currently exist but must remain consistent across observations. Indicate coding scheme here for each of the categories.

Codes:
Academic: Teacher:
Task: Peers:

FIGURE 7.3. Conditional Probability Record (CPR). From T. Steuart Watson and Mark W. Steege (2003). Copyright by The Guilford Press. Permission to photocopy this figure is granted to purchasers of this book for personal use only. See copyright page for details.

CONDITIONAL PROBABILITY RECORD (CPR)

Student: _Mitch Miles_

Date of Observation: _03-16-00_   Observer: _Steuart Watson_

Setting: _Regular Classroom_   Time of Day: _1:15–1:30_

Behavior 1: _Lying and/or rolling on floor_   Behavior 2: _Not Applicable_

	Antecedents			Target Behaviors		Consequences		
	Academic	Task	Teacher	Behavior 1	Behavior 2	Teacher	Peers	Academic
0:15	R	WS	W	—	—	W	Wk	Working
0:30	R	WS	W	—	—	W	Wk	Working
0:45	R	WS	W	—	—	W	Wk	Working
1:00	R	WS	Desk	—	—	Desk	Wk	Working
1:15	R	WS	Desk	√	—	Desk	L	Work stopped
1:30	R	WS	Desk	√	—	Desk	L & R	Work stopped
1:45	R	WS	Desk	√	—	VR	Wk	Work stopped
2:00	R	WS	Desk	√	—	VR	Look	Work stopped
2:15	R	WS	PP	√	—	PG	Wk	Work stopped
2:30	R	WS	PP	√	—	PG	Wk	Work restarted
2:45	R	WS	PP	—	—	PP	Wk	Working
3:00	R	WS	PP	—	—	PP	Wk	Working
3:15	R	WS	W	—	—	W	Wk	Working
3:30	R	WS	W	√	—	W	R	Work stopped
3:45	R	WS	W	√	—	VR	Look	Work stopped
4:00	R	WS	PP	√	—	VR	Wk	Work stopped
4:15	R	WS	PP	√	—	VR	Look	Work stopped
4:30	R	WS	PP	√	—	PG	Wk	Work stopped
4:45	R	WS	PP	√	—	PG	Wk	Work stopped
5:00	R	WS	PP	—	—	PG	Wk	Work restarted

Any of the categories may be coded according to the observer's preferences or the data that currently exist but must remain consistent across observations. Indicate coding scheme here for each of the categories.

Codes:

Academic: R = Reading   Teacher: W = walking around the classroom; PP = physical proximity to target student; VR = verbal reprimand; PG = physical guidance to target student; Desk = sitting at desk

Task: WS = Worksheets   Peers: Wk = working on task; L = laughing at target student; Look = looking at target student; R = reporting behavior of target student to teacher

FIGURE 7.4. Example of a completed Conditional Probability Record (CPR).

4. Behavior (i.e., the defined interfering behavior)
5. Consequence (i.e., the events that followed the interfering behavior)
6. Effect (i.e., change in rate/intensity of occurrence of the interfering behavior)
7. Staff (i.e., the staff person who recorded the data and/or the staff person working directly with the student)

Note: With the FBAOF the observer typically records and briefly describes the interfering behavior within the column labeled "Behavior." A variation of this method is to record both the behavior and the magnitude of the behavior (e.g., frequency, duration, intensity).

Figure 7.5 is a copy of a blank FBAOF.

Questions for the Observer to Consider When Using the FBAOF

Date and time: What was the date and time of the incident? How long did the behavior last?

Setting events: Where did the behavior occur? What tasks/activities was the person participating in? Who was interacting with the student?

Antecedents: What were the specific events that occurred immediately prior to the interfering behavior? What were the specific events that triggered the interfering behavior?

Behavior: What did the person do?

Consequence: What happened immediately after the behavior occurred? If relevant, what did peers or staff do after the behavior occurred?

Effect: What impact did the consequence have on the magnitude of the interfering behavior (e.g., frequency, duration, intensity)?

Staff: Who observed the behavior and recorded this information?

When one is using the FBAOF, it is important to differentiate between a "setting event" and an "antecedent." The setting event is the general situation in which the behavior occurred. The antecedent is the precipitating variable (i.e., the specific event that triggered the behavior). For more information on setting events, see Chapter 10.

It is also important to recognize that with some behaviors it may be very difficult to identify the antecedent. In these cases, the trigger may not be an environmental, social, instructional, or transitional event; rather the trigger may be an internally driven (or individual) variable. In these cases, the phrase "not observed" is recorded.

Example of the Use of the FBAOF

Figure 7.6 illustrates the use of the FBAOF to assess the verbal refusal/ argumentative behavior of a student with a learning disability over the span of 2 weeks. We first described verbal refusal/argumentative in behavioral terms, then asked staff to use the FBAOF each time that screaming behavior occurred. By recording the behavior and relevant contextual

FUNCTIONAL BEHAVIOR ASSESSMENT OBSERVATION FORM (FBAOF)

Setting–Antecedent–Behavior–Consequence–Effect

Student Name _____

Date/Time	Setting Events	Antecedent	Behavior	Consequence	Effect	Staff

FIGURE 7.5. Functional Behavioral Assessment Observation Form (FBAOF). Reprinted with permission from John F. Murphy Homes, Inc. From T. Steuart Watson and Mark W. Steege (2003). Copyright by The Guilford Press. Permission to photocopy this figure is granted to purchasers of this book for personal use only. See copyright page for details.

FUNCTIONAL BEHAVIOR ASSESSMENT OBSERVATION FORM (FBAOF)

Setting–Antecedent–Behavior–Consequence–Effect

Student Name *George Oppose*

Date/Time	Setting Events	Antecedent	Behavior	Consequence	Effect	Staff
3/29 9:50 am	Math class independent worksheets	George was asked to complete worksheet	Verbal refusal/ argued	Ignored George and I walked away	George calmed	TH
3/29 10:02 am	Math class independent worksheets	George was offered instructional support	Verbal refusal/ argued	Ignored George and I walked away	He calmed down	TH
3/30 9:55 am	Math class small group	I offered to assist George with instructional support	He refused and argued with me	Redirected George back to his desk to finish his work	George swore at me, shouted, and argued	TH
3/30 9:56 am	Math class small group	Redirected George to complete his work, task orientation prompt	He swore, argued, and shouted at me	Ignored George and I walked away	He calmed down in about 2 minutes	TH

FIGURE 7.6. Example of a completed Functional Behavioral Assessment Observation Form (FBAOF).

variables, we were able to identify events that appeared to trigger and reinforce the occurrence of verbal refusal/argumentative behaviors. Review of data sheets revealed that verbal refusal/argumentative behavior typically occurred within the contexts of academic tasks (e.g., math worksheets, writing assignments, etc.) and when the student was provided with either a task orientation prompt (i.e., "George, you need to finish your work") or an instructional prompt (i.e., instruction explaining the tasks or to correct an error). Thus, setting events were identified to be academic tasks and antecedents were both instructional and task orientation prompts. When verbal refusal/argumentative occurred, the educational technician who provided prompting responded by walking away. Thus, the consequence following verbal refusal/argumentative behavior was the termination of instructional/task orientation prompts. This typically resulted in an immediate cessation of verbal refusal/argumentative behavior. These findings supported the hypothesis that verbal refusal/argumentative behavior was motivated by negative reinforcement (i.e., verbal refusal/argumentative behavior was "escape motivated" and resulted in the avoidance or cessation of instructional/task orientation prompting).

THE INTERVAL RECORDING PROCEDURE

The IRP is a functional behavioral assessment procedure involving the direct observation and recording of interfering behavior(s) and associated contextual variables at the conclusion of prespecified intervals (usually 5, 10, or 15 minutes). The IRP is essentially a modified scatterplot assessment that goes beyond documenting the occurrence of interfering behavior within particular times of the day to:

- Identifying specific settings/activities/tasks in which interfering behavior occurs
- Recording the magnitude of appropriate behaviors
- Recording the magnitude of interfering behaviors
- Identifying corelationships among appropriate and interfering behaviors
- Identifying corelationships among different interfering behaviors
- Identifying relationships between specific staff and both appropriate and interfering behaviors

Designing the IRP involves the four steps discussed below.

Step 1: Designing Data-Recording Procedures

Identifying interfering and appropriate behaviors
Describing interfering and appropriate behaviors
Identifying and describing the behavior-recording procedure for each interfering and appropriate behavior (e.g., frequency, duration, intensity, and/or performance-based recording procedures)
Identifying intervals (we typically use 15-minute intervals)

Identifying the duration of data recording and the number of intervals (e.g., from 8:00 A.M. to 3:00 P.M.; 28 intervals)

Designing the data-recording form

> *Note 1:* We typically include a column that corresponds with each interval in which recorders document the specific tasks/activities in which the student was engaged or in which he/she was expected to participate (i.e., scheduled, planned, or expected tasks/activities) during the interval.
>
> *Note 2:* We typically include a column that corresponds with each interval in which recorders document the staff/teacher who interacted with the student during the interval.

Step 2: Staff Training

Accurate use of the IRP requires training staff/teachers to implement the procedure with precision. The data derived from implementation of the IRP are only as good as the persons who are collecting the data. If staff/teachers have never used this type of data-recording procedure, we have found the following training model to be very effective:

Review of the labels and descriptions of each target behavior

Review of the data-recording procedures for each target behavior

Role-play scenarios in which staff/teachers practice recording behaviors using the IRP

Supervised practice in the use of the IRP with the target student within naturally occurring situations

Establishment of interobserver agreement: simultaneous and independent recording using the IRP by a second observer

Monitoring of staff/teachers in their implementation of the IRP

Step 3: Implementing the IRP

Implementing the IRP requires that staff/teachers be committed to using this procedure. It is our experience that staff/teachers consistently use the IRP when they find it to be an *effective* and *efficient* process. The IRP is an effective process when it accurately records the occurrence of behaviors. It is an efficient process when it does not get in the way of providing direct services to students.

Step 4: Analyzing the Data

This is an incredibly important step. Simply collecting but not analyzing the data is comparable to:

- Going to a bookstore, searching for a compelling book, then bringing it home and never reading it *or*
- Building a sailboat, but never going to sea *or*

- Training for a marathon, but never running the race *or*
- Making an elaborate dinner, then not joining your friends and family during the feast *or . . .*

You get the idea. Obviously, we consider the analysis of data to be a critical and often rewarding part of the process.

Analyzing Antecedents Associated with Behaviors

This involves reviewing the data sheet for one specific recording period and looking for patterns of occurrence of behaviors related to:

Times of day
Specific tasks/activities
Relationships among target behaviors within intervals
Relationships among target behaviors across intervals
Staff/teachers

Analyzing Trends

This involves graphing the data collected across time (e.g., several days, weeks, or months) and looking for the increase or decrease of behavior across time. Make sure that all raw data are converted to rates (e.g., convert 18 occurrences of self-injury that occurred within 6 hours to 3 occurrences/hour). Graph the data and identify trends in the graphed data (e.g., increasing, decreasing).

Specific Uses of the IRP

As part of a problem-solving process, we have found the IRP to be extremely valuable as a data-recording procedure that can be used prior to, during, and after the implementation of an intervention to document the effectiveness of individualized programming:

Prior to intervention—baseline (documentation of behaviors prior to intervention)
During the intervention—objective documentation of behavior change
After the intervention—objective documentation of generalization and maintenance

We also use the IRP as part of our ongoing direct descriptive FBA process. Presently, we are providing psychological consultation services to several programs that have incorporated the IRP within individualized educational programs (IEPs) and individual program plans (IPPs) with persons with disabilities. In these cases, behavioral data are recorded on an ongoing basis. We have found that analyzing previously completed IRP data-recording forms is extremely valuable as part of the FBA process.

In those cases in which one is conducting an FBA and previously recorded data are either not available (i.e., no one has collected any data) or the data collected are not helpful in identifying contextual variables (e.g., frequency data only without any connection to time of day or task/activity), we typically recommend the use of the IRP. After training staff to use the IRP, we recommend the implementation of the procedure for a sufficient amount of time to allow for:

Documentation of current levels of occurrence of behaviors
Identification of contextual variables

Note: The use of the IRP as a form of direct descriptive assessment does not preclude the use of other forms of FBA. We typically use the IRP as one of our FBA procedures.
Figure 7.7 is a blank IRP data sheet.

Example of the Use of the IRP

The following case illustrates the use of the IRP with a student with Asperger's disorder who received special education services within a middle school program. Figure 7.8 shows the specific behaviors, their definitions, and recording procedures that were developed prior to implementing the IRP.

As you can see, seven behaviors, two appropriate and five interfering, were identified for observation and recording. *Active participation* (AP) behavior was selected as a measure of the student's overall level of engagement throughout the school day. *Initiating social interactions* (ISI) behavior was selected because this historically (i.e., baseline) occurred at very low rates. Both AP and ISI were behaviors that were targeted for improvement within the student's IEP. The remaining five interfering behaviors were identified through indirect FBA interviews and anecdotal observations.

Figure 7.9 depicts a completed IRP data sheet. These data showed that:

- AP varied throughout the school day
- High AP was associated with low levels of interfering behavior
- Low AP was associated with high levels of interfering behavior
- The daily rates/percentages of the target behaviors were as shown in the tabulation

Behaviors:	AP	Verb. Opp.	Nonverb. Opp.	Prop. Dest.	Verb. Agg.	Phys. Agg.	ISI
Rate or %:	66%	4.0/hour	13.2%	1.08/hour	1.70/hour	1 = 0.48/hour 2 = 0.64/hour 3 = 0.16/hour	S = 2.77/hour C = 0.61/hour

- Interfering behaviors occurred most frequently within small group, reading, and spelling
- Initiation of social interactions with staff were much higher than with classmates

The IRP is typically used over a span of several days or on an ongoing basis. Reviewing the data collected over a period of time provides very valuable information in identifying contextual variables and the corelationships among variables.

INTERVAL RECORDING PROCEDURE DATA SHEET

Time	Target Behaviors Recording Procedures Setting and/or activity											Staff
Add each column												
Convert to percent or rate												

FIGURE 7.7. Interval Recording Procedure data sheet. Reprinted with permission from John F. Murphy Homes, Inc. From T. Steuart Watson and Mark W. Steege (2003). Copyright by The Guilford Press. Permission to photocopy this figure is granted to purchasers of this book for personal use only. See copyright page for details.

Active Participation (AP): visual, verbal, motor on-task responding, engaged in the task activity

Recording Procedure: Performance-Based
0 = No AP
1 = 1″ to 2′59″ of AP
2 = 3′ to 5′59″ of AP
3 = 6′ to 8′59″ of AP
4 = 9′ to 11′59″ of AP
5 = 12′ to 15′ of AP

Verbal Opposition (Verb. Opp.): one or more of *verbal* refusal to: (a) participate in tasks/activities, (b) follow teacher directions, and (c) follow school rules

Recording Procedure: frequency of occurrence (record as discrete episodes when occurrences of verbal opposition are separated by 15″ of no verbal opposition)

Nonverbal Opposition (Nonverb. Opp.): one or more of laying on the floor, sitting in chair avoiding eye contact, walking away from staff when asked to (a) participate in tasks/activities, (b) follow directions, and (c) follow school rules. Note: a response latency of 30″ is typical, and nonverbal opposition is only recorded *after* 30″ of nonresponding to teacher/staff directions.

Recording Procedure: Duration (record the length of time of the occurrence of Nonverb. Opp.)

Property Destruction (Prop. Dest.): tearing, throwing and/or damaging own or others' property.

Recording Procedure: Frequency of occurrence (record as discrete episodes when occurrences of property destruction are separated by 15″ of no occurrence of property destruction.)

Verbal Agression (Verb. Agg.): verbal threats (e.g., "I'm going to hit you.")

Recording Procedure: frequency of occurrence (record as discrete events when occurrences of verbal aggression are separated by 15″ of no verbal aggression.)

Physical Aggression (Phys. Agg.): *physical* acts involving hitting, kicking, grabbing of others; spitting on others. These behaviors typically occur as a response set and are recorded as episodes.

Recording Procedure: frequency and intensity of episodes
1 = mild (any single behavior or set of behaviors lasting less than 10 seconds)
2 = moderate (any single behavior or set of behaviors lasting *less* than 1 minute)
3 = severe (any single behavior or set of behaviors lasting *more* than 1 minute)

Initiating Social Interactions (ISI): verbal interactions directed toward teachers or classmates (e.g., initiating "Good morning," requesting help, conversations)

Recording Procedure: frequency and person (i.e., staff or classmate)
S = occurrence of initiating social interaction with teacher/staff
C = occurrence of initiating social interaction with classmate

FIGURE 7.8. Interval Recording Procedure.

Time	Target Behaviors / Recording Procedures / Setting and/or activity	AP 0–5	Verbal Opp. frequency	Nonverb. Opp. duration	Prop. Dest. frequency	Verb. Agg. frequency	Phys. Agg. intensity 1, 2, 3	ISI frequency	Staff
8:30–8:45	arrival routine	5	O	O	O	O	O	s,s	MWS
8:45–9:00	breakfast	5	O	O	O	O	O	s,c	MWS
9:00–9:15	breakfast	5	O	O	O	O	O	s	MWS
9:15–9:30	small group—circle	3	III	3'30"	O	O	O	s	MWS
9:30–9:45	small group—circle	2	IIII	4'20"	1	1	1	O	MWS
9:45–10:00	Reading (DTT)*	1	II	30"	1	III	2	O	MWS
10:00–10:15	Reading (DTT)	O	II	14'30"	O	O	O	O	MWS
10:15–10:30	Break—snack	5	O	O	O	O	O	s	MWS
10:30–10:45	Break—ind. play	5	O	O	O	O	O	s,c,s	MWS
10:45–11:00	Math—DTT worksheets	3	I	O	1	O	1	O	MWS
11:00–11:15	Math—group	5	O	O	O	O	O	O	MWS
11:15–11:30	Math—group	5	O	O	O	O	O	O	MWS
11:30–11:45	Lunch—prep.	5	O	O	O	O	O	O	MWS
11:45–12:00	Lunch	5	O	O	O	O	O	s,c	TD
12:00–12:15	Brush teeth	5	O	O	O	O	O	s,s	TD
12:15–12:30	Recess	5	O	O	O	O	2	O	TD
12:30–12:45	Music	3	O	O	O	O	O	O	TD
12:45–1:00	Music	2	O	O	O	O	O	O	TD
1:00–1:15	Spelling worksheets	1	III	2'40"	II	IIII	2	O	TD
1:15–1:30	Spelling worksheets	O	II	12'00"	1	1	1	O	TD
1:30–1:45	Break—ind. play	5	O	O	O	O	O	O	TD
1:45–2:00	small group—coop play	2	II	O	1	1	O	O	TD
2:00–2:15	small group—coop play	1	O	O	O	O	2	s,c	TD
2:15–2:30	Reading (DTT)	3	1	30"	O	O	O	s,s	TD
2:30–2:45	Reading (DTT)	O	III	15'0"	O	O	3	s	TD
2:45–3:00	Prep. go home	5	O	O	O	O	O	s,s	TD
Add each column		86	25	51'30"	7	11			
Convert to percent or rate		86/130 66%	3.8/hour		1.08/hour	1.70/hour	#1's = 3.48 #2's = 4.69 #3's = 1.16	s = 2.77/hour c = 0.61/hour	

*DTT: discrete trial teaching sessions

FIGURE 7.9. Example of a completed Interval Recording Procedure data sheet.

COMPARING AND CONTRASTING THE FBAOF AND THE IRP

The FBAOF and IRP are both examples of direct descriptive FBA procedures. There are specific advantages and disadvantages of each:

- The FBAOF is definitely more efficient. The recordings are only made when interfering behavior occurs. In contrast, the IRP is used in an ongoing basis and, as such, requires the observer to record behaviors at the conclusion of each interval.
- The FBAOF requires some training, but generally folks are able to use this procedure accurately following verbal explanation, written explanation, and modeling. The IRP requires much more extensive training, particularly when observers are using performance-based recording procedures.
- The FBAOF, through the recording of specific antecedents and consequences associated with each occurrence of interfering behavior, provides more specific contextual data than the IRP.
- In contrast to the FBAOF, the IRP provides more information about the magnitude of each behavioral incident, the corelationships among specific variables, the situations in which interfering behavior does not occur, and occurrences and magnitude of appropriate behaviors
- Both the IRP and the FBAOF are useful as an ongoing measure of student behavior.
- The FBAOF is typically used to assess one behavior. A separated form is used for each behavior. The IRP allows for the collection of data for several behaviors on one form. Reviewing the form allows one to get a "snapshot" of the students performance throughout the school day.

Is one procedure better than another? Which should I use? In many cases we have used both procedures! Blending the results of both assessments tends to yield a rich source of data that enhances our understanding of the variables that influence the display of interfering behavior and the conditions in which we can provide positive behavioral supports.

Troubleshooting

If the results of the combination of indirect and direct descriptive FBA procedures are suspect or if the data-based intervention proves to be unsuccessful, then additional assessments may be recommended. But before we go there, let's consider a few factors that may have impacted the validity of the assessment–intervention continuum. At this point, we suggest considering the following questions:

- Did the interview address *all possible* variables (antecedents, individual, and consequences) that might influence the display of interfering behavior?
- Were there any sources of error in the assessment, such as those described in previous chapters, that may have contaminated the results?
- Was a solid conceptual framework based on behavioral principles used as the foundation for understanding behavioral functions?

- Was the intervention based on the results of the functional behavioral assessment?
- Was there consistency across assessment procedures in identifying antecedent, individual, and consequence variables?
- Was a collaborative problem-solving process used in the design of the intervention?
- Was there a systematic plan for evaluating the effectiveness of the intervention?
- Did the folks who were responsible for implementing the intervention:

  Have any input in the design of the intervention procedures?
  Have confidence in (i.e., "buy into") the efficacy of the intervention procedures?
  Implement the intervention with precision?

If there is a resounding "YES" (from most parts of the country), "AYYAHHH" or "YUP" (from the Mainers), "YOU BETCHA" (from the Midwesterners), or any other positive affirmation, then the team may very likely need to consider revisiting the indirect and direct descriptive FBA processes or conducting more formalized assessments. If the latter is the case, then this is where functional behavioral analysis procedures are typically recommended.

We want to make it clear that *functional behavioral analysis* methodologies are certainly indicated in some cases. Indeed, in our clinical work there are times when we use functional behavioral analysis procedures after we have conducted indirect and direct descriptive FBAs. For example, the case of Eric Trout (Chapter 9) includes several FBA procedures, including a functional behavioral analysis. However in this book we have made a conscious decision to emphasize indirect and direct descriptive FBA procedures for the following reasons:

- The vast majority of referral issues faced by school-based practitioners can be adequately addressed through indirect and direct descriptive FBA procedures.
- The level of description needed to accurately explain all of the complexities, pragmatics, procedural issues, and ethical issues related to conducting functional behavioral analyses is beyond the scope of this book.
- It has been our experience as faculty members who teach graduate-level courses covering FBA procedures that teaching functional behavioral analysis methodologies requires a combination of didactic and clinical instruction that includes (1) assigned readings, (2) lecture/discussion, (3) modeling, (4) role play, and (5) in vivo guided practice under the supervision of an experience behavior analyst.

In those situations in which functional behavioral analyses are called for and the school-based practitioner is not experienced or competent in conducting this level of assessment, we recommend the following:

- Refer the student to a professional who has training and experience enabling him/her to competently conduct functional behavioral analyses.
- Refer the student to a professional who has training and experience enabling him/

her to competently conduct functional behavioral analyses; the school-based practitioner should participate in the evaluation under his/her supervision.

SUMMARY

In this chapter we have described several direct descriptive FBA procedures. It has also been our experience that in most cases an assessment process that includes both indirect and direct descriptive FBA procedures is sufficient in assessing and understanding behavioral functions. Moreover, assessments based on this comprehensive blend of procedures usually leads to the development of effective interventions.

Following is a case example in which indirect and direct descriptive FBA procedures were used in the assessment of a student with an emotional disability. The example illustrates and explains the application of several of the assessment procedures that we often use in conducting FBAs. This case example is not intended to be an example of an FBA report (we offer those examples earlier in this chapter and in Chapters 8 and 9). Rather, the case of Dawn is offered to show how the integration of indirect and direct descriptive FBA processes result in a thorough understanding of the student's behaviors and their controlling variables.

CASE EXAMPLE: INDIRECT AND DIRECT DESCRIPTIVE FBA

Relevant Background Information

Dawn was a 9-year, 5-month-old third-grade student enrolled in a self-contained program for students with emotional disabilities. In the previous 4 years, psychological evaluations had been conducted on three occasions as part of comprehensive psychoeducational evaluations recommended by the multidisicplinary team. Referral issues included concerns/questions regarding the following: developmental delays, social skills delays, academic skills delays, and interfering behaviors (e.g., screaming and aggressive behaviors). The three psychological evaluations were conducted by three different school psychologists in May 1998, April 2000, and September, 2001. These evaluations included the following assessments:

1. Intellectual assessment (e.g., the Wechsler Intelligence Scale for Children, 3rd ed.)
2. Adaptive behavior assessment (e.g., the Scales of Independent Behavior—Revised)
3. Anecdotal observation (e.g., one 15-minute classroom-based observation)
4. Behavior rating scales (e.g., the Achenbach Teacher's Report Form)
5. Projective assessment (e.g., the House–Tree–Person Test, the Thematic Apperception Test, the Tasks of Emotional Development)

Additional assessments (e.g., norm-referenced achievement testing, speech/language evaluations, occupational therapy evaluations) were conducted by other members of the team.

Furthermore, psychiatric evaluations/consultations were conducted in June 2000 and September 2001.

Based on these evaluations, the following labels/diagnoses were offered:

1. Pervasive developmental disorder—not otherwise specified
2. Obsessive–compulsive disorder
3. Oppositional–defiant disorder
4. Mixed receptive–expressive language disorder
5. Autistic disorder (autism spectrum disorder)
6. Anxiety disorder

Critique of Previous Assessments

The previous psychological evaluations could be described as "traditional psychological assessments" and, as such, are typical of the school-based psychological evaluations that are routinely conducted by thousands of practitioners each year. These assessments were primarily norm referenced and, while providing valuable information about Dawn's current levels of functioning compared to other children of the same age, provided little useful information for developing interventions to address interfering behaviors. Although the psychological evaluations did a good job of documenting that Dawn had a "disability," confirmed that the interfering behaviors she exhibited were unusual for a child of that age, and determined that these interfering behaviors were disruptive to her acquisition of skills, this information was not particularly useful in designing individually tailored interventions. In fact, review of the psychological reports and Dawn's IEP revealed little if any direct connection between documents.

Current Disposition

The multidisciplinary team had convened meetings to review Dawn's case on nine occasions over the past 3 school years. Review of minutes of these meetings indicated that on several occasions Dawn's screaming behavior was described as "attention seeking" and as "self-stimulating." The team recommended the use of a "time-out" procedure to address screaming behavior. The team decided that if Dawn exhibited aggressive behavior toward classmates she should be sent home from school. The team also recommended the use of sensory integration techniques as a way of decreasing screaming and aggressive behaviors.

Although the team did not collect data on specific problem behaviors, it did record how many times Dawn had been sent home because of aggressive behaviors and the number of times that time-out had been used. During the first 10 weeks of the 2001–2002 school year, Dawn had been sent home on 12 occasions because of aggressive behavior and had been sent to the time-out area 24 times. The team frequently referred to Dawn's behavior as being "out of control" and reported that problem behaviors had increased in frequency, duration, and intensity.

In mid-November, a team meeting was held to review Dawn's case. During that meeting, Dawn's behaviors were discussed at length. Much of the discussion focused on what to do when Dawn screamed or became aggressive. A variety of interventions were proposed, including sensory diets, token economies, and the continued use of time-out, among others. The team also discussed the option of out-of-district residential placement to "address Dawn's severe behavioral, academic, and social/emotional needs." Dawn's parents objected to sending Dawn home and asked the school team to develop alternative interventions. At this point, the multidisciplinary team was asking for help: interfering behaviors were escalating, the interventions used by staff were not effective, and sending Dawn home was not acceptable. Dawn was referred for a comprehensive FBA. Because the school psychologist who regularly provided psychological services to students within the school program did not have training or experience in conducting FBAs, a referral for the evaluation was made to another psychologist within the district who did have a background in conducting FBAs with students with developmental disabilities.

Prior to initiating the FBA, the latter psychologist met with Dawn's family. During the meeting, Dawn's parents made several astute observations and asked some very good questions. For example, "Dawn has been evaluated by school psychologists three times already. She's been diagnosed to death. Do we really need another psych evaluation?" and "What do you plan to do that would be different from what the other folks did?" and "How will your assessments help us to help Dawn?" Read on and see how the school psychologist used the FBA process to address these question and concerns.

The FBA Process with Dawn

Step 1: Indirect Assessment

The initial phase of assessment was conducted through interview of the special education classroom teacher (Ms. Smith), special education technician (Ms. Jones), and Dawn's parents. The purposes of this interview were to:

1. Specify interfering behaviors that interfere with Dawn's acquisition and/or performance of academic, social, and daily living skills
2. Describe those behaviors in concrete terms
3. Identify antecedents or "triggers" of interfering behaviors (e.g., times of day, events, situations in which interfering behaviors typically occur)
4. Identify individual variables that are related to the occurrence of interfering behaviors (e.g., receptive language delays, health problems, academic skills)
5. Identify consequences that occur following interfering behaviors (e.g., social attention from classmates or staff, cessation of tasks, access to activities)
6. Identify reinforcers (e.g., tangibles, preferred activities, or social reinforcers)
7. Describe communication skills (e.g., expressive skills)

The interviews included the use of the following assessment procedures:

- The Functional Behavioral Assessment Screening Form (FBASF)
- The Antecedent Variables Assessment Form (AVAF)

- The Individual Variables Assessment Form (IVAF)
- The Consequence Variables Assessment Form (CVAF)
- The Behavioral Stream Interview (BSI)

RATIONALE

Conducting these interviews served several purposes:

- Information gained during the interviews resulted in the identification and description of each of the interfering behaviors.
- The information gained from conducting the initial interviews was useful in identifying those variables that *might be associated* with the occurrences of interfering behavior.
  Note: at this point of the assessment, the information gathered through interviews was considered to be preliminary data and functional relationships (cause–effect relationships) were hypothesized.
- The interview was also very useful in helping interviewees understand that interfering behavior is oftentimes situation specific. This shifted the focus from the student as being an "interfering child" (suggestive of intrapsychic determinants of behavior) to a model whereby behavior might be viewed as a result of what is oftentimes a complex set of *interacting* environmental and individual variables.
- As in most cases, direct observations of the referred student *followed* the behavioral interviews. The information gained from the interview was very helpful in determining:
  1. Which behaviors to observe and record
  2. What type of direct observation procedures to use (e.g., A-B-C, behavioral stream observations)
  3. What type of data-recording procedure to use (e.g., frequency, duration, interval, performance-based), and
  4. The settings in which to conduct the observations (e.g., reading, recess)

ASSESSMENT RESULTS

Identification and Description of Interfering Behaviors. The results of these assessments indicated that the interfering behaviors of concern were screaming and aggression. Screaming was defined as loud yelling of words or emitting screeching sounds (e.g., "EEEEEEEHHHHH"). Aggression was defined as hitting, kicking, biting, scratching, or gouging of others.

Antecedent Variables. Reported *triggers* of screaming were academic tasks, errors when completing tasks/assignments, physical contact initiated by others, and instructional feedback (particularly corrective feedback). Reported *triggers* of aggression were physical contact initiated by others.

Individual Variables. Reported individual variables associated with interfering behaviors were severe expressive language and social skills delays, sensitivity to touch from others, difficulty in accepting criticism or corrective feedback, and anxiety when in novel situations or when given feedback from teachers.

Consequence Variables. Reported consequence variables of screaming were cessation of instructional tasks and cessation of instructional feedback. Reported consequence variables of aggression were cessation of social interactions, particularly those that included physical contact.

During interviews with school staff and Dawn's parents, it was reported that aggressive behavior almost always occurred when others initiated physical contact. Moreover, aggression was typically part of a response chain that included screaming behavior. An example of a response chain is as follows:

Setting event: Dawn was in the self-contained classroom. The expectation was to complete an academic assignment. Dawn was off-task.
Antecedent: The educational technician used gesture and verbal prompts to redirect Dawn to task.
Behavior: Dawn engaged in screaming behavior
Consequence: The educational technician used gesture and verbal prompts to redirect Dawn to task.

In this example, the consequence (i.e., "The educational technician used gesture and verbal prompts to redirect Dawn to task") for the previous occurrence of screaming also serves as the *antecedent* for subsequent occurrences of screaming.

Antecedent: The educational technician used gesture and verbal prompts to redirect Dawn to task.
Behavior: Dawn engaged in screaming behavior.
Consequence: The educational technician directed Dawn to the time-out area. Time-out was used at this point because it was determined that Dawn's screaming behavior was disruptive to the other students within the classroom. The behavior management plan developed to address screaming behavior specified that time-out be used in these circumstances.

The time-out procedure was initiated with a verbal prompt of "Dawn, your screaming is bothering the other students. You need to go to time-out."

Antecedent: As with the previous consequence, this consequence of time-out also served as the antecedent to more screaming behavior.
Behavior: Dawn engaged in screaming behavior. She did not stand up from her chair to walk to the time-out area.

Consequence: The educational technician initiated the time-out with a verbal prompt of "Dawn, your screaming is bothering the other students. You need to go to time-out" *and* a physical prompt in which the educational technician placed her hand on Dawn's shoulder and attempted to physically guide her to stand.

As with the previous consequence, this consequence as served as the antecedent to more interfering behavior.

Antecedent: The educational technician initiated the time-out with a verbal prompt of "Dawn, your screaming is bothering the other students. You need to go to time-out" *and* a physical prompt in which the educational technician placed her hand on Dawn's shoulder and attempted to physically guide her to stand.

Behavior: Dawn engaged in screaming behaviors. She did not stand up from her chair to walk to the time-out area. Dawn also exhibited aggression (i.e., pushed, hit, and kicked the educational technician).

Consequence: The educational technician backed away. Essentially, she withdrew the verbal and physical prompts.

Antecedent: The educational technician withdrew the verbal and physical prompts to time-out.

Behavior: Dawn discontinued screaming and aggression behaviors. She picked up a book and opened it to a section featuring presidents of the United States.

Consequence: The educational technician monitored Dawn but did not interact with her.

In this example, a response chain was in place in which screaming and aggression occurred sequentially. Screaming behavior appears to be motivated by negative reinforcement (i.e., avoidance of instructional demands) and aggression appears to be motivated by negative reinforcement (i.e., avoidance of social/tactile demands). When two behaviors have the same function, they are said to be members of the same response class. The response class is determined by the function, as opposed to the topography, of behavior.

With Dawn, critical questions remained regarding the variables associated with aggression:

- Is physical contact with Dawn a predictor of aggression? In other words, would any physical contact, regardless of related events, result in aggression?

OR

- Does aggression only occur when physical contact is provided after an occurrence of screaming behavior?

OR

- Does Dawn exhibit aggression when physical contact is provided when she is engaged in preferred activities?

These questions were posed to members of the team. The answer was that aggression never occurred outside of physical contact provided in the context of a behavioral incident in which screaming was occurring. Therefore, it was hypothesized that aggression only occurred during situations in which tactile prompts were provided following an incident of screaming behavior.

Step 2: Direct Descriptive Assessment

Based on interviews with school staff, direct descriptive assessments were conducted to (1) document the occurrences of interfering behavior, (2) document and investigate possible functional relationships, and (3) record the current level of occurrence of interfering behaviors. The following procedures were used:

BEHAVIORAL STREAM OBSERVATION AND RECORDING

The school psychologist, observing Dawn within predetermined settings based on interviews with school staff, conducted this assessment. By discussing with the classroom teacher optimal times for observing Dawn within classroom settings in which interfering behavior typically occurred, the school psychologist was able to increase the probability of observing and recording interfering behaviors.

Behavioral stream observation and recording involved watching and keeping a record of behavioral incidents, as well as keeping track of the sequential flow of antecedents, behaviors, and consequences that constitute such a behavioral incident. Following are examples of descriptions of behavioral incidents using this procedure:

> *Example 1: Screaming.* Dawn was sitting at her desk completing a writing assignment ⟶ The educational technician approached Dawn and offered instructional support (i.e., corrective feedback regarding her writing sample) ⟶ Dawn screamed loudly ("EEEEHHHH!!!") ⟶ The educational technician quickly walked away ⟶ Dawn stopped screaming and returned to the writing task.
>
> *Example 2: Screaming.* Dawn was completing a reading assignment with teacher assistance ⟶ The teacher corrected her word substitution error ⟶ Dawn screamed ("EEHH") ⟶ The teacher provided a mild verbal reprimand ("No screaming, please") and pointed to the assignment ⟶ Dawn screamed louder and longer ("EEEEHHHH!!!") ⟶ The teacher discontinued instruction and offered to help another student ⟶ Dawn stopped screaming but did not return to task; she opened a book to pages of pictures of Abraham Lincoln (highly preferred activity).

Both of these examples of screaming support the hypothesis that screaming behavior is motivated by escape from academic demands and teacher corrective instruction. In addition, both examples point to another hypothesis, one that was not identified in the interview process; namely, that screaming behavior appears to also be related to access to tangible reinforcers (e.g., a book with pictures of Abraham Lincoln).

Aggressive behavior was not observed during the scheduled observation sessions. Because aggressive behaviors were not observed and to more fully evaluate screaming and aggressive behaviors, additional assessment procedures were implemented.

Note: It is not uncommon for the school psychologist to schedule an observation session and position him/herself within the classroom to observe and record specific behavior, only to find that the behaviors of concern did not occur at all during the observation session. In these cases, we recommend that the classroom teacher and/or educational technician observe and record the defined target behaviors. The following ongoing FBA procedure is one we have found to be very effective in the evaluation of interfering behaviors:

FUNCTIONAL BEHAVIORAL ASSESSMENT OBSERVATION FORM

This procedure involved the use of the FBAOF in which school staff recorded observed occurrences of aggressive and screaming behaviors on a form that included:

- The time of day
- Setting events (e.g., math, science, recess, small-group reading, staff)
- Antecedents (i.e., environmental triggers)
- Interfering behaviors
- Immediate consequences
- The effect that the consequences had on the frequency, duration, or intensity of the behavior
- The staff person who observed and recorded the behavioral incident

The FBAOF was used for 5 school days. Review of the completed FBAOFs involved analyzing each of the data-recording forms. Analysis involved review of the number of times that interfering behavior occurred and the variables that were associated with each occurrence of interfering behavior. The results of this analysis are as follows:

- Aggressive behaviors occurred 4 times
- Screaming behaviors occurred 68 times
- 94% of occurrences of screaming occurred within the context of academic situations

Note: the FBAOF did not consistently identify specific antecedents associated with screaming behaviors. However, 72% of occurrences of screaming behavior were related to direct instruction that included corrective feedback:

- 6% of occurrences of screaming occurred during nonacademic situations (e.g., lunch, recess, hallway).
- 97% of occurrences were followed by the discontinuation of teacher instructions or academic tasks/demands
- 100% of occurrences of aggression occurred within the context of academic pro-

gramming when Dawn was engaging in screaming behavior and when she was physically redirected; also, 100% of these behaviors were followed by the discontinuation of physical contact, teacher instruction, or academic expectations

Results

Indirect and direct descriptive FBA procedures were used to identify hypotheses about the variables that trigger and maintain interfering behaviors. The results of the FBA were used to generate the following hypotheses:

Hypothesis 1: Screaming behavior appears to be primarily motivated by negative reinforcement (i.e., "escape" from corrective instructional feedback).

Hypothesis 2: Screaming behavior appears to be secondarily motivated by positive reinforcement (i.e., access to preferred tangibles/activities).

Hypothesis 3: Aggressive behavior appears to be motivated by negative reinforcement (i.e., "escape" from physical redirection to a task following occurrences of screaming behavior).

Recommendations

Based on the results of the FBA, the school psychologist recommended the following interventions:

1. Given Dawn's reaction to physical prompts provided by staff, the use of physical prompting to redirect Dawn to a task is strongly discouraged.

2. Given that Dawn's screaming behavior typically occurs during academic situations in which she has received corrective instructional supports, the following suggestions are offered:

a. Teaching Dawn to use self-editing and self-monitoring strategies within academic tasks might well be an effective means of increasing accuracy in completion of assignments, thereby decreasing (and perhaps eliminating) corrective instructional feedback.

b. Functional communication training strategies might be employed that include teaching and reinforcing Dawn's use of appropriate language as a replacement for screaming behaviors. Because the function of screaming is "escape," teaching her to request a break, to request that the teacher not provide corrective feedback, or another functionally related response could be given consideration.

c. Differential reinforcement of other behavior (DRO) procedures might be used in which Dawn is reinforced (e.g., by opportunities to read picture books about presidents of the United States for several minutes, with tokens that later could be exchanged for preferred activity/tangible rewards or social reinforcement) for the nonoccurrence of screaming behaviors at prespecified intervals (e.g., 15 minutes, class periods).

3. The FBAOF might be used to monitor the occurrence of screaming behaviors and to evaluate the effectiveness of such interventions.

4. Direct behavioral consultation in the design, implementation, and evaluation of the effectiveness of a positive behavioral support plan incorporating the recommended interventions is suggested.

Final Case Disposition

The aforementioned intervention strategies were developed and implemented with Dawn. The interventions were a smashing success. To make a long story short, the implementation of the intervention package resulted in marked reductions in screaming and aggressive behaviors. In fact, within the first week of implementation of the intervention package, aggressive behaviors were eliminated! Screaming behaviors were reduced by 65% during the first week of implementation and occurred at very low rates thereafter. For example, by the end of the school year screaming behavior occurred three and four times during the months of April and May, respectively. Dawn's levels of academic engagement, appropriate social behaviors, work completion, and task accuracy also increased markedly.

8

Supporting Documentation

Two of the most frequently asked questions about the FBA process are "What type of documentation is needed?" and "How much documentation do I need?" In actual practice, the answer to both questions is that the type and extent of documentation that is needed depends upon the following factors:

- The complexity of the case
- The procedures used
- The likelihood of legal proceedings arising out of the FBA
- School district policies and procedures
- State department of education requirements
- What is generally considered to be best practice in the field

It is far beyond the scope of this book to review and critique typical school district policies and procedures that relate to FBAs and individual state departments of education requirements. Instead, it is our hope that after reading this book the practitioner will be able to judge for him/herself the adequacy of the procedures his/her particular district has in place. Therefore, we will limit our discussion of supporting documentation to the first three and last bullets from the list above.

COMPONENTS OF A FUNCTIONAL BEHAVIORAL ASSESSMENT REPORT

At a minimum, the FBA report should include the following:

- Identifying information (e.g., name, age, school/agency, date of report)
- Reason for referral
- Assessment procedures
- Assessment results
- Identification of interfering behaviors

- Description of interfering behaviors
- Current level of occurrence of interfering behaviors
- Identification of antecedent variables (or "triggers")
- Identification of individual variables
- Identification of consequence variables
- Hypothesized function(s) of interfering behaviors
- Examples that illustrate how antecedent, individual, and consequence variables influence the occurrence of interfering behaviors
- Considerations (or recommendations)

The FBA report might also include the following:

- *Survey of reinforcers:* identification of variables that serve to reinforce behaviors
- *Behavioral deficits:* identification of behaviors or skills that the student needs to learn or needs to perform consistently
- *Implementation and evaluation of recommended intervention(s):* description, implementation, and evaluation of interventions that are based on the FBA results

FUNCTIONAL BEHAVIORAL ASSESSMENT DOCUMENTATION FORM

One basic requirement for *all* FBAs is that there must be in place one form that captures important details such as the date on which the FBA was initiated, the procedures utilized, the date on which the FBA was completed, and the outcome of the FBA. In essence, this form should serve as a cover sheet for a student's FBA file. It is not meant to replace a written FBA report; rather, it is a means by which to summarize and provide easy access to the most salient information for a particular student. We have included one in Figure 8.1 to serve as a sample documentation form that we use. This is not meant to be a perfect example of an FBA documentation form. Instead, it is offered as a model for those wishing to construct their own form.

FUNCTIONAL BEHAVIORAL ASSESSMENT REPORT— BRIEF VERSION

The length of the FBA report depends upon two primary factors: (1) the complexity of the case and hence the various procedures actually used in the FBA, and (2) the likelihood that a legal proceeding will arise out of the case. In the brief version of an FBA report, the main thrust is on giving overviews of information rather than in-depth findings of each procedure. The following report is just one example of a brief FBA report. To assist the reader with writing FBA reports, we have double-columned this section to provide supporting rationale for the information included in the report as well as the implications for the FBA.

Student Name _____   School _____

Grade _____   Teacher _____

Date Referred for FBA _____   Referred by _____

Operational Definition of Target Behavior(s)

1 _____

2 _____

Operational Definition of Replacement Behavior(s)

1 _____

2 _____

Date FBA Initiated _____

Date FBA Procedures Completed

Record Review _____   Parent Interview _____

Teacher Interview _____   Student Interview _____

Functional Behavioral Assessment

    Screening Form _____   Behavioral Stream Interview _____

Antecedent Variables Assessment Form _____   Individual Variables Assessment Form _____

Consequence Variables Assessment Form _____   A-B-C Observation _____

Task Difficulty Antecedent Analysis Form _____   Conditional Probability Record _____

Functional Behavioral Assessment

    Observation Form _____   Interval Recording Procedure _____

Other _____

Date FBA Completed _____

Hypothesized Function(s) of Behavior(s) _____

_____

_____

Date Team Meeting Held to Discuss FBA Results _____

Date FBA Report Written _____

Date Positive Behavior Intervention Plan Written _____

Date Behavior Plan Implemented _____   Follow-Up Dates _____

Final Disposition of Referral (Describe) _____

_____

FIGURE 8.1. Functional Behavioral Assessment Documentation Form. From T. Steuart Watson and Mark W. Steege (2003). Copyright by The Guilford Press. Permission to photocopy this figure is granted to purchasers of this book for personal use only. See copyright page for details.

EXAMPLE 1: FUNCTIONAL BEHAVIORAL ASSESSMENT REPORT

Identifying Information

Student: Ward Cleaver
Date of Report: 10-05-01
Date of Birth: 06-14-93
Age: 8 years, 3 months
School: Beecher Elementary
Grade: 3
Teacher: Teresa King

This part of the report is very straightforward and may include as much demographic and descriptive information as is required by the district and/or state department.

Reason for Referral

Ward was referred to the building-level teacher support team for an FBA by his classroom teacher because of his repeated verbal outbursts in class. Verbal outbursts were subsequently defined as "screaming and yelling at the teacher that may or may not include inappropriate language and physical threats."

Because this is a brief report, there is no need to provide extremely detailed information regarding the initial referral. An operational definition of "verbal outbursts" should also be included at this point.

Assessment Procedures

Record review
Teacher interview using the FAIR-T
Parent interview using the FAIR-P
Direct behavioral observations in classroom
Task difficulty analysis
Curriculum-based assessments

Although you may choose to list the assessment procedures in alphabetical order, we prefer to list them in the order they were completed. Doing so allows the reader to see the flow of the FBA process. Under "direct behavioral observations," you may also list the actual forms that were completed during the observation (e.g., Conditional Probability Record, Interval Recording Procedure) and the specific settings in which the observations were conducted.

Assessment Results

Ward's *record review* indicated a history of low grades across multiple academic areas and low standardized test scores in reading, math, and language arts. In addition, his disciplinary reports indicate that he has been sent to the principal on numerous occasions for disrupting class. Both the *teacher* and *parent interviews* indicated that Ward was defiant and verbally abusive when tasks were assigned to him, particularly tasks that were difficult. Ms. King

Beginning with the record review, the school psychologist should begin constructing hypotheses about the possible function of the behavior as well as identifying potential antecedent stimuli. In this example, the record review indicated that Ward's academic skills might be suspect given his low grades and poor standardized test performance (a possible antecedent condition). The disciplinary data also indicated that he was frequently removed also indicated that if she reminded him to "get to work" or to "get busy," he often yelled at her and used inappropriate language. Ms. King reported that her typical response to Ward's verbal outbursts were to either ignore him, send him to stand in the hall, or send him to the principal's office. She has also contacted his parents on several occasions to pick him up from school for being particularly disruptive.

Direct behavioral observations confirmed the interview data in that, when academic tasks were presented to Ward, he screamed loudly at Ms. King, called her names, and threatened to hit her. A conditional probability analysis indicated that his verbal outbursts occurred 88% of the time when he was presented with an academic assignment and never when given a behavioral request (e.g., clean up around your desk, put the art materials back in the drawer).

Curriculum-based probes were administered for reading, math, and spelling. Ward was found to be lacking skills in each of these areas. For instance, his instructional reading level was first grade and he was able to add only 1-digit-by-1-digit problems. His spelling was also at a first-grade level.

from his classroom or school contingent upon the verbal outbursts (a possible negatively reinforcing consequence). An important piece of information obtained from the interviews is that both the parents and teachers believed that he was defiant when difficult tasks were presented. This information, along with the data from the record review, has profound implications for planning the remainder of the FBA.

The information gleaned from the observation further strengthened the potential relationship between academic tasks and verbal outbursts. A very strong relationship was observed and documented with the conditional probability analysis between academic demands and verbal outbursts.

Given that his verbal outbursts were observed to occur only when Ward was presented with an academic task and it was his teacher's impression that only difficult academic tasks preceded verbal outbursts, a task difficulty analysis needed to be conducted. This type of analysis may be described as a *structural analysis* because the emphasis is on identifying antecedent stimuli that reliably evoke the problematic behavior. Before the structural analysis could be conducted, however, a curriculum-based assessment needed to be done to identify the academic materials to be used in the analysis. The analysis was then conducted by having the teacher systematically provide Ward with either difficult assignments or easy assignments and the school psychologist recording his behavior. Based on the results from the curriculum-based assessment, those tasks were selected that Ward demonstrated he could complete (easy tasks) and he could not (difficult tasks). These were then used in the task difficulty analysis. The data from the structural analysis are very consistent with the data obtained from the other methods in that a reliable antecedent for Ward's verbal outbursts is difficult academic material. Although a consequence analysis has not been conducted, it appears from the existing data that the function of Ward's verbal outbursts is escape/avoidance. That is, contingent upon his outbursts, Ward's teacher engages in behavior that allows him to either escape or avoid having to do the academic task. At this point, the school psychologist has two options: (1) conduct a brief experimental analysis to confirm the hypothesis that escape/avoidance is indeed the function of his outbursts, or (2) stop here and design a treatment plan based on the data collected thus far.

Hypothesized Function of Behavior

Based on information gathered during this FBA, it appears that Ward's verbal outbursts are triggered by being presented with academic tasks that exceed his skills and are maintained by negative reinforcement (i.e., *escape/avoidance* of these tasks).

The title of this subsection begins with "Hypothesized" because a functional analysis was not done to demonstrate a causal relationship and to acknowledge that the function might not be stable over time and/or circumstances. Note that the trigger or antecedent variables were mentioned as well because of their strong relationship to treatment planning.

Positive Behavior Support Plans

1. Remedial instruction will need to be provided in the areas of reading, math, and spelling to improve Ward's skill in each of these areas.
2. Academic tasks that are consistent with Ward's instructional level should be provided by Ms. King instead of academic tasks that are too difficult for Ward at this time.

3. Ward should not be sent to the principal's office or be sent home when he exhibits a verbal outburst. Instead, Ms. King should wait until his verbal outburst is finished and then calmly re-present the academic task. If he exhibits another verbal outburst, then he may be removed, along with his task, to a quiet room to complete the task. The major point to remember here is to not

The first two recommendations acknowledge Ward's lack of basic skills in each of these areas and the results of the functional behavioral assessment that indicated difficult tasks as an antecedent for the target behaviors. Further assessment may need to be completed in these areas including error analysis of the previously administered CBM probes and an academic functional behavioral assessment (see Witt & Beck, 1999).

Recommendation 3 is derived from the results of the functional behavioral assessment that indicate *escape/avoidance* to be the primary function of Ward's target behaviors. The recommended procedures are called *escape extinction* (not allowing him to escape the academic task; recommendation 3) and *differential reinforcement of incompatible behavior* (allowing him to take a brief break when he allow him to escape the task when he exhibits verbal outbursts.

4. When Ward completes academic tasks, he should be allowed to take a short break (i.e., 5 minutes) to engage in a more preferred task that is acceptable to his teacher and does not cause disruption in the class.

5. The difficulty of academic assignments should be gradually increased as Ward becomes more skilled in each of the subjects. The indicator of moving too rapidly will probably be an escalation in Ward's inappropriate behaviors.

6. Data should continue to be collected on each of Ward's inappropriate behaviors to determine if the support plan is effective or if modifications are needed.

finishes his work without incident; recommendation 4).

Teachers and parents often express concern when someone recommends that easier academic assignment be given, even if only for a short while. Thus, this recommendation is offered to show that our goal is not only to reduce Ward's inappropriate behaviors but to increase his academic proficiency as well. This recommendation satisfies part of the IDEA that says a positive behavior support plan must have documentation to show that a plan has been implemented and that modifications have been made if the plan was not effective.

EXAMPLE 2: FUNCTIONAL BEHAVIORAL ASSESSMENT REPORT

Student: Hal
Age: 6–0
Date of Birth: 07/19/96
Grade: 1
School: Tyler Elementary School
Dates of Evaluation: April 10 and 17, 2002
Report Date: April 30, 2002

Reason for Referral

Hal was referred for psychological evolution by the Tyler Elementary School pupil evaluation team (PET). The PET requested an FBA addressing concerns regarding behaviors that Hal was exhibiting within the school setting.

Assessment Procedures

Indirect FBA

- The Functional Behavioral Assessment Screening Form (FBASF)
- The Antecedent Variables Assessment Form (AVAF)
- The Individual Variables Assessment Form (IVAF)
- The Consequence Variables Assessment Form (CVAF)
- The Behavioral Stream Interview (BSI)

Direct Descriptive FBA

- Anecdotal observation
- The Functional Behavioral Assessment Observation Form (FBAOF)
- The Interval Recording Procedure (IRP)
- The Conditional Probability Record (CPR)

Assessment Results

The results of indirect and direct descriptive FBA indicated that Hal exhibited the following interfering behavior:

Screaming:

- Screaming is vocalizations of "EEE" in isolation or paired with other vowels with each incident (or "episode") separated by 10 or more seconds.
- Current level of occurrence (frequency recording procedure): 37.8 occurrences per day

Antecedent variables (or "triggers") associated with screaming:

- Transition to and from tasks/activities
- Unstructured times/activities (e.g., free play, walks, community outings)
- Brief pauses during instructional activities (e.g., staff preparing materials for next activity, staff recording data)

Individual variables associated with screaming:

- Mood (e.g., increased arousal such as when happy or excited but never when angry or upset)
- Hal's display of stereotyped motor movements often occur prior to the occurrence of screaming (e.g., combinations of pacing, jumping, and turning; shaking and tilting of head from side to side repeatedly)

Consequence variables that appear to reinforce screaming:

- Sensory induction (i.e., auditory stimulation)
- Sensory reduction (i.e., arousal reduction)

Hypothesized function(s) of screaming behavior:

- Automatic positive reinforcement (arousal induction)—*Example:* When Hal is engaged in an instructional activity and the teacher pauses to select another teaching task, Hal exhibits screaming behavior. *Example:* During unstructured leisure situations, Hal exhibits screaming behaviors.
- Automatic negative reinforcement (arousal reduction)—*Example:* When Hal appears to be very excited, he often exhibits screaming behavior.

Considerations for the PET

1. The following suggestions are offered as strategies to decrease the probability of the occurrence of screaming that occurs during transition and unstructured situations:

- Increase fluency in the delivery of instructional activities, thereby decreasing unstructured time within instructional sessions
- Gradually introduce incidental teaching and generalization probes of skills acquired during discrete trial teaching sessions during unstructured and transition activities
- Use a picture/symbol activity schedule during transitions within and between tasks/activities to inform Hal of upcoming events and to provide opportunities for increased participation during unstructured situations.

2. When Hal exhibits screaming behavior the following strategies are suggested:

- Planned ignoring of Hal's screaming behavior
- Redirection of Hal to planned structured activities and/or the picture/symbol activity schedule
- Reinforcement of his participation in structured activities

3. Functional communication training (FCT) procedures are suggested. FCT involves teaching Hal functional language skills as a replacement for screaming behavior. For example, this could include modeling "I'm happy," "This is fun," or "I'm excited" when Hal exhibits screaming behavior during unstructured activities/transitions. Reinforce Hal's approximations of verbal responses. *Note:* Consultation with the speech pathologist regarding appropriate communication interventions is recommended.

4. Continued implementation of the IRP as a way of documenting the occurrence of screaming behavior and as an ongoing FBA is supported. The IRP might also be used to record appropriate behaviors.

5. Behavioral consultation in the design, implementation, and evaluation of positive behavioral support interventions is offered.

Terry Longsleeves
School Psychologist

EXAMPLE 3: FUNCTIONAL BEHAVIORAL ASSESSMENT REPORT

Identifying Information

Name: Larry White
Parents' Names: Carter and Emily White
Age: 6.5
Date of Birth: 03/17/93
Grade: 1
School: Percy Park Elementary School, Percy, MS
Date of Report: October 14, 1999

Referral Information

Larry was referred by Dr. Letsmakea Deal of the Percy School District because of concerns regarding his physically aggressive and verbal threatening behaviors that are currently occurring at school. Dr. Deal requested assistance with behavioral programming and with determining if his behaviors are related to any of his diagnosed disabilities.

Methods of Functional Behavioral Assessment

Child interview   Record review
Parent interview   Direct behavioral observation
Teacher interview   Review of behavior logs/discipline reports

Results of Functional Behavioral Assessment

Although a large amount of information was obtained during each of the procedures listed above, only information that is pertinent for either the FBA or behavioral programming is provided.

Parent Interview

Larry's parents were interviewed at the Counseling and School Psychology Lab on the campus of Mississippi State University on September 20, 1999, for 2.5 hours. They both acknowledged that they are well aware of Larry's propensity for both verbal and physical aggression. The aggressive behavior started around age 4 and was directed toward other children and Larry's teacher. Because of his aggressive behavior, Larry was dismissed from five preschools. He began kindergarten in Harrison County, MS, at age 5, and continued to evidence "aggressive outbursts" and threatened to shoot the principal. Despite these behaviors, Mr. and Mrs. White indicated that the school worked closely with Larry and provided a "nurturing environment" which led them to view his initial school experience as positive. They reported that when he became upset, he was allowed to leave the classroom and go talk to the principal. According to the Whites, this resulted in a gradual decrease in Larry's outbursts.

During December 1998, Larry and his family moved to Percy, MS. Upon entering Percy Park Elementary School to finish his kindergarten year, his parents noted that his aggressive outbursts increased once again. They also noted that the school had difficulty in dealing with his behavior. He is currently in a first-grade class and is evidencing frequent and intense verbally and physically aggressive behaviors. He has been suspended several times thus far this year for his behavior. Sometimes, contingent upon verbal or physical aggression, he is removed to a "quiet room" where he is allowed to calm down before returning to class. The Whites indicated that he is more likely to aggress when someone either interrupts his work or provides correction while he is working. They also indicated that being physically touched when he is angry only exacerbates his aggression.

His parents noted that Larry has a hypersensitivity to textures including certain types of clothes, hard surfaces, and hard or crusty foods. At age 4 they began to notice both vocal and motor tics, which led to him being diagnosed as having Gilles de la Tourette's syndrome. He is also diagnosed with attention-deficit/hyperactivity disorder (ADHD) and obsessive–compulsive disorder (OCD). Larry is currently on Luvox (25 mg/day) and Depakote (375 mg/day).

Larry's parents indicated that he continues having difficulty with sleeping, which may impact his school behavior. They noted that he did not begin sleeping completely through the night until 30–36 months of age and that he still does not sleep restfully. He grinds his teeth while asleep and is groggy upon awakening.

Record Review

Leonard Spock, PhD, indicated in a report dated February 2, 1999, that Larry required a 504 plan to address his behavioral and emotional issues. He attributed Larry's sensitivity to criticism and difficulty in adapting to doing things in different ways to his OCD. He recommended adapting the environment to meet some of Larry's sensitivities (e.g., time-outs on a carpeted step versus a wooden chair), offering choices, assigning responsibilities, and avoiding direct criticism. When Larry becomes agitated, Dr. Spock recommended that he be given some method to release his "pent-up anxiety." He also recommended some type of reward system for work.

In a report dated May 6, 1999, Lester Pyle, MD, noted that Larry displayed the following symptoms: aggressive outbursts, hyperactivity, poor school performance, repetitive object counting, biting, fighting, motor tics, throwing objects, yelling, fits of rage, and hitting teachers and other students. He further indicated that Larry posed a long-term risk to himself and others and that he needed a highly structured, closely supervised educational environment that has few students and a high teacher–student ratio. At that time, Larry was taking Prozac, Depakote, and Risperdal.

Glenn Closely, MD, indicated in a report dated August 15, 1999 that, due to his Gilles de la Tourette's syndrome, Larry will sometimes blurt out words over which he has no control. She also attributed his desire for perfection, aversion to being touched when angry, and aversion to certain textures as being related to his OCD. She recommended that adults back off when he is angry, allow him a chance to verbalize his observation of the conflict, and then perhaps draw a picture of his feelings and write out how he feels.

Review of Behavior Logs/Discipline Reports

In examining the behavior logs provided by the school, it is apparent that Larry has had a number of problems since beginning first grade. Instead of recounting these incidents in this report, the information will be reframed using an A-B-C format that is consistent with a descriptive functional behavioral assessment.

Date	Antecedent	Behavior	Consequence
8/16/99	Head-down time	Larry talked about breaking desk: "I can break this desk, you know."	Teacher talked to him to try to get him to lay his head down.
		"I am going to bring my shotgun and kill you. I can, you know." "I'm going to beat your butt."	Teacher told him he would have to put his name on the pad.
		Larry growled.	Teacher told him he had a check beside his name.
		Larry continued making threats.	Teacher told him they were going to the office.
	Teacher took him by the hand to go to the office.	Larry kicked the teacher.	Teacher took him to the office and Mrs. Smith was called.

Date	Antecedent	Behavior	Consequence
8/18/99	Music/PE	Larry refused to participate.	Teacher asked him if he wanted to talk about it.
		Larry growled	Teacher took him outside to talk and gave him a hug.
8/20/99	In line at the water fountain	Larry threatened students from another class.	Teacher asked him if he needed to talk about it.
		Larry held his breath.	Teacher blew into his face.
		Larry almost started crying.	Mrs. Nyberg hugged him.
8/23/99	Handwriting worksheet Repeatedly writing Larry on his paper	Teacher reminded him to write his complete name before going to the next line.	Larry told her that he was going to write all of his "Larrys" before writing his last name.
	Teacher told him to write his complete name in a row.	He said he knew how to write his name.	Teacher said that was wonderful.
	Teacher restated the request for him to write his whole name.	Larry raised his pencil like a shotgun.	Teacher knelt beside him and asked if he needed to go to the hall to talk and calm down.
		Larry moved the pencil closer to the teacher.	Teacher told him to go to the hall.
		Larry got up and walked toward the door.	Teacher told him to give her the pencil.
		Larry threw down the pencil and left the room.	Teacher talked to him for a couple of minutes.
		Larry verbally threatened the teacher.	Teacher carried him to the principal's office.
8/25/99	Writing numbers 1–10	Larry stated that he did not have to do it that way.	Teacher asked him if he needed to go to the hall to talk.
	Teacher reminded the class to write numbers consecutively.	Larry began to crumple his paper.	Teacher went to get Mrs. Smith.
8/26/99	Writing station	Larry started drawing instead of writing.	Teacher reminded him not to draw.
	Teacher helped him form a sentence and prompted him to write it.	Larry said that he did not want to write.	Teacher gave a prompt to write.

Date	Antecedent	**B**ehavior	Consequence
		Larry growled.	Teacher asked him if he needed to go to the hall and talk and calm down.
		He growled again and broke his pencil in the teacher's face.	Teacher called Mrs. Maxwell to come to the room.
	Mrs. Maxwell told him that he needed to come with her.	Larry would not get up.	She warned him that if he did not get up, she would carry him to the office.
	Mrs. Maxwell took him by the hands.	Larry kicked her.	Mrs. Maxwell removed him from class.
	Mrs. Maxwell let go of his hands and attempted to talk to Larry.	Larry began swinging at her and hitting her.	Mrs. Maxwell took him to the office.
8/31/99	Larry was playing on the tower in the playground; another child tried to get on.	Larry told her "No" and blocked her.	The child moved Larry's hand.
		Larry punched her in the nose.	Teacher told him to come down and talk about what happened.
9/1/99	Larry was in the cafeteria; teacher on duty gave a sticker to a child sitting beside Larry.	Larry swung at the teacher and said he could knock her butt off.	Larry was removed from the cafeteria to the office; teacher told him that could go back to the classroom if he apologized.
9/13/99	From behavior log checklist	Larry said the worksheet was boring and not fun.	Larry was removed from class for 15 minutes.
9/14/99	From behavior log checklist	Larry hit the teacher and attempted to harm himself with scissors.	He was removed to the quiet room for the remainder of the day.

Teacher Interview

Mrs. Kotter, Larry's classroom teacher, was interviewed by phone on September 30, 1999. She noted that his behavior problems seem to occur more frequently when he is working on or has been assigned a task that involves paper and pencil. The following sequence, as related by Mrs. Kotter, is one that is typical of Larry's behavior and is used here as only one example to illustrate a behavioral chain:

Antecedent	Behavior	Consequence
Teacher tells Larry, "I need you to write this sentence," or when he has to copy from the board or color, or he has to generate an idea and write it, or has to finish a sheet to do an activity	Larry lays head down on desk, throws paper on the floor.	Teacher allows him to lay his head down or verbally encourages him to do his work.
	Larry slides desk around, bounces desk, yells out, verbally threatens.	Teacher tells him he can either do his work or his name will be written on the pad.
	Verbal threats increase.	He is removed from the classroom.

Direct Behavioral Observation

Larry was observed in his classroom by two separate observers, Wanda Hemp and Dr. Mike Richards, on October 5, 1999. During one part of the observation in which the class was transitioning to reading at their desk, Larry was observed to be out of his seat during 75% of the intervals. (*Note:* a 15-second partial interval recording procedure was used.) During those intervals in which he was out of his seat, 50% of those resulted in either teacher or aide verbal attention. Thus, the probability that Larry received attention for engaging in out-of-seat behavior was .50. At the end of this observation, he began scooting his desk around the back of the room. This evoked a good deal of verbal attention from both the teacher and the aide.

The next observation began during a snack period in which Larry sat quietly and was out of his seat only 16% of the intervals. He did not call out or disturb anyone during snack time. The remainder of this observation occurred during a math worksheet assignment. Larry was off-task during 45% of the intervals. Thus, he was on-task for 55% of the intervals. Most of his off-task behavior involved looking around the room or laying his head down on his desk. When Larry was off-task, the teacher/aide attended to him during 30% of those intervals. Conversely, when he was on-task, they attended to him during 6% of the intervals.

An A-B-C log was also completed during the classroom observations. These are summarized below:

Antecedent	Behavior	Consequence
Teacher told him to throw his trash in the trash can.	Larry threw his trash in the trash can.	
Aide gave him a direction.	Larry looked down.	Aide walked away.
Aide gave him a direction.	Larry looked away.	Aide returned to her desk.
Teacher said, "I am going to count to 2 and then I am going to write your name on the pad if you are not facing forward."	Larry sat with his back to the teacher.	Teacher continued with the lesson.

Antecedent	**B**ehavior	**C**onsequence
Teacher told Larry to return his desk to the proper place.	Larry put his head on his desk.	Larry got his snack and a piece of art paper from the teacher.
Larry was doing written work at his seat.	Larry made several negative comments.	Teacher told him that he could do the work.
A classmate walked by his desk.	Larry growled.	Teacher told him not to growl.

An interesting behavioral sequence occurred in which Larry was leaning out of his desk; the teacher told him to get in his seat; he then said, "I have an idea"; the teacher said, "I don't want to know what it is"; to which Larry replied, "I'm going to kill you," and the teacher responded by saying, "That's enough." Apart from the formal observations in which data were recorded for specific behaviors, other interactions were also noted. For instance, Larry was extremely quiet and compliant while drawing and coloring during snack time. In the afternoon, the teacher was reading to the class. Larry was extremely still and quiet during this time, even more so than most of his classmates. Larry was also attentive and behaved appropriately during a large-group instructional period where the teacher was doing a lesson on patterns at the board and calling on various children to come to the board and point to the correct answer.

Child Interview

Larry was interviewed on October 5, 1999 for the purpose of conducting a reinforcer preference assessment. A preference assessment is considered to be essential when designing a school-based intervention where reinforcement strategies will be used to increase appropriate behaviors. Eighteen items/events to be used in the preference assessment were gleaned from interviews with Larry's teacher, teacher aide, principal, and parents. Each of the 18 items were paired with each other and presented to Larry in a forced-choice format. The results of the assessment are as follows, with higher numbers indicating stronger preference:

1.	Popsicle	15
2.	Play a game for 5 minutes with Mrs. Maxwell	15
3.	Play a game for 5 minutes with Mrs. Kotter	13
4.	5 minutes of outside play	13
5.	Being read to for 5 minutes by Mrs. Meadows	11
6.	Play a game for 5 minutes with Mrs. Meadows	10
7.	Be the classroom helper	10
8.	Listen to music for 5 minutes	10
9.	Two stickers	9
10.	1 piece of candy	9
11.	Being read to for 5 minutes by Mrs. Smith	7
12.	5 minutes of computer time	7
13.	Being read to for 5 minutes by Mrs. Wiggins	6
14.	Break from work for 5 minutes	5
15.	Talk with Mrs. Maxwell for 5 minutes	5
16.	Being read to for 5 minutes by Mrs. Kotter	4
17.	5 minutes of drawing/coloring	4

Determination of Function

Based on the information presented here, including historical data (from behavior logs/discipline reports), anecdotal data (from interviews), and direct observation data, it appears that the primary function(s) of Larry's aggressive behaviors are *attention* and *escape*. Further, it appears that the primary function of his verbally aggressive/inappropriate behavior is attention, while escape seems to be the primary variable maintaining physically aggressive behavior. However, it is likely that both attention and escape are functional for verbal and physical aggression. In other words, Larry uses inappropriate language primarily because adults in his environment respond quickly and reliably when he does so. He physically aggresses primarily because doing so results in the cessation of an unpleasant task (e.g., a paper–pencil task) or removal from an aversive situation (e.g., the classroom). In addition there is a definite pattern, or behavioral chain, that starts with a command or direction that Larry does not follow, which results in an adult either reprimanding him or talking to him in some manner, which then results in even more refusal and inappropriate language. Occasionally these sequences end in physical aggression.

Manifest Determination

It seems unlikely that Larry's inappropriate verbalizations are due to his Gilles de la Tourette's syndrome, primarily because they occur in response to specific environmental stimuli and are not stereotypic, rapid, or nonrhythmic. As for the other conditions being related to either his verbal or nonverbal behaviors, it is extremely difficult to say with certainty that they are or aren't. Based on the diagnostic criteria for ADHD and OCD, one could make a valid argument that his behaviors are indeed related to these disorders. On the other hand, one could make an equally valid argument that stimuli in the environment are evoking and maintaining these behaviors and are thus unrelated to either ADHD or OCD. For purposes of school-based *treatment*, it does not matter whether or not these behaviors are determined to be related to a particular diagnostic category. What is known is that if certain changes are made in Larry's environment, behavior changes will soon follow.

General Recommendations

1. Despite the intensity of Larry's inappropriate verbal behavior, it appears that he can be maintained within the regular classroom environment if appropriate behavioral support is given to his teacher.

2. Based on the observation and interview data, it is likely that if his verbal behavior and noncompliance can be successfully addressed, his physical aggression will diminish as well.

3. The focus of intervention should be on:

   a. Reinforcing compliance with commands/directions
   b. Not reinforcing noncompliance
   c. Reinforcing appropriate verbal behavior
   d. Not attending to inappropriate verbal behavior
   e. Using the results from the preference assessment to guide selection of reinforcers
   f. Disallowing escape from unpleasant activities contingent upon inappropriate verbal and/or physical behavior
   g. Allowing escape from unpleasant activities contingent upon appropriate verbal and/or physical behavior

4. Continue with the 10-minute morning transition time with Mrs. Maxwell. This seems to be helping to transition Larry from home to school.

5. Make certain that instructions and directions are followed-up to increase compliance. Do not give a direction and then walk away. Give the direction, wait for compliance, assist as necessary, and reinforce compliance. For example, if it is snack time and Larry has moved his desk from its appropriate location, he should not get his snack until he returns the desk. This is only one example, and the basic principle should be followed throughout the day.

6. On a daily basis, monitor Larry's target behaviors and provide him feedback on successful performance. It is best, from an intervention perspective, not to point out difficulties but rather to focus on the positives.

7. Also on a daily basis, monitor to what degree the intervention is actually implemented.

Comments Regarding Current Behavioral Programming

The comments made in this section are relative to the behavior intervention plan (BIP) that was to have started on September 13, 1999. The purpose of this section is not to criticize the existing plan but rather to use the data from the current assessment, which obviously was not available when the BIP was written, to highlight effective and ineffective strategies.

1. It is fine to offer Larry choices, but do not offer him the opportunity to escape as one of those choices. For example, do not say you can either do your work or you can go to the office with Mrs. Smith. Instead, say something like "You can either do your work now and then you may _____, or you can choose not to do your work and not get _____." It is still a choice for Larry but one that does not run the risk of reinforcing inappropriate behavior. Be forewarned, however, that Larry's inappropriate behavior will escalate for a brief period of time because he is no longer receiving reinforcement for previously reinforced responses.

2. If adults are going to talk with Larry about his feelings, etc., then this should be done contingent upon *appropriate* behavior and not inappropriate behavior. That is, Larry should not get access to one-on-one adult attention for using inappropriate language or by being physically aggressive.

3. Do not give Larry hugs contingent upon inappropriate behavior. Hugs are fine, but make certain that hugs are given for appropriate behaviors.

4. To the greatest extent possible, do not remove Larry from the classroom contingent upon inappropriate behavior. Doing so reinforces his behavior by allowing him to escape the classroom. If he absolutely must be removed from the classroom, do so without talking to him, counseling him, or correcting his behavior. As soon as he has calmed down, return him immediately to the classroom and reissue the command or direction or have him finish the assignment on which he was working.

It is hoped that the information contained in this report is helpful in understanding Larry's behavior as well as in designing interventions that take into account the resources available at the school and district and the needs of the teacher. If I can be of further assistance, please do not hesitate to call.

_____   _____

Mike Richards, PhD   Date

SUMMARY

In this chapter we have provided some basic supporting documentation forms and examples of FBA reports. In the chapters that follow, you will find additional supporting documentation including other examples of FBA reports and positive behavior support plans. There is no one best FBA report format or behavior support plan. You must use the one that are best suited for the teams with which you work and the types of interfering behaviors that are being addressed.

9

Putting It All Together . . . Where Science Meets Art

Or, Linking Assessment to Intervention

> Your past forms you, whether you like it or not. Each encounter and experience has its own effect and you're shaped the way the wind shapes a mesquite tree on a plain.
>
> —LANCE ARMSTRONG (Cyclist)

Years ago Dan Reschly made a statement that went something like this: "The only good assessment is the one that results in effective intervention." That premise has been a driving force throughout our entire professional careers. From our perspective, assessments that result only in the identification of a diagnosis or special education placement are inadequate. They may be necessary, but with regard to developing effective interventions they are woefully insufficient. We refer to these types of diagnostic assessments as *administrative evaluations.* These evaluations meet the administrative needs for funding (e.g., Medicaid, third party) and/or eligibility for services (e.g., special education placement). You know the drill and could recite it while in a coma. The student is referred, you conduct the assessment, you write the report, you attend the team meeting, eligibility is determined, you close the file, and you make a mental note to see the student again in 3 years.

In contrast, FBAs are conducted for the primary purpose of identifying the variables that contribute to interfering behaviors, with the results used to design individually tailored interventions. We refer to these types of assessments as *clinical evaluations.* FBAs have clinical utility when they result not only in the design and implementation of interventions but in those interventions that lead to socially significant behavioral outcomes. Sounds great, huh? Well, in theory this makes perfect sense and when done correctly this process is incredibly effective. However, linking interventions to assessment results is not

143

a straightforward process. Indeed, this is the stage of the assessment–intervention continuum where science meets art. Just as FBA is the science of human behavior, the design of interventions is a creative endeavor that includes the consideration of a myriad of potential proactive and reactive strategies. Consequently, we cannot begin to provide an adequate description of all the interventions that could be used to address the array of interfering behaviors that occur within school settings in this chapter.

"But wait a minute!" you exclaim and ask, "I thought that the FBA would tell me which behavioral interventions to use to address interfering behavior?" Well, on one level it does. On another level it does not. Let's consider both of these levels. At the most basic level, the results of the FBA often tell us more about *what not to do* than *what to do*. Consider the case of Tara, where the FBA pinpointed that oppositional behavior (e.g., arguing with teachers, refusing to complete tasks) occurred when she was asked to complete academic assignments. The team decided that the consequence to oppositional behavior would include verbal redirection to tasks. If redirection did not result in compliance and the behavior became "too disruptive," a time-out procedure was recommended. This intervention package was implemented for 3 weeks and resulted in a marked increase in oppositional behaviors. Based on the results of the FBA, the school psychologist offered the hypothesis that oppositional behavior appeared to be motivated by negative reinforcement (i.e., escape and/or avoidance of academic demands). She explained that the results of the FBA indicated that time-out, although designed and intended to reduce oppositional behavior, actually strengthened (i.e., increased the frequency of) Tara's oppositional behavior. In this example, the results of the FBA clearly showed that time-out was contraindicated. In short, the FBA tells us what not to do but does not necessarily tell us what to do. So, how would we deal with oppositional behavior given the scenario just described? Following is a list of strategies that we have used with students to effectively address negatively reinforced oppositional behaviors:

- Escape extinction (i.e., redirection to task, thereby eliminating the escape/avoidance reinforcer)
- Functional communication training (i.e., teaching and reinforcing a functionally equivalent communicative response as a replacement for oppositional behavior)
- Differential reinforcement of incompatible behavior procedures (DRI)
- Differential reinforcement of other behaviors procedures (DRO)
- Modification of academic expectations (e.g., reduced workload)
- Instructional supports to decrease the "demands" of the instructional materials
- Self-monitoring of both appropriate and problem behaviors
- Self-editing procedures to increase accuracy of task completion
- "Premack" procedures[1] to reinforce task completion and accuracy

---

[1]In many cases a high probability behavior can reinforce a low probability behavior. For example, a behavior that is observed to occur frequently (e.g., a preferred behavior such as playing a computer game) can be used to follow and reinforce a lower frequency behavior (e.g., nonpreferred behavior such as completing assignments, cleaning one's room). When the high frequency behavior (e.g., playing basketball with friends) is made contingent on the completion of the lower frequency behavior (e.g., practicing the piano), the lower frequency behavior will be increased (Kazdin, 2001).

RESPONSE COVARIATION

Response covariation is observed to occur when an intervention addressing behavior *A* results in a change in behavior *B*. Most of our interventions addressing problem behavior focuses on *increasing* participation within assigned tasks and activities. These interventions either involve reinforcing behaviors that are within the person's repertoire or developing skills to increase the individual's range of behavioral assets. When target behaviors are incompatible with the interfering behaviors, the increase in the former is typically paired with a decrease in the latter. When two behaviors are so related, we refer to this as an *inverse relationship* (i.e., as one behavior increases the other behavior decreases). The model of response covariation is one of the foundations of positive behavioral support plans.

- High-probability response sequence[2] procedures to establish "behavioral momentum" prior to assigning tasks
- Academic skill remediation to decrease the aversiveness associated with the task

Wow! That's an incredible array of interventions. Which one is likely to be most effective and how do I determine which one to use. Read on to find out.

POSITIVE BEHAVIORAL SUPPORT INTERVENTIONS

Historically, interventions addressing problem behaviors have been reactive. Reactive interventions include strategies that are implemented *after* problem behavior occurs. Reactive interventions answer the following questions: "What should we do when problem behavior occurs?" or "What do we do when she does _____?" In one sense reactive behavioral interventions are based on "an eye for an eye" philosophy and emphasize the *reduction* of problem behaviors. However, from our perspective, the reduction or elimination of problem behavior is necessary but hardly sufficient. We need to design not only interventions that eliminate problem behaviors but also interventions that result in the

---

[2]High-probability response sequence or establishing behavioral momentum. In many cases providing an individual with access to a series of high probability activities can be used to increase low frequency behavior. Unlike the Pemack principle in which the high frequency activity is offered *following* the low rate behavior, a series of high frequency behaviors are offered *before* the targeted low rate behavior to establish "behavioral momentum" as a means of increasing subsequent responding. McComas, Wacker, and Cooper (1998) increased compliance behavior in a 22-month-old child during a complex medical procedure by first cueing the child to the following sequence: "touch your head," "say 'Mom,'" and "blow Mom a kiss" immediately followed by "hold still."

In this case, the first three requests were high probability responses (i.e., within the child's repertoire). The final request was a low probability response and one that typically resulted in interfering behaviors. When the cue of "hold still" was *preceded* by the three high probability requests, compliance was increased.

acquisition of socially meaningful behaviors. Positive behavioral support (PBS) methodologies are designed to do just that. So, what do we mean by positive behavioral supports? Koegel, Koegel, and Dunlap (1996, p. xiii) described these PBS interventions thus:

> Positive behavioral support refers to the broad enterprise of helping people develop and engage in adaptive, socially desirable behaviors and overcome patterns of destructive and stigmatizing responding. The term typically refers to assistance that is provided for people with developmental, cognitive, or emotional/behavioral disabilities; however, the principles and approaches have much greater generality. Positive behavioral support incorporates a comprehensive set of procedures and support strategies that are selectively employed based of an individual's needs, characteristics, and preferences. These procedures are drawn from the literatures in operant psychology and applied behavior analysis as well as other disciplines and orientations that offer demonstrable improvements in a person's behavior and manner of living.

Also, PBS refers to interventions:

- That consider and modify the contexts within which interfering behaviors occur
- That address the functionality of the interfering behaviors
- That can be justified by their outcomes (i.e., outcomes that are acceptable to the individual, the family, and the supportive community

COMPONENTS OF POSITIVE BEHAVIORAL SUPPORT PLANS

At a minimum, a PBS plan should include the following:

- Identifying information
- Goals of the plan
- Identification and description of interfering behaviors
- Hypothesized function of interfering behaviors
- Identification and description of intervention components
- Antecedent modification
- Replacement behavior
- Procedures for teaching replacement behavior
- Procedures for reinforcing replacement behaviors
- Reactive procedures (if applicable)
- Description of data-recording procedures

The PBS plan might also include the following:

- *Supports for teachers/staff:* identify the resources that will be available as support for team members who will be implementing the positive behavioral support plan.

- *Training procedures:* identify the types of training procedures that will be used to make sure that team members implement the interventions with precision.
- *Treatment integrity:* identify procedures used to make sure that the intervention is implemented with precision over time, across staff, across settings, etc.
- *Evaluation of interventions:* identify the procedures that will be used to evaluate the effectiveness of the intervention.
- *Programming for maintenance and generalization:* identify the procedures that will be used to promote ongoing maintenance and generalization of intervention effects.

SELECTING INTERVENTIONS

Again, the results of the FBA do no presribe specific interventions. The FBA points you in the right direction. Now you're faced with an overwhelming menu of behavioral interventions from which to choose (like the list generated above for Tara). You've been there before—so many choices, so little time. So what do we recommend? First, consider *all* of

---

A WORD OR TWO ABOUT TIME-OUT

Or, Time to Set the Time-Out Record Straight

Time-out is one of the most overused and misunderstood reactive procedures to address problem behavior. Technically speaking, the term is "time-out from reinforcement." Time-out from reinforcement is a Type II punishment technique and is designed to weaken (or reduce) behavior. When used correctly, time-out from reinforcement typically involves removing the person from a reinforcing environment and placing the person in a neutral setting (i.e., an environment that is devoid of reinforcement) contingent on the occurrence of a prespecified problem behavior. When implemented consistently, the problem behavior eventually is eliminated. However, in cases where the interfering behavior is motivated by negative reinforcement (i.e., escape from or avoidance of nonpreferred stimuli/situations/tasks/persons) the use of time-out actually strengthens as opposed to weakening the problem behavior.

You may ask, "How can that be? Time-out is a form of punishment. How can punishment reinforce behavior?" In behavior analysis there's an old saying that goes something like this: "Time-out from reinforcement is effective to the degree that the time-in environment is reinforcing." In cases in which the time-in environment is not reinforcing and perhaps aversive (e.g., oral reading for a student with a reading fluency disorder), using time-out when problem behavior occurs results in the removal of the individual from the nonpreferred situation. In such a case, the use of time-out designed to reduce behavior actually results in the strengthening of the behavior. When we discover situations like that we generally use another old saying found in the behavior analysis archives that goes something like this: "STOP USING TIME-OUT!"

the variables that influenced the occurrence of the interfering behavior. And, for each variable that contributes to the occurrence of the interfering behavior, a specific intervention needs to be developed. In the following subsection we provide examples that illustrate how the results of the FBA can be used to guide the identification of intervention strategies. Given the complexities of human behavior and the vast array of evidence-based interventions, the following examples are offered as a sampling of possible interventions.

Antecedent Variables

When antecedent variables are identified as contributing to the occurrence of problem behavior, consider the following strategies:

Antecedent Modification

Antecedent modification this involves modifying the antecedent to reduce the probability of problem behavior.

EXAMPLE

Aggressive behavior occurred when staff physically intervened to stop a student's self-injurious behavior. Aggression was determined to be motivated by negative reinforcement. Self-injury occurred during unstructured situations and was determined to be motivated by automatic positive reinforcement. Antecedent modification included (1) reducing unstructured situations by teaching independent and small-group leisure skills and (2) discontinuing the use of physical blocking when self-injury occurred. These modifications resulted in a marked decrease in self-injury and an elimination of aggressive behavior.

EXAMPLE

Disruptive behavior occurred when a student was given a worksheet full of math problems to complete independently at his seat. A comprehensive FBA indicated increased compliance with academic requests when the teacher reduced the length of the math assignment and when she helped the student with the first problem or two on the worksheet. Thus, the intervention consisted of decreasing the length of the work assignment by at least half and assisting the student with the first problem on the worksheet. These very simple academic adjustments resulted in elimination of this student's rather severe disruptive behavior. As the student's compliance increased and continued, the length of the worksheets was very gradually lengthened until he was completing an entire worksheet without disruption.

Teaching Coping Skills

There are some situations in which one simply cannot rearrange the environment or modify the environmental triggers. In these cases we have found that teaching the student to cope with or tolerate the environmental triggers is an effective strategy.

EXAMPLE

A student with a diagnosis of anxiety disorder reported that she became extremely tense, irritable, and antisocial (e.g., screaming at peers, yelling obscenities) when passing in the hallways of her high school between classes. Although one alternative could be to allow her to walk from class to class either immediately prior to or after the scheduled passing time, this meant that she would miss instructional times and had the potential of being stigmatizing. The school psychologist implemented a relaxation training intervention with the student that resulted in significant decreases in her anxiety and her subsequent antisocial behaviors during passing times.

Social Skills Deficits

EXAMPLE

A student's disruptive behaviors (e.g., irrelevant comments during class discussion, laughing loudly, throwing spit balls at classmates) were determined to be motivated by positive reinforcement (i.e., social attention from peers). An individual variable that was contributing to this student's disruptive behavior was his social skills deficits. Additional assessments (i.e., social skills assessments) were conducted and, based on those results, specific skills were targeted for training. Teaching of age-appropriate social skills that resulted in an increase in prosocial interactions with classmates resulted in a decrease in the student's disruptive behaviors.

Academic Skills Deficits

EXAMPLE

A student's oppositional behaviors (e.g., refusal to read aloud, throwing materials, hitting classmates) occurred during small-group oral reading instruction. This oppositional behavior was determined to be motivated by negative reinforcement (i.e., escape or avoidance of difficult tasks). Additional assessments (i.e., curriculum-based assessments) indicated that, although he was in the fourth grade, his reading skills were barely at the second-grade level. Based on these assessments, direct instruction in basic reading skills including phonics and sight words resulted in his increased reading accuracy and comprehension. As the student's reading skills improved, his oppositional behaviors decreased.

Consequences

Relative to designing interventions, the identification of the variables that reinforce interfering behaviors is important in two ways:

First, as discussed previously, this information tells us *what not to do*. Knowing what not to do then becomes a critical component of the intervention. Knowing what not to do usually involves using an extinction procedure. Extinction is a procedure in which the team makes a determined effort to avoid providing the reinforcing consequence contingent on the occurrence of the interfering behavior. To be really precise, if reinforcing

---

FUNCTIONAL COMMUNICATION TRAINING

With many individuals, expressive communication skills are often associated with occurrences of interfering behaviors. In these cases, teaching communication skills as a replacement for interfering behaviors has been shown to be very effective. This type of procedure is referred to as functional communication training (FCT). Teaching communication skills that are functionally equivalent with the interfering behavior is typically more effective than just teaching expressive language skills in general. For example, with a student diagnosed with an expressive language disorder whose disruptive behavior is motivated by social attention, teaching the student to request attention using an FCT strategy (e.g., sign language, picture/symbol exchange) leads to the same functional outcomes (i.e., attention) as self-injury. Over time, the student will display increased use of appropriate means of requesting attention and a significant reduction of attention-seeking self-injury.

---

attention is withheld contingent upon an interfering behavior, we are using *attention extinction*. If we are withholding a reinforcing tangible contingent upon the occurrence of an interfering behavior, we are using *tangible extinction*. If we are preventing escape or avoidance contingent upon interfering behavior, then we are using *escape extinction* or *avoidance extinction*. This level of terminological precision is sometimes necessary to remind everyone on the team the exact nature of the intervention. In short, when we are using any type of *extinction*, we do not provide the reinforcing consequence anymore. That is easier said than done, however. One of our general rules when using extinction is to ask this question: "Can we still withhold _____ if the behavior becomes five or ten times worse than it is now?" If the answer is no, we tend not to use extinction.

The second way in which the identification of the variables that reinforce interfering behavior is important is that we have identified a reinforcing consequence that may be applied to other types of behavior. This is of critical significance. We often hear comments such as "We can't find anything with which to reinforce Steven" and "Nothing seems to motivate him." Really?!? Remember, all behavior is reinforced by something in some way or other. The variables that are reinforcing consequences of *interfering behavior* can also be used to reinforce *appropriate behavior*. Consider the following examples:

Positive Reinforcement

Positive reinforcement may be used to increase appropriate behavior, thereby decreasing interfering behavior.

EXAMPLE

Maggie's inappropriate behavior in the grocery store was determined to be reinforced by eventual access to candy. When she went to the grocery store with her father, she often whined, cried, and shouted, "Candy . . . candy, I want candy, I NEEEEED candy." Her father, in an attempt to be stern, consistently said "No candy" during the initial phases of grocery shopping. However, after a few minutes of Maggie's constant verbal bombardment, he usually broke down and provided Maggie with an edible treat (tangible reinforcement). Of course, at his point she stopped whining and fussing. In this example, Maggie's whining/fussing behaviors are motivated by positive reinforcement in the form of *access to a tangible*. Perhaps just as important for understanding this interaction is that Maggie's father's strategy of providing a treat was negatively reinforced (i.e., when he gave her the treat her disruptive behavior stopped). Thus, we can see why Maggie's annoying behavior persisted when in the grocery store and why her father gave in.

The solution to this "double-whammy" reinforcing situation was easy. Because Maggie's behavior was motivated by tangible reinforcement (candy), her father simply provided her with a treat as soon as they entered the grocery store. The treat was a small box of animal crackers (cookies). While not candy, this was still a form of edible reinforcement and a treat for Maggie. Eventually, this procedure was modified to include brief shopping and prompting Maggie to use appropriate verbal skills: "Dad, cookies please." Guess what? . . . No more whining and fussing while shopping.

Negative Reinforcement

Negative reinforcement may be used to increase appropriate behavior, thereby decreasing interfering behavior. Steege and Northup (1998) and Steege et al. (1990) described interventions addressing escape-motivated interfering behavior in which negative reinforcement (i.e., brief escape from task contingent on appropriate behavior) was used to both increase appropriate behavior (e.g., math tasks and communication skills, respectively) and to decrease interfering behaviors (e.g., oppositional and self-injurious behaviors, respectively).

EXAMPLE

Sara's disruptive behavior in the classroom was determined to be motivated by negative reinforcement (i.e., escape from and avoidance of math worksheets). The team developed a procedure that included providing Sara with brief breaks following the accurate completion of small sets of math problems (see Steege & Northup [1998] for a detailed explanation of this procedure). This resulted in more frequent breaks (i.e., reinforcement), an increase in task completion and accuracy, and a significant reduction in disruptive behavior. In this example, negative reinforcement was used to increase appropriate behavior.

CASE EXAMPLES

In the following pages we have included several case examples illustrating the FBA process. These examples are based on cases in which the authors have conducted FBAs and provided ongoing consultation in the design, implementation, and evaluation of interventions. To protect confidentiality of the individuals identified in the case examples, the reports have been "sanitized" (i.e., names and locations have been changed and are fictitious). Any resemblance to persons living or dead is unintentional.

The following example illustrates a case in which a student, Eric Trout, was referred for a 3-year reevaluation and demonstrates the assessment–intervention continuum. For many years, the Salmon Elementary School student assistance team (SAT) viewed the role of the school psychologist as one of an "evaluator" whose job was to conduct diagnostic assessments to determine a student's eligibility for special education placement. In the case of 3-year reevaluations of students with developmental disabilities, psychological evaluations typically included norm-referenced assessments (e.g., cognitive and adaptive behavior assessments), anecdotal observations and narrations, and record review.

In this case example, the school psychologist decided to offer a more comprehensive evaluation of Eric Trout. In addition to addressing the issue of continued eligibility for special education services, the school psychologist met with team members prior to conducting the evaluation to identify concerns and questions team members had regarding (1) behaviors that interfered with Eric's acquisition of skills and (2) strategies for addressing these behaviors. During the preevaluation team meeting, it was determined that team members were particularly concerned about Eric's stereotypic, self-injurious, and tantrum behaviors.

The following case example includes:

- A sanitized example of a psychological evaluation report (extended report version)
- A sanitized example of a functional behavioral assessment report (brief version)
- A sanitized example of a positive behavioral support (PBS) plan
- Three graphs documenting the effectiveness of specific interventions designed to (1) increase participation in tasks/activities, (2) decrease stereotypic behaviors, (3) decrease self-injury, and (4) decrease tantrum behaviors

EXAMPLE OF A PSYCHOLOGICAL EVALUATION REPORT (EXTENDED REPORT VERSION)

Student: Eric Trout
Age: 7–6
Date of Birth: 10/23/95
Grade: 2
School District: Sebago Lake, ME
School: Salmon Elementary School
Evaluation Dates: April 15, 22, 24, and 26, 2002
Report Date: 11/12/01

Reason for Referral

Eric was referred for psychological evaluation by the Salmon Elementary School student assistance team (SAT). The psychological evaluation was conducted to (1) determine if Eric continues to qualify for special education services, (2) evaluate behaviors that were interfering with Eric's educational progress, and (3) offer recommendations for the design of PBS interventions.

Assessment Procedures

Record Review
Scales of Independent Behavior—Revised
Social Skills Rating System
Indirect FBA:

- Interviews with Ms. Jones (special education teacher)
- Interviews with Mr. and Mrs. Trout
- Functional Behavioral Assessment Screening Form (FBASF)
- Antecedent Variables Assessment Form (AVAF)
- Individual Variables Assessment Form (IVAF)
- Consequence Variables Assessment Form (CVAF)
- Behavioral Stream Interviews (BSIs)

Direct descriptive FBA:

- Anecdotal observations
- Interval Recording Procedure (IRP)
- Structural assessment

Background Information

Eric lives with his parents, Stuart and Sandy Trout, and one elder brother, in Sebago Lake, Maine. Review of records provided by the Department of Behavioral Services indicated that Eric's history is significant for developmental delays, long-standing problem behaviors (e.g., aggression, self-injury, tantrum, stereotypy, refusal to eat solid foods), and the diagnosis of autistic disorder. Prior to entering kindergarten, Eric received home-based developmental therapy services for 20 hours per week over the course of 18 months. He also received biweekly speech/language services.

The most recent psychological evaluation was conducted in May 1999 by Dr. George Curious (school psychologist). The results of intellectual and adaptive behavior assessments indicated that compared to other children of the same age, Eric evidenced significant delays. Dr. Curious indicated that Eric's history was significant for severe impairments in language and social skills. He also indicated that Eric displayed the following problem behaviors: self-injury, tantrum, and stereotypic behaviors. Dr. Curious recommended that Eric receive comprehensive special education support services. In June 1999 the Salmon Elementary School multidisciplinary team determined that Eric was eligible for special education services under the handicapping condition of autism. He was placed in a self-contained program for students with developmental disabilities. Special education supports included speech/language and occupational therapy services.

Presently, Eric attends the Salmon Elementary School on a full-time basis and is enrolled in a self-contained classroom for students with developmental disabilities. He is mainstreamed into recess, lunch, and music. Since the first day of the 2001/2002 school year, Salmon Elementary School staff have expressed concerns regarding Eric's display of stereotypic, self-injurious, and tantrum behaviors. During a preevaluation team meeting, it was determined that the psychological evaluation would focus on the following: (1) assessment of Eric's current levels of adaptive behavior skills and (2) FBA of behaviors that interfere with Eric's educational progress. Behavioral consultation in the design and implementation of positive behavioral support interventions was also requested.

Assessment Results

The Scales of Independent Behavior—Revised (SIB-R) was completed with Ms. Jones and Mrs. Trout serving as informants. The SIB-R is an adaptive behavior assessment that compared Eric's performance to that of same-aged peers. Domains assessed include gross and fine motor, social interactions, language, self-care skills, domestic skills, money, time, and community participation.

Results are reported as standard scores and percentile ranks. An average standard score is 100, with scores from 85 to 115 constituting the broad average range. A score of 50 is considered to be an average percentile rank and would mean that a student's score was higher than or equal to 50% that of similarly aged peers in the norm group. Results are as shown in the accompanying table.

Domain	Standard Score	Percentile Rank
Motor Skills	75	1
Social Interaction and Communication Skills	48	1
Personal Living Skills	68	1
Community Living Skills	62	1
Broad Independence	57	0.2

These results indicated that, compared to other children of the same age, Eric evidenced delays across all domains. Eric's areas of strength within the adaptive behavior domain included visual discrimination skills, visual matching skills, specific personal living skills (e.g., independent toileting), fine motor skills, willingness to try new tasks, recently acquired ability to transition between tasks and settings, and developing expressive verbal language skills. Areas of relative weakness included reciprocal social interactions, cooperative play with peers, independent leisure/play, community living skills, and specific self-help skills (toothbrushing, bathing, and bed making, among others).

To further assess social skills delays that were identified through adaptive behavior assessment, the Social Skills Rating System (SSRS) was administered, with Ms. Jones serving as the informant. The SSRS utilizes rating scales to provide a broad assessment of a student's social behaviors. The SSRS is a norm-referenced assessment in which the results of Eric's performance were compared to that of male peers of the same age to yield Standard Scores and Percentile Ranks. Results indicated that Eric received a Standard Score of 60 and a Percentile Rank of 1, and he is described as having significantly below-average skills when compared to those of same-aged peers.

The results of social skills assessment suggested that Eric evidences relative social skills strengths with regard to his social interest and desire to interact with others. Assessment results indicated that the following skills are particular areas of weakness for Eric: group participation with peers, imitation of appropriate behavior of peers, ignoring peer distractions, using free time in an acceptable way, initiating conversations with peers, inviting peers to join activities, and cooperating with peers without prompting. During interviews regarding Eric's social behaviors, Ms. Jones and Mrs. Trout reported that Eric typically avoids eye contact with others, rarely responds to social interactions that have been initiated by peers/classmates/siblings, rarely initiates social interactions with others, and prefers to manipulate and be occupied with inanimate objects. They reported that Eric has marked weaknesses in independent leisure and cooperative play skills.

Indirect FBA included administration of structured interviews to assess current areas of behavioral concern, relevant antecedents (or "triggers") to problem behavior, relevant internal/individual variables, and relevant consequence variables. This involved the use of the following assessment forms:

- The Functional Behavioral Assessment Screening Form (FBASF)
- The Antecedent Variables Assessment Form (AVAF)
- The Individual Variables Assessment Form (IVAF)
- The Consequence Variables Assessment Form (VAF)
- Behavioral Stream Interviews (BSIs)

The interviews were conducted with Ms. Jones and Mrs. Trout serving as informants.

Identification and Description of Interfering Behaviors

The following behaviors interfere with Eric's acquisition of academic, social, and adaptive living skills:

1. *Stereotypic behaviors*—defined as hand flapping; scratching, rubbing, pounding, or tapping of objects/surfaces
2. *Self-injurious behaviors*—defined as harm to self including hitting of head/face with open hand or closed fist, separated by 10 seconds of no-hitting behaviors
3. *Tantrum behaviors*—defined as a response set including two or more of the following: screaming, crying, flopping to the floor, or throwing materials, separated by 30 seconds of no-tantrum behaviors

Identification of Antecedent, Individual, and Consequence Variables

The following *antecedent* variables were identified as "triggers" (i.e., variables that occurred prior to the onset of interfering behaviors):

1. Unstructured time appears to contribute to the occurrence of stereotypic behavior.
2. Language-based instructional activities contribute to the occurrence of stereotypic behaviors.
3. Physically prompting Eric to stop stereotypic behaviors contributes to the occurrence of self-injurious behaviors and tantrum behaviors

The following *individual* variables were identified as factors that appear to contribute to the occurrence of interfering behaviors:

1. Social skills deficits
2. Expressive and receptive communication skill delays
3. Delays in independent and cooperative leisure skills

The following variables were identified as *consequences* of interfering behaviors (i.e., variables that follow the occurrence of interfering behaviors):

1. Sensory consequences (arousal induction) appear to be a result of stereotypic behaviors.
2. Withdrawal of staff physical prompting typically occurs following self-injurious and tantrum behaviors.

Direct descriptive FBA included (1) anecdotal observations and behavior-recording procedures, (2) the interval recording procedure (IRP), and (3) structural assessments. The results of anecdotal observation and recording indicated that stereotypic behaviors occurred at high rates across multiple classroom settings, activities, and staff. Self-injury was observed to occur less frequently, but it also occurred across settings, activities, and staff. To document the occurrence and to identify antecedent conditions associated with these behaviors, the IRP was implemented for several school days. The IRP is an ongoing functional behavioral assessment and monitoring system where Eric's behavior was monitored and recorded every 15 minutes throughout his school day. Prior to implementing the IRP, each interfering behavior was described and a corresponding data recording was identified for each behavior. Training sessions with Ms. Jones and one educational technician involved both role play and coaching in how to complete the IRP. The results of documentation of interfering behaviors using the IRP are as shown in the accompanying table:

Behavior	Description	Data recording	Current levels of occurrence
Stereotypy	Hand flapping; scratching rubbing/ pounding/tapping objects or surfaces	Performance-based (0, 1, 2, 3, 4, 5)	61% daily average
Self-injury	Occurrences of harm to self including hitting head/face with open hand or closed fist	Frequency (recording of each discrete event)	7.85 occurrences/hour
Tantrum	A response set including two or more of the following: screaming, crying, flopping to the floor, throwing materials	Duration (recording the length of each occurrence of tantrum behaviors)	8.75 minutes/hour

Note. Current level of occurrence (CLO) was determined by averaging behavioral data from April 16, 2002 through April 26, 2002.

Review of the completed IRP data indicated that stereotypic behaviors occurred across a wide range of conditions. Stereotypic, self-injurious, and tantrum behaviors occurred at the highest levels during unstructured and language-based instructional situations and at lower levels during structured situations and when Eric was engaged in functional tasks that involved experiential learning activities. To further evaluate these behaviors, functional behavioral analysis procedures were implemented.

Structural Assessment

To further evaluate interfering behaviors, a structural assessment was conducted. The structural assessment involved observing Eric within *naturally occurring classroom situations* and recording occurrences of appropriate and interfering behaviors using a 6-second partial-interval recording procedure. Eric was observed within the following situations: free play (no instructional expectations were placed on Eric and no social interactions were provided), individual visual–motor (VM) instructional tasks, and individual language-based (LB) instructional tasks. Within each situation, active participation was defined as Eric's visual, verbal, and/or motor on-task behavior. The previous definitions of self-injurious, stereotypic, and tantrum behaviors were used during these observations. The results of the structural assessment are shown in the following table (data are presented as percentage of occurrence).

Setting	Active participation	Self-injury	Stereotypy	Tantrum
Free play	12%	0%	74%	0%
Individual VM instructional tasks:	68%	2%	12%	0%
Individual LB instructional tasks:	22%	24%	66%	12%

During the structural assessment it was observed that Eric exhibited higher levels of stereotypic behavior when prompted to participate in language-based instructional tasks (e.g., expressive labeling) and free-play situations. Conversely, he exhibited lower levels of stereotypic behavior during visual–motor tasks (e.g., putting together a puzzle, performing a visual discrimination task). Also self-injurious and tantrum behaviors occurred at much higher levels during the language-based instruction but at very low (2%) to no occurrences during the visually based and free-play situations.

An additional structural analysis was conducted to further evaluate these findings. This additional assessment involved observing and recording Eric's behavior across naturally occurring classroom situations using a 6-second partial-interval recording procedure. Results are shown in the following table.

Setting	Active participation	Stereotypy	Self-injury	Tantrum
Language-based tasks	18%	84%	16%	21%
Visually based tasks	89%	14%	0%	0%
Language-based tasks	12%	78%	0%	16%
Visually based tasks	94%	12%	2%	0%

These results confirmed the hypothesis that high levels of stereotypic behavior were associated with language-based instructional tasks/activities. Conversely, active participation was much higher during visually based instructional tasks/activities. These data also revealed another finding, namely, that self-injury occurred at higher levels during language-based tasks as compared to visually based instructional situations.

Note: During these observations it was found that self-injury occurred only when the educational technician physically prompted Eric to disengage from stereotypic behaviors. Also tantrum behaviors occurred following physical prompts (i.e., response interruption) to block occurrences of self-injury.

Based on the results of FBA procedures, the following hypotheses are offered:

Hypothesized Functions of Interfering Behaviors

STEREOTYPY

Stereotypic behaviors appear to be motivated by automatic positive reinforcement (i.e., sensory consequences, arousal induction).

Example. When "alone" and not engaged in functional tasks/activities, Eric exhibited hand flapping and tapping of objects/surfaces. It is highly likely that stereotypic behaviors are also motivated by negative reinforcement (i.e., escape/avoidance of nonpreferred tasks/activities)

Example. When prompted to participate in language-based instruction, Eric exhibited high levels of stereotypic behavior and low levels of active participation.

SELF-INJURY

Self-injurious behaviors appear to be motivated by negative reinforcement (i.e., escape/avoidance of nonpreferred social interactions, such as prompting by staff to disengage from stereotypic behaviors) *and* positive reinforcement (i.e., continued opportunity to engage in stereotypic behaviors).

Example. The educational technician was attempting to implement a language-based instructional activity. Eric exhibited high levels of stereotypic behavior. The educational technician physically prompted Eric from stereotypic tapping of objects and cued him to the task. Eric immediately exhibited self-injury (i.e., hit his face with a closed fist). The educational technician withdrew the physical prompt. Eric immediately stopped self-injury and began to exhibit stereotypic behavior.

TANTRUM

Tantrum behaviors appear to be motivated by negative reinforcement (i.e., escape/avoidance of nonpreferred social interactions, such as physical intervention from staff to interrupt or block self-injurious behaviors) *and* positive reinforcement (i.e., continued opportunity to engage in stereotypic behaviors).

Example. During a free-play situation, Eric exhibited stereotypic behaviors. The educational technician provided physical prompts to redirect Eric from tapping objects. Eric exhibited self-injury (i.e., he hit himself on the side of his head with a closed fist several times). The educational technician blocked the self-injury with her hand and attempted to stop Eric from hitting himself. He flopped to the floor, screamed, and threw objects. Eric was physically directed to a time-out area where he exhibited high levels of stereotypic behaviors.

The results of assessments indicated a response chain involving stereotypic, self-injurious, and tantrum behaviors. It was hypothesized that interventions that focused on decreasing stereotypic behaviors would also result in reductions in self-injurious and tantrum behaviors.

Implementation and Preliminary Evaluation of Intervention

Based on the results of the assessment it was determined that Eric demonstrated strengths in visual discrimination and visual matching skills. It was also noted that Eric was in the early stages of learning to use visual communication strategies under the direction of Ms. Peabody (a speech/language pathologist). In collaboration with Ms. Peabody, an intervention involving dialogue displays (DDs) was implemented. The DDs included picture symbols (with the paired written word) depicting the content of the language-based instructional tasks/activities, rules regarding appropriate behaviors, and a symbol that indicated a direction to stop engaging in stereotypic behaviors. The team agreed to implement the DD procedures on a trial basis. To evaluate the efficacy of this intervention, an alternating treatments design was used in which the DD procedures were used within the context of three language-based instructional sessions but were not used in three comparable language-based instructional sessions. Active participation, stereotypy, self-injury, and tantrum behaviors were recorded using a 6-second partial-interval recording procedure.

Note: Because self-injury typically occurred during attempts to physically redirect Eric from stereotypic and tantrum behaviors occurred when staff attempted to block self-injury, staff were instructed not to provide contingent physical redirection or response interruption procedures when Eric displayed stereotypical behaviors.

The results are shown in the accompanying table. These results demonstrated that the implementation of the DD procedure within the context of language-based instructional tasks/ activities resulted in much lower levels of stereotypic behavior and higher levels of active participation compared to comparable instructional sessions in which the DD procedures were not implemented. Also by not providing physical redirection contingent on self-injury, the levels of self-injury were very low to nonexistent. In fact, there were no occurrences of self-injury during those situations in which the DD procedures were used. Moreover, by not blocking self-injury, tantrum behavior was eliminated.

Situation	Active participation	Self-injury	Stereotypy	Tantrum
Language-based (no DD)	16%	0%	80%	0%
Language-based (with DD)	59%	0%	27%	0%
Language-based (no DD)	14%	0%	69%	0%
Language-based (with DD)	72%	0%	20%	0%
Language-based (no DD)	21%	2%	74%	0%
Language-based (with DD)	83%	0%	10%	0%

Psychological Impressions and Considerations for the Team

The results of adaptive behavior and behavioral checklists indicate that compared to other children of the same age, Eric evidences delays across all domains. He exhibits stereotypic, self-injurious, and tantrum behaviors that significantly interfere with his acquisition of academic, social, personal living, community living, and social skills. While over the past year he has gained numerous skills, he continues to display many of the characteristics within the autism spectrum. The diagnosis of autistic disorder is offered. Eric appears to continue to meet the criteria for special education services under the handicapping condition of autism.

The results of adaptive behavior and social skills assessments indicate that Eric is in need of comprehensive social skills training programs. Social skills instruction that focuses on increasing reciprocal social interactions with teachers and classmates and cooperative play skills are supported. Social skills instruction will need to incorporate individualized and group instruction as well as role-play and live practice of a variety of identified social skills. The following types of instructional procedures are suggested:

- Discrete trial teaching methods to teach specific social skills
- Incidental teaching procedures within naturally occurring situations as methods of teaching and generalizing social skills
- Social skills instruction to focus on the acquisition and generalization of socially meaningful skills within self-contained, community, home, and mainstream settings
- The use of behavioral coaching models of instruction to teach and generalize social skills within mainstream classroom settings
- The utilization of a team composed of the special education teacher, special education consultant, school psychologist, and speech/language pathologist to work collaboratively following a problem-solving process so as to develop, implement, and evaluate social skills interventions

The results of FBA of interfering behaviors indicate that these behaviors appear to have multiple functions. Accordingly, interventions addressing these behaviors need to take into consideration the respective triggers, internal/individual variables, and consequences for each target behavior.

It is expected that increasing Eric's repertoire of prosocial behaviors within the context of an educational setting that is relevant, effective, and efficient will result in marked decreases in stereotypic, self-injurious, and tantrum behaviors.

The use of the time-out from reinforcement contingent on the occurrence of interfering behaviors, especially those behaviors motivated by negative reinforcement, is *not supported*.

In general, interventions incorporating the following strategies are supported:

- Planned ignoring of interfering behaviors
- Differential reinforcement of appropriate behavior (DRA)
- Differential reinforcement of incompatible behavior (DRI)
- Embedded instruction procedures using both high probability response sequence and Premack principle procedures are recommended to establish "behavioral momentum" and to reinforce active participation

Continued development of the application of DD procedures is suggested as a method for decreasing stereotypic behavior that interferes with Eric's active participation within instructional settings. Further evaluation of the effectiveness of this intervention needs to be conducted across a variety of instructional situations.

Systematic instruction focusing on teaching Eric independent play, cooperative play, and reciprocal social interactions is suggested as the primary means to decease stereotypy during free-play situations.

Physical redirection and/or physical response interruption procedures when Eric is exhibiting stereotypic and tantrum behaviors should only be used in those situations in which Eric is in danger of harming himself. Use of a picture schedule/picture rules procedure will provide Eric with visual cues of expected behaviors. Redirection involving gesturing to the picture schedule or picture rules is suggested as an alternative to physical prompts during most situations.

Ongoing data recording using the interval recording procedure (IRP) is suggested as a method of documenting current levels of occurrence of behaviors. It is recommended that the IRP be expanded from its present use of documenting only interfering behaviors to include the documentation of appropriate behaviors (e.g., active participation, initiation of social interactions with peers).

Ongoing behavioral consultation to include (1) ongoing FBA of interfering behaviors and (2) design, implementation, and evaluation of positive behavioral support interventions is suggested.

Ima Angler, EdS, NCSP
School Psychologist

There are many situations in which a comprehensive psychological evaluation and extended report are not indicated. For example, the SAT might request an FBA only. In these situations, the psychological report is more direct and to the point. The following report is offered as a sample of a brief version of an FBA report. This report is based on the case of Eric Trout, but this time the SAT requested only an FBA. The report includes the minimum requirements of an FBA report:

- Identification and description of behaviors
- Identification of antecedent, individual, and consequence variables
- Hypothesized function(s) of behaviors
- Possible intervention strategies

EXAMPLE OF A FUNCTIONAL BEHAVIORAL ASSESSMENT REPORT (BRIEF VERSION)

Student: Eric Trout
Age: 7–6
Date of Birth: 10/23/95
Grade: 2
School District: Sebago Lake, ME
School: Salmon Elementary School
Evaluation Dates: April 15, 22, 24, and 26, 2002
Report Date: 11/12/01

Reason for Referral

Eric was referred by the Salmon Elementary School student assistance team (SAT) for functional behavioral assessment of behaviors that interfere with Eric's educational progress.

Assessment Procedures

Indirect FBA
Direct descriptive FBA

Identification, Description, and Current Levels of Occurrence of Interfering Behaviors

Stereotypic Behaviors

Defined as hand flapping; scratching, rubbing, pounding, or tapping of objects/surfaces (CLO: 61%).

Self-Injurious Behaviors

Defined as harm to self including hitting of head/face with open hand or closed fist separated by 10 seconds of no-hitting behaviors (CLO: 7.85 occurrences/hour).

Tantrum Behaviors

A response set including two or more of the following: screaming, crying, flopping to the floor, throwing materials separated by 30 seconds of no-tantrum behaviors (CLO: 8.75 minutes/day).

Identification of Antecedent, Individual, and Consequence Variables

The following *antecedent* variables appear to serve as "triggers" (i.e., variables that occurred prior to the onset of interfering behaviors):

1. Unstructured time appears to contribute to the occurrence of stereotypic behavior.
2. Language-based instructional activities contribute to the occurrence of stereotypic behaviors.
3. Physically prompting Eric to stop stereotypic behaviors contributes to the occurrence of self-injurious behaviors and tantrum behaviors.

The following *individual* variables were identified as factors that appear to contribute to the occurrence of interfering behaviors:

1. Social skills deficits
2. Expressive and receptive communication skill delays
3. Delays in independent and cooperative leisure skills

The following variables were identified as *consequences* of interfering behaviors (i.e., variables that follow the occurrence of interfering behaviors):

1. Sensory consequences (arousal induction) appear to be a result of stereotypic behaviors.
2. Withdrawal of staff physical prompting typically occurs following self-injurious and tantrum behaviors.

Hypothesized Functions of Interfering Behaviors

Stereotyped Behaviors

Stereotypic behaviors appear to be motivated by automatic positive reinforcement (i.e., sensory consequences, arousal induction).

Self-Injury

Self-injurious behaviors appear to be motivated by negative reinforcement (i.e., escape/avoidance of nonpreferred social interactions, such as prompting by staff to disengage from stereotypic behaviors) *and* positive reinforcement (i.e., continued opportunity to engage in stereotypic behaviors).

Tantrum Behaviors

Tantrum behaviors appear to be motivated by negative reinforcement (i.e., escape/avoidance of nonpreferred social interactions, such as physical intervention from staff to interrupt or block self-injurious behaviors) *and* positive reinforcement (i.e., continued opportunity to engage in stereotypic behaviors).

Impressions and Considerations for the Team

The results of FBA of interfering behaviors indicate that these behaviors appear to have multiple functions. Accordingly, interventions addressing these behaviors need to take into consideration the respective triggers, internal/individual variables, and consequences for each target behavior.

A positive behavioral support (PBS) plan needs to be developed that takes into account the results of the FBA. The PBS plan might include the following strategies as a way or preventing the occurrence of interfering behaviors and of increasing appropriate and prosocial behaviors:

- Planned ignoring of interfering behaviors
- Differential reinforcement of appropriate behavior (DRA)
- Differential reinforcement of incompatible behavior (DRI)
- Embedded instruction procedures to establish "behavioral momentum" and to reinforce active participation
- Dialogue displays (DDs)
- Systematic instruction teaching Eric independent play, cooperative play, and reciprocal social interactions
- Picture/symbol schedules
- Picture/symbol classroom rules
- Systematic instruction teaching Eric reciprocal social skills

Ongoing data recording using the interval recording procedure (IRP) is suggested as a method of documenting current levels of occurrence of behaviors. It is recommended that the IRP be expanded from its present use of documenting only interfering behaviors to include the documentation of appropriate behaviors (e.g., active participation, initiation of social interactions with peers).

Ongoing behavioral consultation to include (1) ongoing FBA of interfering behaviors and (2) design, implementation, and evaluation of positive behavioral support interventions is suggested.

Ima Angler, EdS, NCSP
School Psychologist

The following positive behavioral support (PBS) plan was developed through a collaborative problem-solving process involving the school psychologist, special education teacher, speech/language pathologist, educational technician, and special education consultant. The plan was based on the results of the FBA processes outlined in the previous reports and tailored to address the unique needs and characteristics of Eric Trout.

EXAMPLE OF A POSITIVE BEHAVIORAL SUPPORT PLAN

Student: Eric Trout
Age: 7–6
Date of Birth: 10/23/95
Grade: 2
School District: Sebago Lake, ME
School: Salmon Elementary School
Report Plan Date: 11/19/01

Goals of the Positive Behavioral Support Plan

The overall goals of the PBS plan are to increase functional skills and to decrease interfering behaviors. It is expected that by (1) modifying the antecedents that "trigger" interfering behaviors, (2) teaching Eric functional skills, and (3) reinforcing his participation in tasks/activities his functional skills/active participation will increase and interfering behaviors will be reduced and eventually eliminated.

Stereotypic Behaviors

Definition: hand flapping; scratching, rubbing, pounding, or tapping of objects/surfaces
Function: stereotypic behaviors appear to be motivated by automatic positive reinforcement (i.e., sensory consequences, arousal induction)

Antecedent Modifications to Reduce Probability of Stereotypical Behaviors

- Modify the daily schedule to reduce unstructured situations
- Modify the daily schedule to reduce language-based instructional situations
- Picture/symbol schedules
- Picture/symbol classroom rules
- A picture/symbol token board
- Dialogue displays (DDs)
- Social coaching during unstructured situations
- Systematic instruction during unstructured situations
- Social skills instruction

Replacement Behaviors

- Increase active participation in tasks and activities
- Increase reciprocal social interactions

- Increase independent play skills
- Increase cooperative play skills

Reinforcement Procedures

- Social reinforcement contingent on appropriate behaviors
- Token reinforcement program (tangible and activity rewards)

Reactive Procedures

- Planned ignoring
- Gesture redirection to picture/symbol schedule
- Gesture redirection to picture/symbol rules

Data Recording

- Performance-based recording of active participation
- Performance-based recording of stereotypic behaviors

Self-Injurious and Tantrum Behaviors

Note: Self-injurious and tantrum behaviors appear to be members of the same response class. These behaviors typically occur when physical prompts are used to either interrupt or redirect Eric from stereotypic behaviors.

Self-Injurious Behaviors

Definition: harm to self including hitting of head/face with open hand or closed fist, separated by 10 seconds of no-hitting behaviors

Tantrum Behaviors

Definition: a response set including two or more of the following: screaming, crying, flopping to the floor, or throwing materials, separated by 30 seconds of no-tantrum behaviors
Function: self-injurious and tantrum behaviors appear to be motivated by negative reinforcement (i.e., escape/avoidance of nonpreferred social interactions, such as prompting by staff to disengage from stereotypic behaviors) *and* positive reinforcement (i.e., continued opportunity to engage in stereotypic behaviors).

Antecedent Modifications to Reduce Probability of Self-Injurious and Tantrum Behaviors

- Avoid use of physical redirection and response interruption of stereotypic behaviors

Replacement Behaviors

- Increase active participation (AP) in tasks and activities

Reinforcement Procedures

- Social reinforcement contingent on appropriate behaviors
- Token reinforcement program (tangible and activity rewards)

Reactive Procedures

- Planned ignoring
- Gesture redirection to picture/symbol schedule
- Gesture redirection to picture/symbol rules

Data Recording

- Performance-based recording of active participation
- Frequency recording of self-injurious behaviors
- Duration recording of tantrum behaviors

Active Participation

Definition: visual, verbal, and/or motor engagement in task, activities, and assignments

Supports for Staff

Positive Behavioral Support Team

This is a team composed of the special education teacher, special education consultant, school psychologist, and speech/language pathologist. The team will use a collaborative problem-solving process to develop, implement, and evaluate positive behavioral support (PBS) interventions.

Staff Training

All staff assigned to working with Eric will be trained to implement each of the PBS interventions. Staff will also receive instruction in the recording of each of the target behaviors. Staff training will include the following:

- Written descriptions of each intervention and data-recording procedure
- Modeling and discussion regarding the implementation of interventions and data recording procedures
- Performance feedback

Ongoing consultation will be provided to staff by the school psychologist.

Evaluation of the Effectiveness of the Interventions

The effectiveness of PBS interventions will be evaluated using single-case experimental design methodology. Using the aforementioned data-recording procedures, target behaviors will be recorded prior to (i.e., baseline) and during the implementation of the intervention package. A case study (A-B) design will be used.

The school psychologist will be responsible for the evaluation component of the PBS plan. See Figure 9.1 for an alternative way of structuring the PBS plan that was developed by Eric's team.

Following is an example of a Consultation Summary Report. This report is used to:

- Document the consultation services provided by the school psychologist
- Summarize the current disposition of the case
- Report current levels of occurrence of interfering and appropriate behaviors
- Document the effectiveness of the interventions

EXAMPLE OF A CONSULTATION SUMMARY REPORT

Student: Eric Trout
Age: 8–2
Date of Birth: 10/23/94
Grade: 3
School District: Sebago Lake, ME
School: Salmon Elementary School
Report Date: January 5, 2003

Consultation Services Provided

Behavioral consultation services were provided within the context of a collaborative problem-solving process. Consultation services were provided throughout the following stages:

1. Functional behavioral assessment of behaviors (see previous reports)
2. Design of positive behavioral support interventions (see the foregoing PBS plan)
3. Implementation of PBS interventions
   - Staff training in intervention strategies
   - Staff training in data collection
   - Observation of staff implementation of the strategies and data collection procedures (treatment integrity)
   - Weekly team meetings to discuss intervention strategies, review data, and to make modifications as needed
4. Evaluation of the effectiveness of the interventions
   - Weekly analysis of data
   - Graphing of data

Staff Training and Supports

Staff training was conducted prior to implementing the intervention procedures. Staff training included reviews of the FBA report and the PBS plan, discussions of the PBS interventions, role play of PBS interventions and data-recording procedures, and guided practice in implementation of the procedures.

Performance feedback was provided to staff during implementation of intervention procedures to improve treatment integrity. Through observations of staff and weekly consultation meetings it was determined that staff implemented the intervention strategies consistently and accurately.

Student: Eric Trout
Date of Birth: 10/23/95
School District: Sebago Lake, ME
School: Salmon Elementary School

Age: 7–6

Grade: 2

Goals of the Positive Behavioral Support Plan

The overall goals of the Positive Behavioral Support (PBS) plan are to increase functional skills and to decrease interfering behaviors. It is expected that by: (1) modifying the antecedents that "trigger" interfering behaviors, (2) teaching Eric functional skills, and (3) reinforcing his active participation in tasks/activities, his functional skills/active participation will increase and interfering behaviors will be reduced and eventually eliminated.

Interfering behavior	Definition	Function	Antecedent modifications	Replacement behaviors	Reinforcement procedures	Reactive procedures	Data recording
Stereotypy	Hand flapping; scratching, rubbing, pounding, or tapping objects/surfaces	Automatic positive reinforcement (arousal induction)	Modify daily schedule to reduce: unstructured situations and language-based instruction Picture/symbol schedules and classroom rules Dialogue displays Social coaching/systematic instruction of social skills during unstructured situations	Increase active participation (AP) in tasks and activities Increase reciprocal social interaction skills Increase independent play skills Increase cooperative play skills	DRI: social and token reinforcement contingent on behaviors that are incompatible with stereotypic behaviors DRA: social and token reinforcement of appropriate behaviors	When stereotypy occurs implement: • planned ignoring of stereotypy • redirection to the picture schedule procedure • redirection to the picture/symbol classroom rules	Performance-based recording of active participation (AP) Performance-based recording of stereotypic behaviors

The results of the FBA indicated that self-injurious and tantrum behaviors are members of the same response class. These behaviors typically occur when physical prompts are used to either interrupt or redirect Eric from stereotypic behaviors.

Interfering behaviors	Definitions	Functions (for both self-injury and tantrum)	Antecedent modifications	Replacement behaviors	Reinforcement procedures	Reactive procedures	Data recording
Self-injury	Harm to self including hitting of head/face with open hand or closed fist	Negative reinforcement (i.e., escape/avoidance of nonpreferred social interactions, such as prompting from staff to disengage from stereotypy)	Avoid use of physical redirection and response interruption of stereotypy	Increase active participation (AP) in tasks and activities	DRI: social and token reinforcement contingent on behaviors that are incompatible with stereotypic behaviors	When self-injury or tantrum behaviors occur implement: • planned ignoring of self-injury and tantrum behaviors	Frequency recording of self-injury
Tantrum	Response set including two or more of: screaming, crying, flopping to floor, throwing materials, separated by 30 seconds of no tantrum behaviors	Automatic positive reinforcement (i.e., continued opportunity to engage in stereotypy)	Use verbal and gesture redirection cues		DRA: social and token reinforcement of appropriate behaviors	• redirection to the picture schedule procedure • redirection to the picture/symbol classroom rules	Duration recording of tantrum

Supports for Staff

Positive Behavioral Support Team. This is a team composed of the special education teacher, special education consultant, school psychologist, speech/language pathologist, and mainstream teacher. The team will use a collaborative problem-solving process to develop, implement, and evaluate the positives of the PBS plan.

Staff Training. All staff assigned to working with Eric will be trained to implement each of the PBS plan interventions. Staff will also receive instruction in the recording of each of the target behaviors. Staff training will include the following: (1) written descriptions of intervention procedures (e.g., DRI) and data recording procedures, (2) modeling and discussion of each component of the PBS, and (3) ongoing performance feedback and consultation from members of the PBS team.

Evaluation of the Effectiveness of the PBS Plan

The effectiveness of the PBS plan will be evaluated using single-case experimental design methodology. Using the aforementioned data recording procedures, target behaviors will be recorded prior to (i.e., baseline) and during the implementation of the PBS plan. The school psychologist will be responsible for analyzing collected data, including graphing of data on a regular basis.

FIGURE 9.1. Example of a Positive Behavioral Support Plan.

Implementation

During the baseline and intervention phases, data were recorded for each of the target behaviors according to the procedures outlined in the PBS plan. Following a 3-week baseline, the interventions strategies outlined in the PBS plan were implemented. To date, these interventions have been implemented for 21 weeks.

Outcomes

Included here are graphs that depict the effectiveness of the PBS plan for Eric. Figure 9.2 shows both his active participation and his stereotypic behaviors. Figures 9.3 and 9.4 show his tantrum and self-injurious behaviors, respectively.

In general, these data support the overall effectiveness of the PBS plan. Each of the behaviors showed marked improvement compared to baseline levels. While stereotypic behaviors continue to occur daily (approximately 30%), these behaviors occurred at much higher levels prior to the implementation of the PBS plan (65%). Both self-injury and tantrum behaviors currently occur at much lower rates compared to baseline levels.

We view active participation (AP) as a critical component of any student's educational program. AP is directly related to on-task behavior (i.e., engagement in the educational process). Eric's AP has increased from a baseline level of 45% to current levels of 80–85%. This is a marked increase in AP.

Report Summary

These data document the effectiveness of the PBS plan in both increasing appropriate behaviors and in reducing interfering behaviors. The current support team has done an excellent job of implementing the PBS plan with Eric. Continued implementation of the PBS plan is suggested.

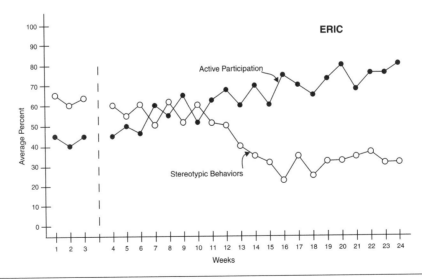

FIGURE 9.2. Effectiveness of the PBS plan. Note the decline of Eric's stereotypic behaviors and increase in his active participation after the intervention strategy was implemented. (Baseline behaviors are shown at the left.)

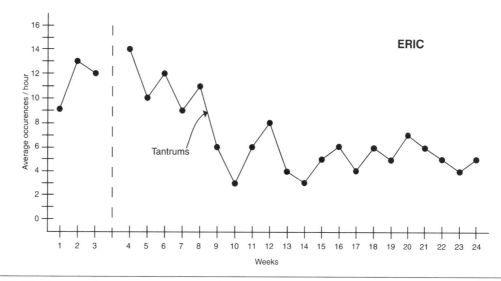

FIGURE 9.3. Decline in Eric's tantrum behaviors after implementation of the PBS plan. (His baseline behavior is shown at the left.)

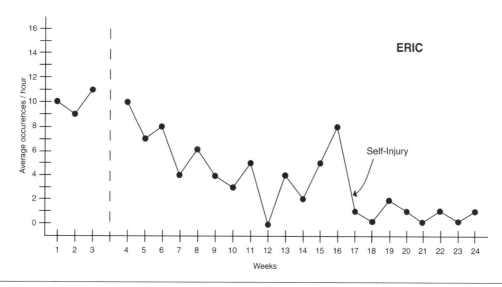

FIGURE 9.4. Decline in Eric's self-injurious behaviors after implementation of the PBS plan. (His baseline behavior is shown at the left.)

Review of the effectiveness of the PBS plan needs to be conducted on an ongoing basis. It is important to keep in mind that strategies that have been effective with Eric in the past may not be effective in the future. Also, behaviors that were motivated by a specific function at one point in his life (e.g., behaviors motivated by negative reinforcement) may be motivated by a different function (e.g., positive reinforcement) in the future. Consequently, ongoing FBA of interfering behaviors and ongoing evaluation of the effectiveness of interventions is recommended.

Ima Angler, EdS, NCSP
School Psychologist

SUMMARY

This has been a lengthy chapter—for us as well as you. How's that for stating the obvious? We have attempted to illustrate how the results of a functional behavioral assessment are linked to the intervention process as well as the documentation efforts that are required of every school-based team. We did not attempt to describe in excruciating detail the components of every type of intervention that is available for several reasons. First, doing so would have been akin to providing a cookbook of interventions, which is of little value to most practitioners and goes directly against our philosophical grain. Second, there are some excellent practice-oriented books that describe various types of interventions, particularly those that are grounded in applied behavior analysis (ABA). Third, the size of this chapter would have been quadrupled had we gone into minute detail regarding the selected interventions. Fourth, we wanted you to understand the rationale for choosing or designing interventions so that you could produce your own interventions rather than merely pulling one from this book. If you understand the rationale and basic principles of linking a particular intervention to the results of your functional behavioral assessment, that is winning the battle that will ultimately win the war against interfering behavior.

10

Extraenvironmental Variables
That Influence Function

How many times has a teacher or other school staff member told you that "I can tell what kind of day Jerrell is going to have the minute he walks in the door"? If our experience is any indication, then you are probably told this exact statement or something like it many times each school year. Unbeknownst to the person predicting Jerrell's day, he/she is actually attempting to link events that have occurred outside of the school setting to Jerrell's in-school behavior. It should come as no surprise that events that occur at Jerrell's home in the morning or on his bus ride to school, as just two possible examples, could have a profound effect on his subsequent behavior. We all know from our own experience that events that occur in one situation often impact our mood, responding, or feelings in another situation. Events that occur apart from the immediate environmental context but that have an effect on behavior in that environment are sometimes called "establishing operations" or "setting events" (see the two boxes below for a more in-depth discussion of these terms). Briefly, an establishing operation is any stimulus or event that both increases the momentary strength of a stimulus as a punisher or reinforcer and simultaneously increases behaviors that are associated with either avoiding the punisher or accessing the reinforcer. A setting event may be defined as any contextual factor or condition that influences behavior. This term is very broad and can include any number of events. Sometimes, in the professional literature, authors mistakenly refer to establishing operations as setting events and vice versa. It is of not much concern to us whether these events are labeled as establishing operations or setting events. We are much more concerned with practitioners understanding these types of stimuli and how they can impact school behavior and, by extension, the FBA process. Because these events occur outside of the school setting, we prefer the term *"temporally distant events"* so that one does not have to be concerned with labeling or distinguishing between setting events and establishing operations (Ray & Watson, 2001). *Note: It is important to mention that both setting events and establishing operations may occur in the same environment as the interfering behavior. In these cases, they are some-*

ADVANCED DISCUSSION ON ESTABLISHING OPERATIONS

Jack Michael first introduced the term *establishing operation* in 1982. He described it as an antecedent event where "any change in the environment which alters the effectiveness of some object or event as a reinforcer . . . simultaneously alters the momentary frequency of the behavior that has been followed by that reinforcement" (pp. 150–151). Michael later differentiated an establishing operation from an antecedent that triggers behavior (the A in an A-B-C analysis that is called a discriminative stimulus). A discriminative stimulus is a stimulus that has a history of correlation between a behavior and the availability of reinforcement. An establishing operation, on the other hand, actually *establishes* the effectiveness of a reinforcer and does not merely signal that reinforcement is available. To better elucidate the concept of establishing operations and how they are present in our everyday lives, Pierce and Epling (1995) offer an interesting analysis of television commercials and how they exert influence over our behavior:

> Television commercials are said to influence a person's attitude toward a product. One way to understand the effects of commercials is to analyze them as establishing operations. In this case, an effective commercial alters the reinforcement value of the product and increases the likelihood of purchasing the item or using it if available. For example, dairy farmers advertise the goodness of ice-cold milk. Those who are influenced by the commercial are likely to go to the fridge and have a glass of milk. Of course, this immediate effect of the commercial depletes the amount of milk you have on hand, and eventually you buy more milk. (pp. 37–38)

This is but one example of an establishing operation and how what happens in one setting influences our behavior in another, temporally distant setting. Other establishing operations that occur on a daily basis might include being sick the night before going to work, having an argument with your significant other before going to the office, having had a migraine the previous evening, hearing a song on the radio on your way to work that is associated with very pleasant memories, etc. So you see, establishing operations are hard at work in your daily life—it's just that most people don't know what to call them and have difficulty describing how these temporally distant events are impacting their behavior.

times referred to as "temporally proximate events." In the following paragraphs, we hope to provide clear descriptions and examples of each of these and how they might be included or considered as part of a comprehensive FBA.

ESTABLISHING OPERATIONS

Perhaps the clearest examples of establishing operations are deprivation and satiation. If you have been deprived of water for a period of 24 hours and are really thirsty, two things happen from an operant perspective: (1) water is, for the moment, a very powerful rein-

ADVANCED DISCUSSION ON SETTING EVENTS

Kantor (1959) was the first person to use the term *setting events* to describe the contextual conditions that influence the stimulus–response relationship. He viewed them as immediate circumstances that influence which stimulus–response sequences in an individual's repertoire will occur in a given situation. According to Kantor, setting events can be internal (e.g., feeling sick) or external (e.g., the classroom). Bijou and Baer (1961) provided an interesting example to illustrate the effects that setting events can have on behavior:

> A mother who routinely puts her eighteen-month old son in a playpen after his afternoon nap finds that during the next hour the baby plays with his toys, tries some gymnastics on the side of the pen, engages in vigorous vocal play, and does not fuss at all. Consequently, the mother has free time for an extra cup of tea and a few telephone calls. One day, however, the baby is kept awake during his entire nap [period] by the unusual and persistent noise of a power mower on the lawn outside the bedroom window. When his mother puts him in the playpen this time (in the setting event or context of sleep deprivation), he whimpers, cries, is generally fussy, and does not play. (p. 26)

In the above example, all of the stimuli associated with the playpen are the antecedents (discriminative stimuli) for play time and the nap is the setting event. In the absence of the setting event (i.e., the nap), the toddler's behavior is fussy instead of playful, even in the presence of the same antecedents. Another example to help us understand the role of setting events in our behavior is to observe the same person's behavior across several very different situations, like a place of worship, a sporting event, and the beach in which the same antecedent is presented (e.g., a stranger placing their hand on the small of your back and speaking to you). The behavior of the observed individual will vary in each situation, although the antecedent is identical, because of the influence of all of the contextual factors (i.e., setting events) on behavior.

forcer, and (2) the likelihood of exhibiting behaviors that have been associated with obtaining water in the past are momentarily increased. Thus, the two criteria for an event to be considered an establishing operation (in this case being deprived of water) have been met. Let's take a look at another example with more direct relevance for in-school behavior:

Consider the case of Taneka, a normally developing kindergarten student who lives with her foster parents and six other foster children. Four of the six foster children are younger than she and demand a great deal of time and attention from the foster parents. Interviews with both Taneka and the foster parents confirmed that she did not obtain a great deal of adult attention at home. Thus, we can say that Taneka is experiencing a state of "adult attention deprivation." At school, Taneka engaged in a variety of disruptive and unusual behavior (e.g., wiping spit and nasal mucous over her entire body in the midst of a tantrum). Subsequent FBA indicated that the function of Taneka's behaviors was adult attention from the teacher, teacher assistant, and principal. Knowing Taneka's living arrangement allowed for a more complete understanding of why adult attention was so potent for her and why she engaged in these highly disruptive and troubling behaviors. Perhaps more importantly, however, this understanding was used in the development of a positive behavioral intervention. Without our going into undue detail regarding all aspects of the intervention, the component of intervention that was relevant for this discussion of establishing operations was that each morning upon arriving at school Taneka spent 15–20 minutes engaging in nonacademic activities (i.e., having fun and enjoying the attention of an adult) with a preferred adult prior to going to her classroom. This was done to eliminate the possible establishing operation of being deprived of adult attention. *Note: We said "possible establishing operation" in the previous sentence because we did not demonstrate a cause–effect relationship between being deprived of adult attention and Taneka's in-school behavior by either a brief or extended functional analysis. The relationship was hypothesized or correlational in nature.* Nonetheless, this extra piece of information was invaluable because it led directly to a critical intervention component and because it allowed us to provide a convincing rationale to the teaching staff on why these behaviors occurred and why certain elements had to be included in the positive behavior support plan.

The findings from the above real case example are very similar to two studies conducted long ago by Gewirtz and Baer (1958a 1958b). (*Remember, we said that many of the concepts used in an FBA are not new. This is just another example of the timelessness of these basic principles*). Without going into excruciatingly painful and perhaps boring detail, we will briefly point out the major components of Gewirtz and Baer's studies. In the first study (1952a), participants were exposed to a 20-minute social deprivation condition in which they were left alone. Next, they played a game where correct responding was reinforced with verbal praise. They found that correct responding was greater in the social praise condition following deprivation than during a baseline condition when no reinforcers were given. In their second study, Gewirtz and Baer (1952b) studied the effects of social satiation on praise as a reinforcer. They did this by assigning 102 first graders to one of three conditions: (1) a deprivation condition exactly like that in their first study, (2) a nondeprivation condition in which the students were allowed to play the game yet received no social praise, and (3) a satiation condition in which the first graders received 20 minutes of social praise and interaction prior to playing the game. Correct responding during each of the conditions was then measured and compared. Not surprisingly, social attention was not a reinforcer for the students who received 20 minutes of social interaction prior to playing the game but was a reinforcer for the students who were deprived of social attention. The findings from the second study are closely related to the applied findings from the above case example of Taneka and should have particular relevance for interventions where adult attention plays a role in the maintenance of interfering behavior.

Other researchers have also investigated the role that establishing operations play in behaviors such as self-injury (Corte, Wolf, & Lock, 1971; Pace, Iwata, Cowdery, Andree, & McIntyre, 1993; Wacker et al., 1990; Zarcone et al., 1993), resistance to treatment of school-related problems (Kolko & Milan, 1983), and obscenity in a male with brain injury (Pace, Ivancic, & Jefferson, 1994). As you can see, however, most of these investigations involved adults, persons with developmental disabilities, and/or low-incidence behaviors. But what about research empirically documenting a process for identifying establishing operations for typically developing children in the school setting? Read on to find the answer.

Quite obviously, there are potent reasons for identifying establishing operations when a practitioner is conducting school-based functional behavioral assessments. Perhaps even more important for the practitioner is the knowledge that the effects which establishing operations have on behavior are powerful tools for understanding and explaining behavior to others. The above case example illustrated both of the advantages of identifying potential establishing operations.

Some studies have examined certain extraenvironmental events and concluded that they qualified as establishing operations. O'Reilly (1995) found a relationship between sleep deprivation and an increase in the frequency of aggressive behavior in the presence of task demands in a 31-year-old male with severe mental retardation. On nights where more than 5 hours sleep was obtained, the participant had fewer instances of escape-maintained aggression than on days when he slept less than 5 hours. Although O'Reilly labeled sleep an establishing operation, he failed to demonstrate that escape from task demands was more reinforcing on sleep-deprived days than on non-sleep-deprived days. For the practitioner, it really does not matter if the event is an establishing operation or a setting event. What matters more is discovering that the extraenvironmental event (in this case, sleep deprivation) is having an impact on school behavior.

SETTING EVENTS

Perhaps more so than establishing operations, setting events can be more cleanly divided into two categories: temporally proximate setting events and temporally distant setting events. Let's take a quick look at studies in each category.

Temporally Proximate Setting Events

This category of setting events simply means that they occur close in time, and therefore usually in the same environment, as the interfering behavior. In an early study, Krantz and Risley (1977) investigated possible setting events for the disruptive behavior of kindergartners during a story-time activity. Their analysis indicated that a period of vigorous play preceded story time that might serve as a setting event for disruptive behavior. To test their hypothesis, they replaced the active play period with a quiet activity prior to story time that resulted in a decrease in disruptive behavior. The results from this study may have particular significance for interfering behaviors that occur in the classroom following unstructured activities, physical education (PE) class, recess, or other high-energy activities.

Another interesting study was conducted by McAfee (1987), who examined the relationship between classroom density and the disruptive behaviors of 918 children with moderate-to-severe disabilities across 72 special education classrooms. Although the data were only correlational in nature, the results indicated that the number of aggressive acts increased as classroom density increased. Likewise, when the amount of space available to each student was increased, the number of aggressive acts decreased.

And, finally, in a study with which most readers can probably readily identify, Talkington and Riley (1971) found that imposed reduction diets were associated with aggressive behavior in 32 adults with mental retardation living in an in-patient facility. Additionally, adults living in the same facility who were not under dietary restrictions had fewer instances of aggressive behavior. Although included under temporally proximate setting events, dietary restriction could be placed under the temporally distant category as well if certain foods were being restricted at home, particularly in the morning before the student comes to school.

Temporally Distant Setting Events

This category of setting events refers to those events that occur apart from the immediate environment in which the interfering behavior occurs. Two of the most interesting studies, and ones that have a high degree of relevance for practitioners, were conducted by Gardner, Cole, Davidson, and Kavan (1986) and Kennedy and Itkonen (1993). In the study of Gardner et al., the physical and verbal aggressiveness of an adult male was targeted for intervention. Using a conventional A-B-C analysis, they were able to identify six antecedents that reliably preceded (i.e., triggered) aggressive outbursts. Because of considerable variability between the stimuli, it was difficult to select one antecedent as the one most closely related to aggressive behavior. Thus, Gardner and colleagues included consideration of setting events to better understand the relationship between each of the antecedents and the man's aggressive behavior. They began with an interview using the Functional Analysis Interview Form (O'Neill, Horner, Ablin, Storey, & Sprague, 1990). Five setting events were identified during the interview: (1) his arguments with peers in the group home or on the bus prior to arriving at the vocational center, (2) his difficulty in arising in the morning, (3) weekend family visits with his brother in the home, (4) the presence of specific staff, and (5) weekend family visits without his brother in the home. Data were kept for 1 month and indicated that setting events that occurred at the group home were related to both physical and verbal aggression at the vocational facility. This was one of the first studies that systematically and empirically explored the impact of events in one environment (i.e., the group home) on the behavior in another environment by events in another environment (i.e., the classroom).

The Kennedy and Itknonen (1993) study examined the role that setting events may play in helping to explain why behavior plans are sometimes ineffective. Two students with developmental delays had been exposed to several different behavior plans with inconsistent results. An analysis of setting events was conducted that included record reviews, structured interviews, and direct observations of the students in their respective classrooms. For one student, awakening late appeared to be a setting event; for the other student, the number of stops that were made on the way to school. Intervention involved implementing a morning wake-up procedure and taking an alternate route that resulted in fewer stops, respectively. Both of the interventions resulted in decreases in all interfering behaviors.

One may logically ask how does awakening late influence subsequent school behavior. Although there a number of possible explanations, consider the following example:

Tess awakens late one morning and receives many high-intensity commands and directions from her parents: "Hurry up and get dressed!"; "Go brush your teeth right now, you don't have much time"; and "The bus is almost here—hurry up and get your backpack together." She may have to rush through breakfast, not get to wear the clothes she wants, nor have time to adequately style her hair. Overall, her morning routine has been seriously disrupted. Now Tess gets to school where she is immediately issued other commands and directions. Perhaps because of the aversiveness associated with the commands delivered at home, she is less likely to comply with commands at school and more likely to engage in behaviors that allow her to avoid those commands and directions (resulting in negative reinforcement).

TEMPORALLY DISTANT EVENTS

Perhaps the most comprehensive study to date identifying the effects of temporally distant events on school behavior was conducted by Ray and Watson (2001). Three typically developing preschoolers evidenced high rates of interfering behaviors. Prior to these authors conducting extended functional analyses, interviews regarding each participant were conducted with school personnel, the primary caregiver, and transportation staff. Based on information gathered during the interviews, a checklist was constructed for each participant of possible setting events or establishing operations (i.e., temporally distant events [TDEs]; see Figure 10.1). Concurrent with the extended functional analyses, the primary caregiver recorded the occurrence or nonoccurrence of each event each day on the checklist. Where appropriate, transportation staff were contacted to determine if a particular event had occurred or not. After all functional analysis and checklist data had been collected, the checklists were examined to determine which events occurred at least 50% of the time. For each participant, one event was identified from the checklist as occurring at least 50% of the days: the TDEs included getting less than 5 hours sleep per night, waking up late, and nocturnal enuresis, respectively.

Results of the functional analyses were analyzed in three ways: (1) overall, (2) with the presence of the TDE, and (3) without the presence of the TDE. Across all three participants, the overall functional analyses were inconclusive. That is, there was no readily discernible dominant function for each participant's interfering behavior. When the functional analysis data were analyzed according to whether or not the TDE occurred, however, interesting results emerged for all three participants. For instance, one participant's interfering behavior was maintained primarily by escape on days when the TDE did not occur and by access to tangibles on days the TDE did occur. This pattern of changing function according to whether or not the TDE occurred was replicated across the other two participants.

The implications of the findings from the Ray and Watson (2001) study on TDEs for school-based practitioners conducting FBAs should be quite obvious:

Child _____ Date _____

Completed by _____

	Yes, it occurred	No, it did not occur
Difficulty awakening	_____	_____
Argument with parents	_____	_____
Argument with older brother	_____	_____
Complained of stomachache	_____	_____
Was spanked	_____	_____
Slept less than 7 hours	_____	_____
Bus was late	_____	_____
Skipped breakfast	_____	_____
Bus was early	_____	_____
Awakened wet	_____	_____
Spent time with uncles previous night	_____	_____

FIGURE 10.1. Sample checklist for temporally distant events. From T. Steuart Watson and Mark W. Steege (2003). Copyright by The Guilford Press. Permission to photocopy this figure is granted to purchasers of this book for personal use only. See copyright page for details.

- They can help us to further understand and explain behavior, especially the variability that frequently occurs in an interfering behavior.
- They provide one viable explanation for why a stimulus (e.g., attention from the teacher) is reinforcing one day and not reinforcing another day.
- They can be integrated into the positive behavioral support (PBS) plan and can help to reduce and prevent the occurrence of interfering behavior.
- They provide a more comprehensive approach to functional behavioral assessment and include events that occur in the home environment.
- If the events occur in the home environment, they provide a good way to get the parents more involved in the assessment and treatment process.

PROCESS FOR IDENTIFYING
AND MEASURING TEMPORALLY DISTANT EVENTS

We do not advocate measuring TDEs in every case of school-based functional behavioral assessment. To do so would place undue burdens on school staff and unnecessarily increase the complexity of the FBA process. We do advocate examining the possible impact of TDEs in any of the following circumstances:

- When the indirect and direct descriptive assessments have not yielded a strong finding
- When the brief or extended functional analyses have yielded mixed or unclear results
- When there is considerable variability in the student's interfering behavior from day to day
- When the student's responsiveness to an otherwise well-designed PBS plan is variable

If any of the above circumstances exist, we suggest that you begin to consider that extraenvironmental events are impacting school behavior. In such cases, we recommend the following process to determine whether TDEs or perhaps temporally proximate setting events are operating:

- Begin by interviewing those who interact with the student most frequently both at school and home. If the student takes a bus to school, an interview with the bus driver may yield important information. You may use the Functional Assessment Interview Form (FAIF) or the Functional Assessment Informant Record—Parent (FAIR-P) to help structure the interview.
- Closely examine the student's physical environment and sequence of scheduling to help identify temporally proximate setting events.
- Possible events that arise from either or both of the above-described procedures might then be organized into a checklist format (see Figure 10.1).

- Conduct direct descriptive functional behavioral assessments by having the appropriate person(s) complete the checklist while simultaneously observing and measuring the interfering behavior, and (if possible) conduct brief functional analyses.
- If establishing operations or setting events seem to be influencing behavior, alter the establishing operations or setting events as part of the PBS plan.

SUMMARY

This chapter was meant as an introduction to the concepts of establishing operations, setting events, temporally distant events, and temporally proximate events and how they may impact not only a student's behavior but also the results of functional behavioral assessments. Although these concepts are certainly not new, they have not been as thoroughly researched as other topics in the applied behavior analysis (ABA) and functional behavioral assessment literatures. We hope that we have given enough information to promote an understanding of these events and how they may be useful for understanding and predicting behavior, particularly behavior that occurs in the school setting. We also hope that the process we have described for assessing extraenvironmental events proves useful within the context of your school-based FBAs. As we mentioned, it is not necessary or time efficient to assess these events as part of *every* FBA. Only under certain circumstances will it be necessary to include an assessment of these events in order adequately to describe and change behavior, circumstances we have already delineated. Spending great amounts of time to analyze the effects of extraenvironmental events in a typical FBA (if there is such an animal as a "typical" FBA) is unwise and will not add significantly to either the FBA or the resulting behavior intervention plan (BIP).

In closing this chapter, perhaps a word of caution is necessary. When one is explaining the results of an FBA that has included consideration of extraenvironmental events, it is best to temper statements of causality linking these events and in-school behavior. This is necessary for several reasons, chief among them that parents may mistakenly believe that you are blaming them, in the case of home-based events, for *causing* their child's interfering behavior at school. It is a prudent course of action to reassure them that they are not to blame for their child's in-school behavior, but rather that certain events occurring at home can set the child up for difficult interactions at school. We have found that providing an adult-related analogy often helps parents understand the role that extraenvironmental events may have on behavior in another setting at a later time. Conversely, school personnel need to understand that it is not only home events that are related to the in-school behavior. Placing undue emphasis on the home events may inadvertently confirm suspicions that the student's interfering behavior is solely the result of "the home" and therefore there is no need to change the interaction he/she has with the student. It is best to summarize the relationship between extraenvironmental events and immediate environmental events as an interaction in which both are contributing equally to the interfering behavior. Doing so provides ample opportunities for both parents and teachers to change their interactions with the child/student.

11

Training School/Agency Personnel to Implement Functional Behavioral Assessments

Perhaps one of the most daunting tasks facing school districts is training building-level personnel to conduct FBAs. After all, the IDEA states that the individualized education program (IEP) team is responsible for a wide range of activities that are subsumed under FBA and positive behavior support (PBS) programming. Because IEP teams are typically composed of personnel located at the building level, it is necessary to train teams at each building who can provide these services. Before discussing training, monitoring, and support strategies that are necessary for these teams to function effectively, we would like to point out some of the problems/concerns around this issue of training IEP teams to conduct FBAs and implement behavioral intervention plans (BIPs).

- *Issue 1:* In small districts where there are only several schools, training school-based teams may pose less of a problem than for larger districts that have tens or hundreds of schools.
- *Issue 2:* There are a myriad of logistical issues that will impact each district regardless of size, including problems such as the following:

When will the training occur?
Who is going to provide the training?
What type of training will district personnel receive?
How will the district compensate personnel to receive training during summer or for substitute teachers if training occurs during school days/hours?
How much training is necessary?
What type of follow-up training is needed?
Are team members provided release time to perform the extra duties required?

- *Issue 3:* Who will be responsible for monitoring the teams for compliance, effectiveness, troubleshooting, determining future training needs, etc?

183

- *Issue 4:* There are no data indicating the most effective means of training school-based teams to conduct FBAs and implement BIPs.
- *Issue 5:* There are no data indicating that school-based teams can actually do what is required of them by law.
- *Issue 6:* Is it OK to hire a couple of outside experts in functional behavioral assessment to do all of the FBAs and BIPs?
- *Issue 7:* Does anyone on the team have the expertise to develop interventions for a wide range of problems that are likely to be encountered in a school setting?
- *Issue 8:* Who is going to be responsible for ensuring that the BIPs are implemented with integrity and that effectiveness data are collected?
- *Issue 9:* How can a team of professionals possibly learn enough during a 2- or 3-day training module to do FBAs in a reliable and valid way, especially when one considers that most behavior analysts and others with particular expertise in functional behavioral assessment have studied for a minimum of several years and have a number of mentored experiences in this area?

All of the issues cited above are ones that we have come across in our collective experience of providing services to a wide variety of school districts in many states. Because of Issues 4 and 5, we do not have data that tell us how to train school teams to be the most effective at implementing FBAs and BIPs. Nor do we have data telling us that these teams are actually conducting "best-practice" and "legally defensible" FBAs. In fact, a dissertation recently completed by one of our graduate students (Dittmer-McMahon, 2001), indicated that some school-based teams do a poor job of conducting FBAs, discerning function based on their data, and designing BIPs.

Given the problems cited above (and no doubt there are many others), as well as the data indicating the difficulty that teams have in conducting FBAs and implementing BIPs, is there anything that can be done? Given that teams must be trained, we offer the following guidelines along with our own overheads accompanied by an explanation of each overhead to facilitate the training process. These overheads are not meant to be immutable. On the contrary, they are provided as guides that will allow you to customize training for your district's school-based teams.

GUIDELINES

- First, we recommend that each building assemble a team of staff that will be relatively stable (i.e., with a low chance of yearly turnover), motivated, and has expertise that, when pooled, will result in an effective unit for conducting FBAs and BIPs. Team members should represent regular education, special education, administration, school counseling, and a behavioral specialist if available. Teams should not be larger than six individuals.

Rationale: Data from the Dittmer-McMahon (2001) study indicated that teams which had the same members over a 2- to 3-year time span performed "better" FBAs than did teams whose members changed more frequently. Likewise, the study found that teams that were constructed based on carefully chosen staff with specific skills (e.g., someone who is a good classroom manager, someone with good knowledge of alternative instructional techniques) were more effective than teams based on either volunteers or mere availability.

• FBA teams need "up-front" training of 2–3 days and then ongoing training of at least 1 day per month during the first year.

Rationale: The up-front training provides the requisite knowledge regarding the basic principles and procedures of FBA and an introduction into positive behavioral programming. The monthly training session allows the teams to bring up cases on which they are currently working to receive feedback and coaching. It also permits the trainer to model effective problem-solving strategies for determining which procedures should be included as part of a particular FBA. In addition, it allows the trainer(s) to determine which teams may need additional assistance and which teams are moving ahead a bit more quickly. These instructional strategies (didactic, modeling, feedback, and coaching) and pacing (some massed instruction and some spaced instruction as opposed to only mass instruction) are consistent with the literature on effective instruction (Sterling-Turner, Watson, & Moore, 2002; T. S. Watson & Kramer, 1995; T. S. Watson, Ray, Sterling, & Logan, 1999).

• Training should be mastery based such that movement from one phase to the next should be based on meeting or exceeding a criterion score. That is, team members should demonstrate a particular skill before moving on to the next skill.

Rationale: Learning to conduct FBAs is the result of an accumulation of separate but related skills, with each building on the previous skill. For instance, one cannot functionally analyze a problem behavior that has not been operationally defined. Therefore, team members should actually demonstrate during training that they can define problems in observable and measurable terms.

• The actual process used by the district, including forms, should be made as simple as possible.

Rationale: In our experience, school districts that have an unwieldy and overly complex system, from initial referral to conclusion, often do not perform even minimal procedures required by law. Keeping everything simple, particularly paperwork, allows the team members to focus their efforts on conducting reliable and valid FBAs instead of merely engaging in activities designed to fill in spaces on a form.

TRAINING SCHOOL/AGENCY PERSONNEL

To assist you in training school/agency personnel in your district, we are providing the actual overheads that we use in our own training. These overheads are certainly not meant to be the Holy Grail of training FBA teams. Rather, they are meant to serve as exemplars as you go about the process of deciding how to train teams and in collecting materials to assist in the training process. Accompanying each overhead is a narrative of the commentary that we use that, again, may serve as a model for information that you may wish to present. The particular model that is presented here has been evaluated in two districts and shown to be effective for teaching basic skills in conducting FBAs. A wider applicability of this training program has not, however, been empirically evaluated.

• Members of the FBA team should provide school/agency-wide training to staff in basic principles of applied behavior analysis, with an emphasis on functions of behavior (see Chapter 4) and FBA procedures.

Rationale: In our experience, the efficiency in conducting and the validity of the FBA is increased to the degree with which school/agency staff members are grounded in the conceptual foundations and are familiar with the FBA procedures.

The training is divided into four sections:

• Overview and Introduction to Functional Behavioral Assessment
• Methods of Functional Behavioral Assessment
• Writing FBA Reports
• Linking Assessment to Intervention

Although these are separate sections, it is important to create links between each of the sections so that team members see the connection between assessment data and intervention, for example.

SECTION I: OVERVIEW AND INTRODUCTION TO FUNCTIONAL BEHAVIORAL ASSESSMENT

Before beginning the formal presentation, we introduce ourselves and welcome everyone to the training. Depending on what the participants have been told and their background, they may not have much, if any, information related to functional behavioral assessments or the training they are about to receive. Therefore, we typically begin by saying something along the lines of the following:

"We would like to begin by welcoming everyone to this 2 (or 3 or however many) day training module on functional behavioral assessment. My name is Dr. Steuart Watson and my copresenter is Dr. Mark Steege. We have been invited by your district to train your school-based teams to conduct functional behavioral assessments and to implement positive behavioral supports. We realize that, for many of you, the term 'functional behavioral assessment' (or FBA) may be new. Perhaps some of you are wondering why you were selected to be part of this team. Although we don't know the exact criteria your district used to select you, we are happy that you are here. This part of the training will last 2 (or 3) days and is divided into four sections: an overview of functional behavioral assessment, a thorough look at the methods associated with FBAs, writing FBA reports, and (most importantly) linking the assessment data to effective interventions. We understand that some of the information we are going to present to you may be contrary to aspects of your previous training, but we ask that you stick with us and learn as much as you possibly can in the next 2 (or 3) days. The training is very content rich and will require you not only to listen but to demonstrate many of the skills that we are going to teach you. With that in mind, are there any questions before we get started?"

Overhead 1

After the introductory statement, we move right into the opening overhead (see page 207), which is a standard definition of functional behavioral assessment. We focus on several terms in the definition:

- *Systematic.* It is systematic because we have specific procedures for conducting functional behavioral assessments and they are not done in a haphazard or one-size-fits-all fashion.
- *Variables.* we make certain that participants understand we are not talking about "inside the person" factors like personality, psyche, or traits. We focus on variables that we can observe and measure.
- *Antecedents.* We provide a definition of antecedents such as "Any event or stimulus that happens before a behavior occurs. The closer in time the event or stimulus is to the actual behavior, the more powerful is the effect it has on behavior." We may also give classroom examples that include things like verbal instructions or comments from other students.
- *Consequences.* We provide a definition of consequences such as "Anything that happens in the person's environment after a behavior occurs. The manner in which the term 'consequence' is used in FBAs does not necessarily mean something negative. In fact, a consequence can be positive, negative, or neutral."
- *Particular environmental context.* We emphasize that a functional behavioral assessment must be conducted in the environment where the behavior occurs in order to accurately identify the variables that are impacting the behavior.

Overhead 2

Perhaps the most obvious question that participants have upon entering the training is "Why is it necessary to conduct functional behavioral assessment?" In anticipation of this rather obvious question, Overhead 2 (see p. 207) is presented. There are four related bullets here:

- *Mandated by the IDEA (Public Law 105-17).* Many, if not all, participants will not be knowledgeable regarding the reauthorization of the IDEA and what it specifically says about when FBAs must be conducted. Therefore, we follow up with Overhead 3, which briefly delineates the circumstances under which an FBA must be conducted. In this overhead, we give a brief overview of the most relevant sections from the IDEA.
- *Leads to effective interventions.* Although this statement appears to be fairly self-explanatory, most participants have been taught to base interventions on the form (topography) of behavior rather than on the function. In other words, "If a child is hitting, then the intervention is [*fill in the blank*]." Thus, we spend a bit of time describing how interventions based on function are actually more effective than those based on form because they take into consideration exactly "how" of "why" the behavior works for the student.
- *Best practice for service delivery.* What we mean here is that psychoeducational services are likely to be more effective and more efficient if they are based on a careful func-

tional behavioral assessment. The way psychoeducational services are currently delivered (refer–test–place) have been empirically shown to be ineffective for the vast majority of students receiving them.

• *Offers legal protection to the school district.* Quite simply, districts that meet their legal obligation to perform functional behavioral assessments when required by law prevent parents from suing for failing to provide the appropriate services. It is important to remember that in an overwhelming majority of due process hearings, parents have won because districts failed either to conduct an FBA or to use appropriate and/or adequate procedures.

Overheads 3a and 3b

We use these two overheads (see p. 208) to acquaint participants with the basic circumstances under which an FBA *should* and *must* be conducted. Although the law makes the distinction regarding "should" and "must," we emphasize that *any* of the circumstances on the overheads should trigger an FBA because it simply is best practice, it leads to effective intervention, and it will protect the district if the behavior becomes worse or parents pursue legal action.

Overhead 4

This overhead prompts us to describe, in layperson's terms, what *function* really means. First, it tells us "why" an individual engages in behavior. "Why" is synonymous with the "causes" of behavior and the way most people talk about motivation. When one is interested in function, one is not very interested in the topography of behavior or what the behavior looks like or the form the behavior takes. That is, it is less important to know that Sallie hits her classmates on the chest with the back of her hand than it is to know *why* she is doing it.

On a related note, no behaviors are really maladaptive. This is a difficult point for many educators to understand, but it is essential for "buying into" the philosophical framework of FBA. We stress that, although a behavior may be inappropriate, it is working for the student in some way. If it is working, then it can not be maladaptive, which literally means "bad adaptation." Any behavior that works for an individual is, by definition, adaptive.

Overhead 5

Remember the true story from Chapter 4 where we asked workshop participants how many functions of behavior there were and the response was "thousands"? Before discussing function any further, it is essential that everyone be on the same terminological page with the actual functions of behavior.

There are three broad functions of behavior, with subcategories within each. Let's first look at the three broad categories—positive reinforcement, negative reinforcement, and automatic sensory reinforcement. At this point, we typically show an overhead of the FBA decision tree and refer participants to their handout (see Chapter 4). We then explain each possible function of behavior.

Note: At this point, we may give brief examples of each of the functions but we do not go into excruciating detail on each. Some of the real-life examples we use for each include the following:

Positive reinforcement. The student who raises her hand frequently during independent seat work just so the teacher will come check on her; the student who makes funny noises in class because all the kids laugh at him when he makes noise. In both instances, the behavior continues because the students are getting positive reinforcement in the form of *attention* from others.

Negative reinforcement. The student who, when given an assignment, gets up to sharpen her pencils, then walks around the classroom twice, then comes to the teacher's desk to ask for more information is delaying (*avoiding*) getting started on her work; the student who, when working on a difficult task that greatly exceeds his skill level, suddenly throws his paper to the ground and sits sullenly in his seat does so to *escape* the difficult task.

Tangibles. The child who pushes another child away so as to get the last dictionary on the shelf does so because he gets a *tangible* object (the dictionary); the kindergartner who cries upon coming to school until the principal gives her a piece of gum does so in part because of receiving a *tangible* item (chewing gum).

Automatic reinforcement/sensory stimulation. A child with a severe visual impairment gouges her eyes with her thumbs because doing so produces bright lights in her visual field, a type of *automatic positive reinforcement (arousal induction).* A student suddenly begins engaging in self-injurious behavior (SIB) that consists of slapping the left side of his face with an open hand; further assessment reveals that he is probably doing so because the slapping results in a decrease in the pain on that side of his face associated with a severely abscessed tooth, a type of *automatic negative reinforcement (arousal reduction).*

Overhead 6

Although it is important to recognize the functions of behavior, it is equally important to recognize what are not functions of behavior. This overhead contains some of the most common misconceptions we have heard in the educational arena about possible functions of behavior. Power, revenge, or control are not functions of behavior; they are labels used to describe the purpose of the target student's behavior based on the behavioral response of someone in the target student's environment. For instance, if the target student manipulates another child into doing something inappropriate, some might incorrectly say that the function of the behavior was power or control. The correct way of describing this interaction is "Jimmy's behavior has been positively reinforced by social attention in the form of compliance by a classmate."

Medical conditions are not functions in that they do not directly evoke or maintain behavior. That said, however, we must acknowledge that medical conditions may be setting events or establishing operations. Children who are sick often behave differently from when they are well. Likewise, certain medical conditions can make any number of reinforcers more potent (see Chapter 10 for a more complete discussion of the role that medical conditions play in an FBA).

Overhead 7

We now focus on a more in-depth discussion of attention and the various sources of attention available in most classrooms. This is not an exhaustive list. Rather, it is meant as a prompt for assessing the assorted means by which attention may be delivered.

The two basic sources of attention in the classroom are the *teacher* and *peers*. Within each of these broad categories are positive and negative attention. Here, positive and negative do not refer to the effects on behavior; rather, they refer to global conceptualizations of attention. For instance, positive attention may be a smile (*nonverbal*), a hug (*physical*), or a sincere statement of praise (*verbal*). Likewise, negative attention could involve a frown (*nonverbal*), a push in the back (*physical*), or a reprimand (*verbal*). We conceptualize attention in this way because many people believe that for attention to be a reinforcer it must be positive. We want people to understand that *any* interaction between humans is potentially reinforcing, whether that interaction is positive or negative in nature.

Overhead 8

This overhead illustrates the most common stimuli that children in schools work to escape or avoid. Again, this is not an exhaustive list but an overall categorization of some of the most likely aversive stimuli. One of the most common things students work to escape or avoid are tasks, most typically academic tasks. Students will often engage in a variety of behaviors to escape or avoid a task that, for some reason, is aversive to them. One of the most frequent reasons why students work to escape/avoid academic tasks is that they do not have the necessary academic skills to complete the task. Other reasons might include that the task is boring or too long.

Students also sometimes escape/avoid behavioral demands such as the teacher's requests to "stay in your seat," "clean up around your desk," and "move from the reading center to the math center." Although most people view social interactions as a very potent source of positive reinforcement, not all social interactions are reinforcing. In fact, interacting with some people can be quite unpleasant (i.e., aversive or punishing). Thus, students will sometimes engage in behaviors that allow them to escape or avoid social interactions with particular adults and/or peers.

We are all aware of some students who either do not come to school at all or are frequently sent home at some point during the day for misbehaving. It is possible that all of the behaviors exhibited by these students to either avoid or escape the school environment are being negatively reinforced because the school, or some specific aspect of the school environment, is aversive.

Overhead 9

Within the school environment, it is unlikely that tangibles are the primary function of most behaviors that you will encounter. This is not because tangibles are not powerful; in fact tangibles are some of the most potent reinforcers around. Rather, it is because there are so few tangibles that are available contingent upon behavior in a typical classroom. That said, however, we will discuss this because we have seen cases where tangibles are the primary function of behavior and where they contribute as a secondary function of behavior.

One of the most potent tangibles is *food*. Consider the case where, each day just before snack time, the first-grade teacher announces, "Get your snacks from your cubby" and the children race to their cubbies. The function of their running and hurrying is to gain quicker access to their snacks, a *tangible*. Sometimes, access to certain *activities* can be reinforcing. For instance, a student may pretend to be finished with her work so that she may work at the computer. In this case, gaining access to the computer was the reason the student pretended to be finished and did not complete her task.

Games are another type of *tangible* that are available in classrooms. One particular situation comes to mind to describe how access to games may reinforce a host of inappropriate behaviors. This was a self-contained elementary classroom for children with moderate disabilities. The teacher was concerned that the children were not able to stay on task for even a minute or two. Observations indicated that, instead of doing their work, the students retrieved games from a nearby shelf to play while the teacher was attempting to teach. In this case, the student's off-task behavior was reinforced by access to games. And, finally, access to *materials* may be reinforcing. In classrooms where there are insufficient materials for everyone, children may push other students, run, or get out of their seats early in order to get dictionaries, paper, glue, etc. before their classmates do.

Overhead 10

This overhead describes the two different types of automatic reinforcement. To make this function more salient for the participants, we offer some examples that they likely have personally encountered:

Automatic Positive Reinforcement

This type of behavior occurs because the behavior itself produces some kind of "good" or "pleasant" feeling (arousal induction). For instance, when you run your fingers through your hair it usually results in a pleasant feeling to your scalp. Thus, running your fingers through your hair has been *automatically positively reinforced*.

Automatic Negative Reinforcement

This type of behavior occurs because the behavior itself results in a decrease or elimination of some kind of "unpleasant" feeling (arousal reduction). For instance, when your neck feels tense, you may rub your neck or move your head slowly from side to side to take away some of the tension. Thus, moving your head from side to side has been *automatically negatively reinforced* by a decrease in tension.

Overhead 11

This is a summary overhead to recap Section I, the "Overview and Introduction to Functional Behavioral Assessment." There is also a test given at this juncture to make certain that everyone is fluent in the basic concepts before moving on to some of the procedures associated with FBAs. We have replicated the test here so that it may be administered at this point. (*Note:* You may wish to establish a minimum criterion score that everyone must pass in order to move on to the next section.)

SAMPLE TEST: BASIC CONCEPTS OF FBA

1. What are the three broad functions of behavior?

2. Function is more important than _____.

3. Name three words that are synonymous with function.

4. What are four reasons why we conduct an FBA?

5. What is functional behavioral assessment?

For each of the following situations, indicate whether you *must* (M) or *should* (S) conduct an FBA:

6. When suspensions or placements in an alternative setting exceed 10 consecutive days or amount to a change in placement. M

7. When a student is placed in an interim alternative educational setting for 45 days when his/her misconduct involves weapons or drugs. M

8. When a student's problem behavior impedes his/her learning or the learning of others. S

9. When a due process hearing officer places a student in an interim alternative educational setting for behavior that is dangerous to him/herself or others. M

10. When a student's behavior presents a danger to him/herself or others. S

11. When a student's suspension or placement in an interim alternative educational setting approaches 10 cumulative days. S

SECTION II: METHODS OF FUNCTIONAL BEHAVIORAL ASSESSMENT

"This section will describe the overall procedure and some of the most likely methods that you will use to conduct FBAs in your schools. Because all of you are already very busy people, our goal is not to make you any more busy than you have to be. Therefore, we focus on methods that are not only accurate but time efficient as well. We will start with some very basic procedures and then add to them as we go along."

Overhead 12

The first thing that must be done when conducting an FBA is to operationally define the target behavior(s) of concern. The rest of the process depends upon this critical first step. Let's take a look at what we mean by operationally defining behavior. Basically, it means that the behavior is stated in observable, measurable terms such that two people could watch the behavior as it occurs and see the same thing. On a related note, you must avoid the temptation to use words that are not descriptive of behavior in your operational definition—words like *angry, frustrated, upset*, or *aggressive*. These words mean different things to different people and are subject to many interpretations.

Overhead 13

Perhaps one of the most difficult tasks that occurs in the early stages of the FBA process is identifying replacement behaviors. In most cases when a student is referred to a teacher support team, the teachers are seeking assistance with a behavior they want to reduce. When you ask them what the goal of treatment is, you may hear something like the following: "I want Betina to stop making strange noises when I am trying to teach and I want her to stop bothering others by whispering their name." Fair enough. Those behaviors can certainly be annoying, particularly when they occur at a high frequency. However, specifying which behaviors you want to get rid of is only half the story. The other half of the story is determining which behaviors you want Betina to engage in instead of the interfering behaviors. Thus, this overhead communicates the follow-up to operationally identifying the interfering behaviors: *identifying replacement behaviors*. Replacement behaviors must be operationally identified as well and can be based on one or more of the following criteria:

• *They are functionally equivalent to the interfering behavior.* "Functionally equivalent" means that they will result in the same outcome (e.g., peer attention, escape from difficult tasks) as the interfering behaviors. Because a functional behavioral assessment has not yet been conducted, you may not yet know the function of the interfering behaviors. That is OK as long as you keep this concept in mind throughout the FBA and BIP processes.

• *They result in socially valid outcomes for the student.* "Socially valid" means that there is some benefit of the behavior beyond the intervention process, and it is socially meaningful for the individual engaging in the replacement behavior. For instance, you may replace a student's nose picking with envelope stuffing. Yes, it is hard to pick your nose and stuff envelopes at the same time, but the skill of stuffing envelopes has little to no social validity for students and is therefore not socially meaningful for them. As a real example of this concept from an applied project we just completed, a second-grade female student was observed to masturbate almost continuously in class. Obviously the teacher wanted her to stop masturbating. When we asked the teacher what she wanted the student to do with her hands instead of masturbating, she replied, "Anything else except THAT!" That left the options for replacement behaviors virtually limitless. We settled, however, on her using her pencil to write as a replacement behavior. We chose this behavior for several reasons: (1) she was right-handed and always masturbated with her right hand, so writing would be incompatible with masturbating; (2) she was observed to complete very little work during class; and (3) writing is a socially meaningful behavior in the context of the classroom.

• *The replacement behavior is incompatible with the interfering behavior.* That is, just like the nose picking–envelope stuffing example from the preceding item, you may select a replacement behavior that precludes the student from engaging in the interfering behavior.

Overhead 14

After operationally defining both the interfering behavior and the replacement behavior, the next step is to figure out how to measure each one. Measurement of behavior is important because (1) it is required on the IEP, (2) it allows us to determine the relative strength of each behavior, (3) it gives us a means of measuring intervention effectiveness, and (4) it serves to help confirm or disconfirm information from other sources (e.g., parents, teachers, students). There are a number of ways to measure a behavior, but the most typical are frequency recording, duration recording, interval recording, momentary time sampling, and permanent product recording. Let's look briefly at each method and when you should/could use them:

• *Frequency recording* involves recording the *number* of times a behavior has occurred. It typically is used to record occurrences of discrete, low-rate behaviors (i.e., behaviors that have a definite beginning and end and which do not often occur). Although frequency recording is often a very accurate method for recording discrete behaviors, it tends to inaccurately estimate behaviors like time on-task that occur for long periods of time, behaviors that occur at a very high rate, and behaviors for which it is difficult to determine exactly when it starts and when it ends.

• *Duration recording* involves recording the *total amount of time* a behavior has occurred. It is most applicable for behaviors that persist for long periods such as on-task and stereotypy. Duration recording is typically done using a stopwatch and can be expressed as a percentage of time. For example, if Bart is out of his seat for 12 minutes of a 15-minute observation, you could say that he is out of his seat during 80% of the observation time. Duration recording is very difficult to use when measuring high-rate, short-duration behaviors and multiple behaviors.

• *Interval recording* involves recording the occurrence and nonoccurrence of behaviors at predetermined units of time (i.e., intervals ranging from several seconds to several minutes or even hours). There are three types of interval recording procedures:

1. *Whole-interval recording* is when a behavior is recorded only if it was observed to occur during the *entire* interval. For example, if the observation interval was 15 seconds in length, was Arvis out of his seat during the entire 15 seconds?
2. *Partial-interval recording* is when a behavior is recorded if it was observed for *any part* of the interval. For example, was Arvis out of his seat at any time during the 15-second interval?
3. *Momentary time sampling* is when the observer looks at the student only at predetermined points in time and records whether or not the interfering target behavior is occurring at the precise moment the observation occurs. For example, was Arvis out of his seat when you looked up at the *end* of the 15-second interval?

• *Permanent product recording* is used when a behavior results in specific *tangible* outcomes. This procedure involves recording the number of products (e.g., the number of math problems completed in a 10-minute classroom session) that a student produces. One particular advantage of this method is that the observer need not be present when the behavior occurs. Conversely, it is sometimes difficult to determine whether the student actually produced the product. For example, a teacher cannot determine whether a student completed his/her own homework or whether someone else completed the assignment.

Overhead 15

Ultimately, the decision upon which recording method to use is driven by three factors:

1. The dimensions of behavior (i.e., topography, frequency, duration)
2. The goals of the intervention
3. Pragmatic considerations such as time, resources, and competency of the observers

For most practitioners, the pragmatic considerations will probably outweigh the other two. Regardless of which procedure you select, make certain that it is done accurately and consistently. *Some data are better than no data.*

Overhead 16

Now we are getting to the "meat" of FBA—the actual how-to-do-it part. The are three very broad methods of functional behavioral assessment.

1. Indirect FBA
2. Direct descriptive FBA
3. Functional behavioral analysis, both the brief and extended versions

Because functional behavioral analysis requires considerable expertise and time, we are not going to cover it in this training session. Rather, we are going to focus on the first two.

Overhead 17

Every FBA that you will do will involve some type of indirect assessment. The most common methods of indirect assessment include record reviews, interviews, and ready-to-use, preconstructed forms.

Overhead 18

Let's start by talking about what you are and are not looking for in a record review. You are not looking at a student's folder to gain historical data. You are looking for clues about his/her learning history and how that learning history may be affecting the occurrence of his/her interfering behavior in the current context. To do this, you look at previous grades and trends in grades, scores on standardized achievement tests, attendance history, disciplinary history, medical and social histories, previous interventions, and IEPs. Essentially, you are looking for the academic, social, and medical variables that may play a role in triggering and maintaining the interfering behavior and that may be tested through more direct means of functional behavioral assessment.

Overhead 19

The next method of indirect functional behavioral assessment involves interviews. A number of people can be interviewed to obtain information regarding the interfering behavior and possible antecedents, consequences, and individual variables including the student, parent, teacher, or other staff member. Perhaps the most important thing to remember about interviewing is to be clear about your objective. For instance, is the purpose of the interview to operationally define the behavior, to gain each person's perspectives on the variables related to the behavior, or to determine the complex sequence of a behavioral interaction?

Note: We sometimes explain the behavioral stream interview (BSI) in this part of the training and give an example. Feel free to use the examples provided in Chapter 6.

Overhead 20

There are a number of forms that can be used to assist in the FBA process. These include the Functional Behavioral Assessment Screening Form (FBASF), the Antecedent Variables Assessment Form (AVAF), the Individual Variables Assessment Form (IVAF), and the Consequence Variables Assessment Form (CVAF). Each of these seeks to identify different kinds of variables, as their respective names imply, that may be impacting interfering behavior.

Note: You may choose to hand out blank copies of each of these forms at this time and briefly review each one.

Overhead 21

The next method of functional behavioral assessment is called direct descriptive FBA. This method involves observing and recording behavior as it occurs in the natural context/setting. During the direct observation, the observer is trying to identify setting events, antecedents, and consequences that occur in relation to the interfering behavior.

Overhead 22

As with indirect assessment, there are a number of preconstructed forms to assist you in the observation process. These forms include the Task Difficulty Antecedent Analysis Form (TDAAF), the Conditional Probability Record (CPR), and the Functional Behavioral Assessment Observation Form (FBAOF). Again, the aims of each of these forms varies. For instance, the TDAAF helps determine if academic antecedents, namely, difficult academic tasks, are reliable triggers for interfering behavior. The CPR helps determine which consequences are most likely to occur contingent upon a behavior. The FBAOF is a more general observational form that assists the observer in identifying antecedent and consequence variables as well as individual variables and setting events.

Note: Again, you may choose to provide handouts of the blank forms at this point and briefly review each one.

Overhead 23

OK, that finishes this section that describes some of the most basic procedures involved in conducting a school-based functional behavioral assessment. Let's take a quick review of what those procedures are:

Note: At this point, we have videotapes of students from that school district exhibiting behavior problems and, using the procedures described above, practice completing them based on information seen in the video. We also use the following written scenarios within small teams of three to five participants to generate discussion, assess their grasp of information thus far, and determine potential areas of weakness. The comments in italic are for the trainers.

Scenario I

Cindy is a 5-year-old child attending kindergarten. She has only been in your class a short time as she moved from Michigan after being removed from her mother's home and placed with her grandmother. Although reports are sketchy, it seems that while she was with her mother she was severely neglected and it is unclear if there was ever any physical abuse. Her first days in your class were marked by extended crying episodes, which were often followed by severely aggressive behavior toward other children and even you. You tried pairing her with a friend when she cried to make her feel more secure and even tried to console her yourself, all to no avail. Due to the crying and aggressive behavior, her pediatrician thought she might be depressed and recommended that she receive an in-patient evaluation at a local psychiatric hospital. She was gone for 2 weeks and the child psychiatrist experimented with several antidepressant medications to get her behavior under control. When Cindy returned to your class, the crying had not gotten any better. In fact, it seemed to have gotten worse.

Based on what you have just read, answer the following questions:

1. What behavior should be targeted for intervention?

Many participants will say the aggression, because it is a dangerous behavior. However, crying is an antecedent for aggression. Thus, the most appropriate target behavior is crying.

2. What behavior-recording method would be most appropriate in this circumstance?

With this question, almost any of the answers would be correct. The important point here is to generate discussion about how each of the recording procedures would be used in this case.

3. What forms might you want to use in your FBA of this case?
4. Based solely on the information above, what is the *most likely* function of Cindy's behavior?

This question will throw participants a loop for two reasons: (a) if they answered question 1 with aggressive behavior, many of them might use words like "control" and "power" to describe the function of Cindy's behavior; (b) because of Cindy's one-time removal from class, many might list "escape" as the function. In fact, the most likely function of Cindy's behavior is "social attention."

5. Given the function of the target behavior, describe a classroom-based intervention.

There is considerable latitude here. Again, you want to focus on decreasing the crying and aggressive behavior but also increasing a more prosocial, adaptive behavior. If participants do not identify a replacement behavior without being prompted, promptly prompt them.

Note 1: Please feel free to add other questions to this list if you so desire.

Note 2: It is of extreme importance during this exercise that the trainer model good "FBA behavior" for the participants. That means talking in FBA language and not allowing participants to get sidetracked by other information in the scenarios.

Scenario II

Wilbur is 11 years old and in the fourth grade. He is generally well-behaved but does not perform well academically. One of the reasons he fails is that he does not get his work done, either at home or school. Even though he is weak in most subjects, particularly reading and math, he is of average intelligence. You are worried that if he does not remediate his academic weaknesses very quickly, he will likely have significant academic trouble throughout the remainder of his school career. You notice that, during his in-class assignments, he sits quietly at his desk for a few minutes and then gets up and walks around the room. You tell him to return to his seat, which he always does, but he is soon up wandering around the room again. He never really bothers the other students, nor does he go to a specific area of the room—he just seems to wander aimlessly.

Based on what you have just read, answer the following questions:

1. What behavior should be targeted for intervention?

Many participants will say that wandering should be targeted and perhaps it should. The problem with targeting wandering is that even if you get him to spend more time in his seat, Wilbur will not likely complete more work because of his poor academic skills. A more viable alternative is to target his academic weaknesses so that such tasks are not so aversive for him. Concurrently, a related target behavior could be the amount of work he is completing.

2. What behavior-recording method would be most appropriate in this circumstance?

*Given the most appropriate behavior to target, the best answer for this question is **permanent product measures** because we want his work output to increase.*

3. What forms might you want to use in your FBA of this case?

Obviously, there is no one correct answer for this question. It is meant to stimulate discussion about the most appropriate forms for a particular case and to give participants an opportunity to provide a rationale for instrument selection.

4. Based solely on the information above, what is the *most likely* function of Wilbur's behavior?

The best answer for this question is that his wandering and not doing work is negatively reinforced by escape from the academic task. Although there may be a secondary attention component because the teacher reminds him to return to his seat, the primary function is escape from academic tasks.

5. Given the function of the target behavior, describe a classroom-based intervention.

Some participants, particularly regular education teachers, will indicate a referral for special education testing as a "treatment." As we all know, referral is not a treatment. What you are looking for here is a program to remediate Wilbur's academic weaknesses and to reinforce gradually increasing amounts of work completion.

Scenario III

Tyrone is a special education student in the third grade. He is above average in most areas except reading. He is currently in a foster home due to physical abuse by his father and stepmother. In previous years, you have taught Tyrone's siblings and all of them had the same problem as Tyrone: extremely aggressive behavior. He is not only physically aggressive, but he also threatens other children and you and uses quite graphic language when he threatens. You have noticed that he tends to be aggressive with the other children whey they are playing with toys that he wants to play with. He typically hits or pushes them, and they give up what they are playing with at the time. When Tyrone threatens, it is usually when you have given him a direction or command and he responds by telling you, "You don't tell me what to do—I'll kick your ass," and other assorted colorful phrases. Not wanting to push him to a physical confrontation, you usually back off with the command and let it go. You often feel bad about doing this, but you know that he is capable of physical aggression.

Based on what you have just read, answer the following questions:

1. What behavior(s) should be targeted for intervention?

This is a tricky one because there are actually two different targets: (a) physical aggression with his classmates and (b) verbal aggression with you. Make certain that these are identified separately because, as will be seen later, they have different functions.

2. What behavior-recording method would be most appropriate in this circumstance?

Again, the important point here is to remember that two different behaviors will need to be recorded and that some creativity may be needed because it may be difficult to accurately record all acts of aggressive behavior against classmates.

3. What forms might you want to use in your FBA of this case?

Again, there is no one correct answer for this question. Take the time to discuss which of the forms would be most appropriate for the case presented.

4. Based solely on the information above, what is the *most likely* function of Tyrone's behavior?

This question adds a new dimension for the participants because each of the target behaviors has a different function. The physical aggression with classmates seems to be motivated by access to tangible positive reinforcement and the verbally aggressive behavior toward the teacher appears to be motivated by escape from commands. It is crucial that participants understand that all types of aggressive behavior may not have the same function, as exemplified in this example.

5. Given the function of the target behavior, describe a classroom-based intervention.

There will need to be two different interventions because of the dual nature of the target behaviors and respective function. It will be of critical importance to address issues related to interventions that may result in a temporary increase in aggressive behavior and how such an increase can be appropriately handled so that more intense forms of aggressive behavior are not reinforced.

SECTION III: WRITING THE FBA REPORT

This section is extremely important because the FBA report is the mechanism by which all of the collected information is compiled, presented, and interpreted. Let's take a look at the basic components of an FBA report.

Overheads 24–25

The next two overheads are going to scare many of you. They are meant to scare; indeed, they are intended to illustrate the type of information that you are going to need to effectively communicate the results of the FBA.

Note: At this point, we refer participants to the two FBA reports that are included in Chapter 8. Using the reports as exemplars, we explain the sections that are listed in the overheads.

Overhead 26

A common question is "How much information do I really need to include in the FBA report?" We think that the length and specificity and detail of the FBA report is dictated by (1) the complexity of the case, (2) the procedures used, (3) the likelihood of legal procedures arising out of the FBA, (4) district policies and procedures, (5) state Department of Education requirements, and (6) what is generally considered best practice in the field. Quite obviously, as the complexity of the case and the number of procedures used increases, there will be a corresponding increase in the length of the report. If there is a high likelihood that parents will pursue some type of legal action against the school district, then it is likely that the FBA report will need to be more detailed than an "ordinary" report.

SECTION IV: LINKING ASSESSMENT TO INTERVENTION

Overhead 27

This is the real meat-and-potatoes section of training. All of you want to know what to do with the information that you have spent hours collecting and interpreting. Before we begin discussing behavior change techniques and matching those to identified function, let's start with some basic principles of intervention planning. First, the primary focus on intervention should be on preventing the occurrence of the target behavior rather than merely relying on reactive, consequence-based strategies. Second, socially valid (socially meaningful) replacement behaviors should be identified for each interfering behavior that is targeted. And, third, teachers and other staff should be given adequate training and support for the interventions that are designed.

Note: The following overheads contain information on the techniques that are used to change behavior. It is far beyond the scope of this book to describe each one. Instead, we would encourage those who wish use them to consult a good behavior modification text, such as Miltenberger (2001), for complete descriptions of each of the procedures. Within each of these different procedures, there is wide latitude in their actual implementation and in the details of the intervention. As we said in Chapter 9, there is a good deal of "art" in designing and implementing effective behavior change programs. The art is in selecting between equally appropriate procedures and making them "fit" a particular classroom environment.

Overhead 28

In those cases where attention is identified as the primary function, there are a number of alternatives available to the practitioner. The list is not inclusive; rather, it is meant to serve as an exemplar for the types of interventions that are most commonly used in classroom settings. This overhead lists four types of differential reinforcement procedures that could be used when attention is maintaining interfering behavior. For instance, you may decide that you are going to provide attention contingent upon demonstration of a functionally equivalent alternative behavior (e.g., raising a hand for assistance vs. calling out) (differential reinforcement of alternate behavior, DRA). DRA refers to reinforcing behaviors that are appropriate and functionally equivalent to the interfering behavior. That is, if the function of the interfering behavior is escape from academic tasks, then a more appropriate response that results in escape from academic tasks should be taught and reinforced. Each of the different differential reinforcement procedures is used in different cases. Using the same example of the student calling out, the only behavior truly incompatible with calling out is to remain quiet, even when assistance is needed—clearly not a desirable goal. Along with using a differential reinforcement procedure, you must also stop providing attention contingent upon the interfering behavior. Not providing attention after having previously done so is called *attention extinction*. It is necessary to use attention extinction to accelerate the decrease of the interfering behavior.

Overhead 29

When the function of interfering behavior is access to tangible reinforcement, one must always be certain when designing an intervention that the student no longer can gain access to the tangible contingent upon interfering behavior (*tangible extinction*). For instance, if a student is hitting another student to gain access to food items, the team must figure out how to prevent—within the context in which the behavior is occurring—the student from getting food contingent upon hitting. Simultaneously, the team must also determine an appropriate replacement behavior that the student can use to gain access to food. In some cases, the student may not have the necessary language skills to access tangibles and may need to be taught that skill or some other functional communication skill that results in the acquisition of tangibles. At least in the initial phases of training, every occurrence of the replacement behavior must be immediately reinforced with a tangible so that learning occurs more rapidly. After a period of steady or increasing demonstration of the replacement behavior, reinforcement may be gradually thinned.

Overhead 30

When the function of interfering behavior is escape/avoidance (i.e., negative reinforcement), one must first determine if the student has the skill to do what he/she is escaping or avoiding. For instance, if a student is being disruptive during reading and his/her reading skills are poor, then at least part of the intervention must address improving his/her reading skills. It is the lack of skill that makes the task aversive in many cases and not the task per se. Along with academic skill remediation, there will need to be a negative reinforcement procedure in place whereby the student's replacement behaviors are reinforced by brief periods of escape or avoidance of the task. If the student has the skill (can do the work and has *demonstrated* through some type of assessment procedure that he/she can in fact do the work) but is not doing the task, this is referred to as a *performance deficit*. In the case of performance deficits, there is inadequate reinforcement available for doing the task. Thus, intervention would focus on two aspects in the case of performance deficits: (1) not allowing escape/avoidance contingent upon interfering behavior and (2) reinforcing replacement behaviors with brief periods of escape or avoidance (see Steege et al., 1990).

Note: One of the most troubling problems with using escape extinction is that there will often be an escalation in the interfering behavior and perhaps in additional aggressive behavior. Teams and support staff must be prepared to deal with these escalations when addressing escape maintained behavior. Procedures for dealing with escalating behavior should be addressed in considerable detail in the positive behavior support (PBS) plan.

Overhead 31

Although not a common occurrence, except perhaps in students with moderate-to-severe disabilities, students sometimes engage in interfering behavior because it results in some type of sensory consequence. In such cases, a number of procedures need to be implemented simultaneously to adequately address these behaviors. First, one must identify a replacement behavior that will result in the same type of sensory reinforcement. In many cases, you will need to *teach* a replacement behavior because of the limited behavioral repertoire of persons with various types of developmental disabilities. To enhance the acquisition of the replacement behavior and to promote its use by the student, you may need to provide extra tangible reinforcement contingent upon the display of the behavior.

Overheads 32–33

Part of the FBA process involves identifying the "triggers" or antecedents of interfering behavior. As such, intervention often involves altering these antecedent events to prevent the interfering behavior from occurring. The next overhead and the ones that follow highlight some possible (but not all) ways that antecedents might be altered. The antecedent manipulation strategies listed on the overheads are for common antecedents for interfering behavior that are found in classrooms.

In some instances, interfering behavior occurs more frequently during teacher-assigned tasks than during student-selected tasks. In such cases, the teacher can give the student the option of working on one of two or more tasks that need to be completed and that are part of the instructional agenda. Giving the student the option to select the work task may increase work output, academic achievement, and decrease interfering behavior. Likewise, highly preferred tasks are less likely to occasion, or trigger, interfering behavior than less preferred tasks. When the FBA reveals that this is the case, the opportunity to engage in the highly preferred task may be used to reinforce the completion of less-preferred tasks.

Overhead 34

It is not unusual to discover that some students find novel tasks more interesting than repetitive tasks. In such cases, you might switch from a repetitive task to a novel task prior to the student engaging in the interfering behavior. Even if the opposite is the case (the student prefers repetitive tasks and these tasks occasion less interfering behavior than novel tasks), the same procedure may be applied wherein access to a repetitive task is used to reinforce participation in a novel task without interfering behavior. Gradually, the amount of time that a student is required to spend engaging in the novel task without interfering behavior may be increased before he/she gains access to a repetitive task.

Overheads 35–36

For some children, interfering behavior occurs more frequently during unpredictable routines than during predictable routines. If this is the case, intervention may simply involve some method by which a student is warned beforehand about changes in schedule or routine instead of having the information "sprung" on them. The method that you decide to use to warn them is probably less important than making sure that it is doable in the targeted setting and that it does not require a great deal of effort on the part of the teacher. As we mentioned earlier, this is the "art" side of intervention planning. The science part is in discovering that unpredictable routines have resulted in more interfering behaviors than have predictable routines.

You may find that different types of academic material result in more interfering behavior. For instance, difficult tasks may be more likely to trigger interfering behavior than easy tasks. Perhaps written tasks for some students are more aversive and are more likely to occasion interfering behavior than oral tasks. In either of these situations, one must determine why certain tasks are difficult (e.g., due to an academic weakness) or why written tasks are more aversive (e.g., due to poor handwriting skills, poor eye–hand coordination) and then work to remedy the underlying problem (the academic skill deficit or the poor handwriting skills) while modifying the tasks so that interfering behaviors are less likely to occur.

Overhead 37

We have found that for children who exhibit oppositional-defiant and/or "escape-motivated" behaviors modifying the presentation of tasks and reinforcers results in an increase in appropriate behaviors and a decrease in interfering behaviors. Embedded instructing involves "sandwiching" difficult tasks between easy tasks. A series of easy tasks results in momentum in responding, which increases the probability of the occurrence of responding during *subsequent* tasks. The presentation of easy tasks or preferred activities following the difficult task serve to reinforce (i.e., Premack principle) the completion of the difficult task.

Overhead 38

This is sort of an all-encompassing overhead because it lists some additional antecedent variables that often trigger interfering behavior. We finish with this to drive home the point that almost anything found in a classroom can serve as an antecedent for interfering behavior. We sometimes ask for examples from participants that relate to each of the points or we draw from our own experience and provide additional examples.

Overhead 39

Documenting the effectiveness is the final step of the FBA process. In most cases, if the intervention results in meaningful behavior change, then the results of the FBA have been validated. Documentation of the effectiveness of the intervention involves the use of single-case experimental designs. At the most basic level (an AB design), the first step is to establish baseline levels of responding and then measure the target behaviors across time. If improvement occurs, then the intervention is likely to have been responsible for the changes in behavior. We say "likely" because a simple AB design is not an experimental design and does not control for possible extraneous variables. For more information on single subject experimental designs, see Steege et al. (2002).

CONCLUSION

This has been a rather long chapter, but it probably needed to be. Effective training of school-based teams to conduct valid FBAs probably represents the single greatest need if this part of the IDEA is to be fully implemented. We are not implying that ours is the best method or the only method for training teams. There are training programs that are available commercially or on the Internet that purport to do the same thing. It behooves the wise practitioner to examine the information that is available and decide which is most appropriate for his/her needs. More than likely, the end product will be a compilation of the many different products that are out there.

We encourage readers to make use of the overheads that we have presented as well as to use the information given in this chapter to construct their own training overheads. The examples we have provided are based on real cases but may be substituted by ones from your own practice that are more relevant for the teams that you are training. In the final analysis, the training will be judged not by how slick the overhead show presentation is, nor by the length of training, but by how well the FBAs are conducted and to what degree the information is used to assist students so that they can benefit maximally from their educational experience.

Overhead 1

WHAT IS FUNCTIONAL BEHAVIORAL ASSESSMENT?

A systematic means of identifying variables that may control a behavior. Both the antecedents and consequences are examined to understand why a behavior occurs in a particular environmental context.

Overhead 2

WHY CONDUCT A FUNCTIONAL BEHAVIORAL ASSESSMENT?

- Mandated by the IDEA (Public Law 105-17)
- Leads to effective interventions
- Best practice for service delivery
- Offers legal protection to district

Overhead 3a

WHEN A FUNCTIONAL BEHAVIORAL ASSESSMENT
MUST BE CONDUCTED

- When suspensions or placements in an alternative setting exceed 10 consecutive days or amount to a change in placement
- When a student is placed in an interim alternative educational setting for 45 days when his or her misconduct involves weapons or drugs
- When a due process hearing officer places a student in an interim alternative educational setting for behavior that is dangerous to him/herself or others

Overhead 3b

WHEN A FUNCTIONAL BEHAVIORAL ASSESSMENT
SHOULD BE CONDUCTED

- When a student's problem behavior impedes his or her learning or the learning of others
- When a student's behavior presents a danger to him/herself or others
- When a student's suspension or placement in an interim alternative educational setting approaches 10 cumulative days

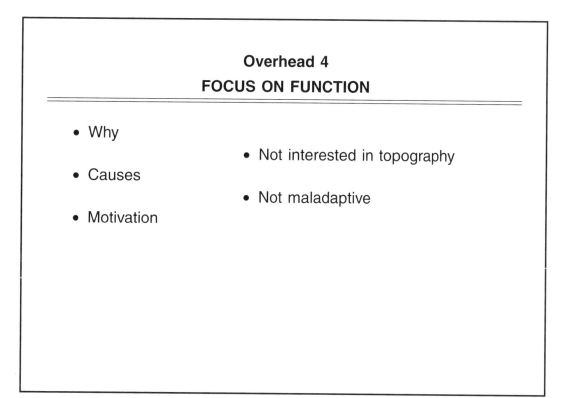

Overhead 4

FOCUS ON FUNCTION

- Why

- Causes

- Motivation

- Not interested in topography

- Not maladaptive

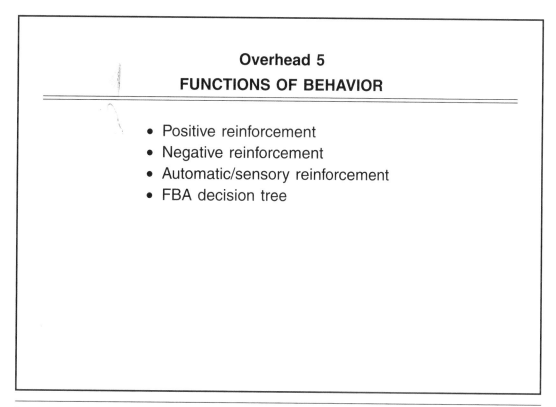

Overhead 5

FUNCTIONS OF BEHAVIOR

- Positive reinforcement
- Negative reinforcement
- Automatic/sensory reinforcement
- FBA decision tree

Overhead 6
NOT FUNCTIONS OF BEHAVIOR

- Power
- Revenge
- Control
- Medical conditions

Overhead 7
ATTENTION

Teacher		Peers	
Positive	Negative	Positive	Negative
Verbal		Verbal	
Physical		Physical	
Nonverbal		Nonverbal	

Overhead 8

ESCAPE/AVOIDANCE

- Tasks/demands
- Activities
- Social interactions
    Peers
    Adults
- Settings

Overhead 9

TANGIBLES

- Food
- Activities
- Games
- Materials

Overhead 10

AUTOMATIC/SENSORY REINFORCEMENT

Positive	Negative
Behavior that results in the attainment of a positive reinforcer that is not mediated by the action of another individual	Behavior that results in the cessation or attenuation of an unpleasant or aversive stimulus and is not mediated by the action of another individual
"Arousal induction"	"Arousal reduction"

Overhead 11

SUMMARY

- What is functional behavioral assessment?
- Why do we conduct an FBA?
- "Must" versus "should" circumstances
- Why focus on function instead of topography?
- What are the four functions of behavior?

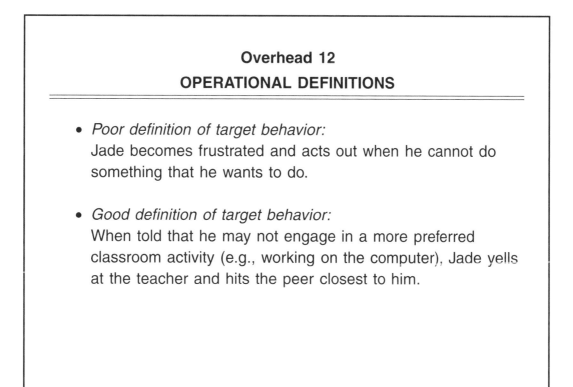

Overhead 12
OPERATIONAL DEFINITIONS

- *Poor definition of target behavior:*
  Jade becomes frustrated and acts out when he cannot do something that he wants to do.

- *Good definition of target behavior:*
  When told that he may not engage in a more preferred classroom activity (e.g., working on the computer), Jade yells at the teacher and hits the peer closest to him.

Overhead 13
REPLACEMENT BEHAVIORS

- Functionally equivalent to the interfering behavior

- Socially valid

- Incompatible with interfering behavior

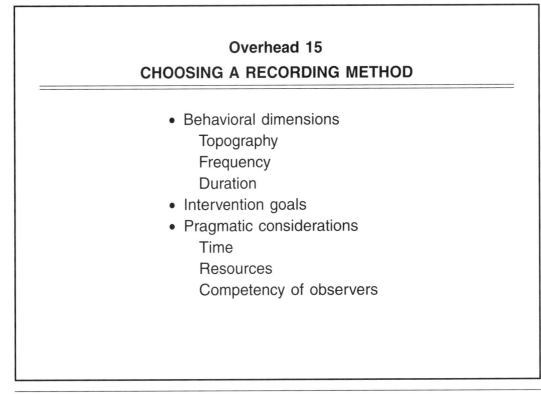

Overhead 14

MEASURING BEHAVIOR

- Frequency recording
- Duration recording
- Partial interval recording
- Whole interval recording
- Momentary time sampling
- Permanent products
- Performance based

Overhead 15

CHOOSING A RECORDING METHOD

- Behavioral dimensions
    Topography
    Frequency
    Duration
- Intervention goals
- Pragmatic considerations
    Time
    Resources
    Competency of observers

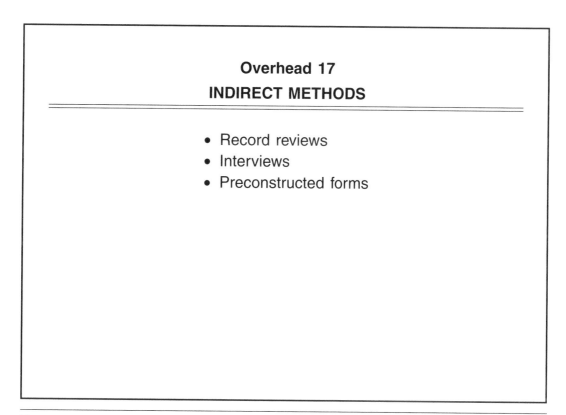

Overhead 16

METHODS OF FUNCTIONAL BEHAVIORAL ASSESSMENT

- Indirect FBA
- Direct descriptive FBA
- Functional behavioral analysis

Overhead 17

INDIRECT METHODS

- Record reviews
- Interviews
- Preconstructed forms

Overhead 18

RECORD REVIEW

- Previous grades
- Achievement tests
- Attendance history
- Disciplinary history
- Medical history
- Social history
- Previous interventions
- Individualized education program (IEP)

Overhead 19

INTERVIEW GOALS

- Operationally define the interfering behavior(s)
- Identify potential antecedents, consequences, and setting events
- Estimates of problem strength
- Determine more appropriate behavioral response
- Determine the sequence of the behavioral interactions

Overhead 20

PRECONSTRUCTED FORMS

- Functional Behavioral Assessment Screening Form (FBASF)
- Antecedent Variables Assessment Form (AVAF)
- Individual Variables Assessment Form (IVAF)
- Consequence Variables Assessment Form (CVAF)

Overhead 21

DIRECT BEHAVIORAL OBSERVATIONS

- Setting events
- Antecedents
- Consequences

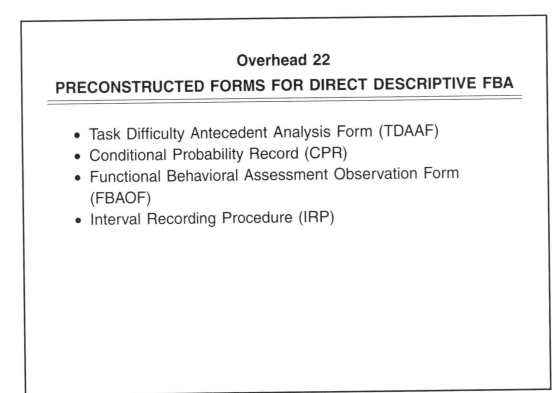

Overhead 22

PRECONSTRUCTED FORMS FOR DIRECT DESCRIPTIVE FBA

- Task Difficulty Antecedent Analysis Form (TDAAF)
- Conditional Probability Record (CPR)
- Functional Behavioral Assessment Observation Form (FBAOF)
- Interval Recording Procedure (IRP)

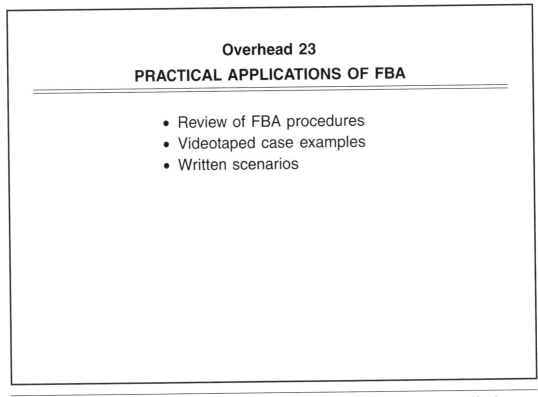

Overhead 23

PRACTICAL APPLICATIONS OF FBA

- Review of FBA procedures
- Videotaped case examples
- Written scenarios

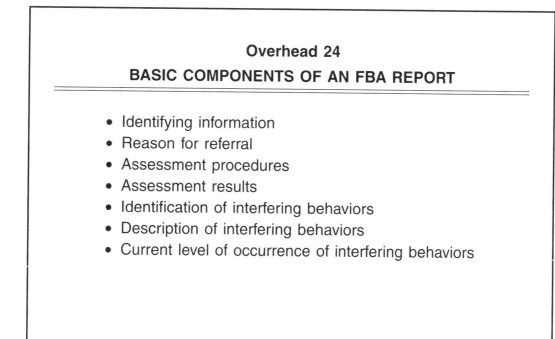

Overhead 24

BASIC COMPONENTS OF AN FBA REPORT

- Identifying information
- Reason for referral
- Assessment procedures
- Assessment results
- Identification of interfering behaviors
- Description of interfering behaviors
- Current level of occurrence of interfering behaviors

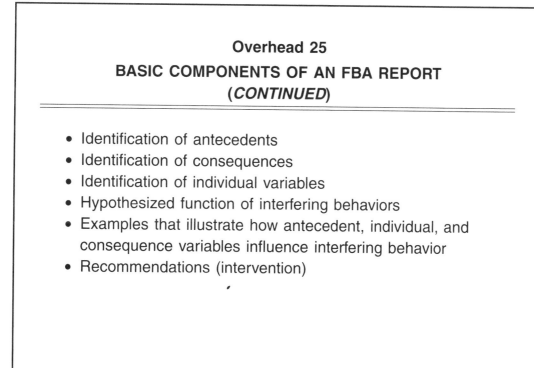

Overhead 25

BASIC COMPONENTS OF AN FBA REPORT
(*CONTINUED*)

- Identification of antecedents
- Identification of consequences
- Identification of individual variables
- Hypothesized function of interfering behaviors
- Examples that illustrate how antecedent, individual, and consequence variables influence interfering behavior
- Recommendations (intervention)

Overhead 26

FACTORS INFLUENCING THE LENGTH OF THE FBA REPORT

- Complexity of the case
- Procedures used
- Likelihood of legal proceedings
- District policies and procedures
- State Department of Education requirements
- Best practice in the field

Overhead 27

UNDERLYING PRINCIPLES OF INTERVENTION

- Focus should be on prevention rather than on reaction
- Socially meaningful replacement behaviors should be identified and reinforced for each interfering behavior
- Teachers should be trained and given adequate support to implement classroom-based interventions

Overhead 28

FUNCTION IS ATTENTION

- Differential reinforcement
    - Alternative behaviors
    - Incompatible behaviors
    - Other behaviors
    - Low rates of responding
- Attention extinction

Overhead 29

FUNCTION IS TANGIBLE

- Tangible extinction
- Reinforce appropriate behavior with tangibles
- Immediate reinforcement with a tangible
- Start on a continuous schedule, then thin to intermittent reinforcement

Overhead 30

FUNCTION IS ESCAPE/AVOIDANCE

- Skill versus performance deficit
- Teach skill or escape extinction
- Reinforce performance with escape
- Be prepared for escalation and aggressive behavior
- High probability response sequence

Overhead 31

FUNCTION IS AUTOMATIC/SENSORY

- Define alternative means of obtaining same/similar reinforcement
- Need to teach new behavior
- May need to enhance with tangibles in the beginning
- Response prevention/blocking

Overhead 32

ANTECEDENT MANIPULATION

- *Task choice:*
    Teacher assigned
    versus
    Student choice

Overhead 33

ANTECEDENT MANIPULATION

- *Task preference:*
    Preferred task
    versus
    Nonpreferred task

Overhead 34

ANTECEDENT MANIPULATION

- *Task novelty:*
    Novel tasks
    versus
    Repetitive tasks

Overhead 35

ANTECEDENT MANIPULATION

Predictable schedule
versus
Unpredictable schedule

Overhead 36

ANTECEDENT MANIPULATION

Teacher presentation of class material:
- Difficult versus easy
- Oral versus written
- Pacing

Overhead 37

EMBEDDED INSTRUCTION

Embedded instruction involves interspersing easy and difficult tasks as a way of increasing academic engagement in low probability (e.g., nonpreferred or difficult) tasks, activities, and situations. It involves as well the pairing of two procedures:

- High probability response sequence: to establish "behavior momentum" to increase the likelihood of a student's participation

- Premack principle: to reinforce appropriate behavior

Overhead 38

OTHER POSSIBLE ANTECEDENTS

- Location of the student's desk
- Density during activity
- Proximity of peers
- Proximity of the teacher
- Noise
- Most previous activity

Overhead 39

DOCUMENTING THE EFFECTIVENESS OF INTERVENTIONS

- Baseline data
- Intervention data
- Single-case experimental designs

Overhead 40

OPTIMAL INSTRUCTIONAL ENVIRONMENTS

Instructional environments that are:

- Relevant
- Effective
- Efficient

result in high levels of appropriate behavior and low levels of interfering behavior.

Overhead 41

BEHAVIORAL SUPPORTS

Interventions that include the following supports:

- Environmental
- Instructional
- Reinforcement contingent on appropriate behavior

result in high levels of appropriate behavior and low levels of interfering behavior.

Overhead 42
SOMETIMES THE _____ STILL HITS THE FAN.

Even with optimal learning environments and well-crafted behavioral supports, interfering behaviors occur. What should be done?

We have found the following set of procedures to be effective in addressing a wide range of interfering behaviors, regardless of function.

When interfering behavior(s) occur, try the following sequence of steps:

- Planned ignoring of the specific behavior (e.g., not commenting on the behavior)
- Redirection to appropriate behavior (e.g., directing the person to the task at hand or to an alternative task/behavior)
- Reinforcement of participation/engagement of appropriate behavior

The procedure incorporates several behaviorally based strategies:

- Extinction (not reinforcing the specific behavior)
- Positive practice (participation in the appropriate behavior following the occurrence of interfering behavior)
- Functional communication training (when the person is redirected to a communication behavior)
- DRI/DRA (reinforcement of alternative or incompatible behavior)
- Premack principle

12

A Baker's Dozen Plus One

The Authors' Responses
to 14 Frequently Asked Questions
about Functional Behavioral Assessment

1. What is a functional behavioral assessment?

FBA is the process for gathering information that can be used to maximize the effectiveness and efficiency of positive behavioral interventions. The following are six primary outcomes of an FBA:

a. Clear description of interfering behaviors
b. Description of the events, times, and situations that trigger interfering behavior
c. Description of the individual differences that contribute to the occurrence of interfering behavior
d. Description of the rewarding outcomes of interfering behavior
e. Development of summary statements or hypotheses specifying the motivating functions of interfering behavior
f. Design of assessment-driven socially meaningful positive behavioral support (PBS) interventions

2. What is the difference between functional behavioral assessment and functional behavioral analysis?

Functional behavioral assessment is a term used to describe any procedure whose aim is to identify the variables that are related to problem behavior. These variables may include setting events and/or establishing operations, antecedents, and consequences. FBA includes all of the procedures we have presented in this book, including functional behavioral analysis. *Functional behavioral analysis* is a specific type of functional behavioral assessment and refers to those situations where specific variables are systematically manipulated in a highly controlled setting to assess their controlling functions on behavior (Gresham, Watson, & Skinner, 2001).

3. What are the qualifications one needs to conduct an FBA?

This one is potentially a very sticky issue because there are no minimum training standards for being qualified to perform FBAs nor does the law specify who should be responsible for conducting FBAs and what their training and background should be. Having said that, it is our opinion that professionals conducting school-based FBAs should have a minimum of graduate academic training in assessment, basic principles of applied behavior analysis (ABA), and PBS interventions. Being realists, however, we understand that this is not possible in many districts. Even in those districts where school psychologists lead the team in completing the FBA, recent data suggests that they may not have the necessary training or skills required to conduct a comprehensive, reliable, and accurate FBA (Shriver & Watson, 2001). Conversely, in some cases special educators, classroom teachers, social workers, speech pathologists, etc. may have the necessary *combination* of academic training and supervised experience to complete a solid and meaningful FBA.

Because it is unlikely that most districts would have one or more persons competent to conduct independent FBAs, we recommend that the FBA be conducted using a team approach. For example, we have found that a team composed of several professionals (e.g., a school psychologist, a special educator, a special education consultant, and a speech pathologist) can result in reliable, accurate, and socially meaningful assessments that result in the design and implementation of effective interventions (Dittmer-McMahon, 2001).

4. How long does it take to complete an FBA?

The amount of time needed to complete the FBA process varies from case to case. The following factors determine the amount of time required to complete a comprehensive FBA:

a. The complexity of the behavior(s) assessed
b. The number of behavior(s) assessed
c. The degree of training and experience of evaluators in conducting FBAs
d. The degree of training and experience of informants participating in an FBA process

Steege and Northup (1998) provided estimates of the amount of time required for an evaluator to complete a comprehensive FBA as follows:

- Indirect FBA (interviews, record review, rating scales): 2–3 hours
- Direct descriptive FBA (direct observations in the natural setting): 2–4 hours
- Brief functional analysis (6–10 observation sessions): 2–3 hours
- Consultation in the design of the PBS plan: 2–3 hours

- FBA report: 2–3 hours
- Total time: 10–16 hours

In most cases, however, it is likely that a brief functional analysis will not be done nor will a comprehensive FBA report be compiled. Thus, the amount of time to complete a typical FBA in the schools may be only 7–11 hours. In fact, this time estimate is highly consistent with survey data indicating the average time of 10 hours that a practitioner spends conducting a traditional psychoeducational assessment and is probably more realistic for most districts than 16 hours. Because school districts are relying on teams composed of staff members to conduct the FBAs, sometimes without release time or additional compensation, it is far more reasonable to expect a briefer model of FBA that is accurate yet time efficient.

There are other situations in which the FBA process may take only a few minutes. Consider the situation of the supervising psychologist within a program serving students with a variety of disabilities in which the following resources are available:

- Teaching and support staff who have extensive training in the principles and applications of ABA
- Ongoing direct descriptive FBA processes of interfering behaviors for each student
- A well-designed intervention plan that is implemented both accurately and consistently
- Accurate and up-to-date graphs showing the student's progress on the behavior intervention plan (BIP)

In these cases, although the initial FBA process may require several hours of assessment and report writing time, follow-up FBAs are much more time efficient.

5. When should we conduct an FBA?

There are a number of situations where an FBA is required by law (as discussed in Chapter 3). There is really no reason to comment further on those situations because the law is clear regarding those circumstances. What are much less clear are the other circumstances under which an FBA should be conducted. Although we described some of those situations in earlier chapters (see Chapters 1 and 3), the real answer to this question is "ALWAYS." Or at least always when there is a behavior that is bothersome to others. This may seem like an exaggerated response, but it's really not. Although we have presented FBA as a systematic process with specific procedures, it can be as simple in some cases as a school psychologist making a brief observation while taking particular care to note potentially relevant antecedents and consequences. We are realists and understand that every problem behavior exhibited by students is not going to be subjected to a full-blown FBA, nor should it be. What we do advocate, however, is that—even when a complete FBA is not required or needed—the school psychologist should, within the context of his/her interviews with teachers and direct observations, strive to identify those antecedents and consequences that seem to be related to the problem behavior (sort of a "mini-FBA"). In such cases extensive documentation is not required, but the school psychologist still has the necessary information to plan an intervention. Thus, we believe that an FBA should be conducted prior to designing interventions and any time when one wishes to understand the motivation of a particular behavior.

We also believe that FBAs should be conducted especially for those children outside of special education who are receiving ineffective disciplinary interventions. For instance, if a child is being sent to the principal's office *frequently* for disrupting the classroom, then it is clear that the disciplinary strategy (being sent to the principal's office) is not working. It has been our experience that few ever stop to wonder *why* a particular strategy or intervention is not working. It just may be that the intervention is not addressing the function of the behavior. In such cases, an FBA is clearly called for to identify the contextual variables and antecedent stimuli that are triggering the problem behavior and the consequences that are maintaining it.

6. Why should we complete an FBA?

It just makes good sense! Important decisions regarding the development and evaluation of interventions with persons who exhibit interfering behaviors should be based on objective and accurate information. Experience has shown that interventions based on subjective, biased, and anecdotal information often result in ineffective programming.

Moreover, although traditional forms of assessment may be useful for purposes of diagnosis or for making placement decisions, the results of these assessments have not been shown to be particularly useful in designing interventions. In contrast, the results of FBAs are used as the basis for developing individually tailored interventions.

Behavior does not occur in a vacuum. Rather, interfering behavior typically occurs in reaction to a complex set of interacting variables (e.g., environmental, individual, instructional, and/or rewarding outcomes). Only by identifying the relationships between the unique characteristics of the individual and the contextual variables that trigger and reinforce behavior can we truly understand human behavior and work in concert with the person served to develop interventions that lead to socially significant and meaningful behavior change.

7. Are FBAs applicable only to persons with autism and mental retardation?

FBA is not applicable only to persons with developmental disabilities. Yes, the early literature on FBA and functional behavioral analysis predominately featured investigations with persons with developmental disabilities within nonschool settings. However, within the past decade, dozens of studies have demonstrated the application of FBA across a wide range of populations (including persons with emotional disturbance, behavioral impairments, and/or learning disabilities; also typically developing students, among others) and behaviors (e.g., self-injury, oppositional–defiant disorder, aggression, food refusal, thumb sucking). For more information, see the annotated bibliography of 102 school-based functional behavioral assessment studies that appeared in *Proven Practice: Prevention and Remediation Solutions for Schools* (Vol. 3, No. 1) by Radford et al. (2000).

A cursory review will reveal studies that include a wide range of populations and presenting problems.

It is equally important to remember that FBA is not limited to the analysis of interfering behavior. For example, Daly, Witt, Martens, and Dool (1997) described an FBA model for evaluating academic performance problems. Given that school psychologists receive numerous referrals for academic skill deficits, it only makes sense to apply the scientific process of FBA to academic problems as well as social behaviors.

8. Aren't most interfering behaviors simply motivated by social attention?

Historically, interfering behaviors have been viewed as being motivated by positive social attention (e.g., smiles, visual attention, verbal comments) or negative social attention (e.g., reprimands). In our collective experience, this hypothesis appears to be tied to institutional models of service delivery with persons with disabilities. The logic goes something like this:

> Persons living in institutions were neglected and bored. Acting-out behavior was sometimes the only way these folks could get attention. Any form of attention (both positive and negative) was better than no attention at all. Consequently, folks living in institutions typically exhibited interfering behaviors as a way of getting attention. Although there may be some merit to this hypothesis, it is erroneous to assume that students in school settings are acting out solely to get attention. First of all, schools are nothing like the segregated institutions of past decades. True, students may be bored and feel "neglected," and in those situations interfering behaviors may be motivated by access to attention. However, it is our experience that interfering behaviors within schools are motivated by the full range of motivating conditions and many times are reinforced by multiple sources.

Also, when we say that behavior is motivated by social attention we need to be more descriptive. For example, is the behavior motivated by social attention from the teacher because having obtained the teacher's attention the student is able to receive academic support? Or, is "getting a reaction" from classmates or teaching staff reinforcing in and of itself?

9. What about those students whose behavior is driven by a "need to control"?

The answer to this question involves first asking, "What do you mean by control?" If "control" refers to the individual's motivation to (a) have access to preferred objects, activities, persons, etc., and/or (b) avoid or terminate undesirable social interactions, tasks/activities, persons, etc., and/or (c) induce or reduce internal states of arousal, then we answer with a resounding "YES! YOU BETCHA!" and "RIGHT ON!" You probably see that the word "control" really does not convey what the person is controlling by his/her behavior. Thus, you must look at what outcome the controlling (i.e., interfering) behavior results in (a) positive reinforcement, (b) negative reinforcement, or (c) automatic reinforcement.

10. What about behaviors that appear to be "out of the blue?"

When folks use the phrase "out of the blue" in discussing interfering behaviors, what it really indicates is that they have not been able to identify a predictable pattern of antecedents, individual, or consequence variables associated with interfering behaviors. In many cases, such statements say much more about their level of knowledge and skills about behavior analysis and FBA processes than it does about the individual and the interfering behavior.

By conducting a comprehensive and thoughtful FBA, the variables that drive interfering behavior becomes self-evident. When behaviors are considered to be "out of the blue," it is akin to sailing on the ocean in a dense fog without the use of instrumentation. When in fog, the prudent sailor checks his/her bearings, consults the charts, listens carefully for the sounds of other boats, the crashing surf, foghorns, bells, etc., and if so equipped uses radar, or GPS (Global Positioning System) devices to assist with navigation. Similarly, when confronted with interfering behaviors, the prudent practitioner uses all of his/her available tools and resources to investigate the situation at hand and to formulate a plan of action.

11. I am confused about the term "negative reinforcement." Isn't that the same thing as punishment?

OH, NO, here we go again! This is probably one of the most common misconceptions and terminological snafus in all of behavior analysis. Obviously the answer is no—they are actually opposites of one another. Negative reinforcement *strengthens* a behavior, whereas punishment *weakens* a behavior. Let's break down the term "negative reinforcement" to better understand. The root of the word "reinforcement" (i.e., reinforce) means to strengthen. The negative part refers to something aversive or unpleasant being removed after a behavior. Thus, when a person engages in a behavior that results in the removal of something unpleasant, we say that the behavior has been negatively reinforced.

In contrast, punishment occurs when what happens after a behavior weakens that behavior. There are two kinds of punishment: positive and negative. Positive punishment occurs when something is *added* to the environment contingent upon a behavior (e.g., a hard smack on the bottom for not obeying a command). Negative punishment is (*do you want to offer a guess here?*) when something is taken away after a behavior that weakens that behavior (e.g., removing a toy when the child hits another child with the toy).

12. When I conduct an FBA, am I not analyzing the behavior of the teacher and other students just as much as that of the target student?

Absolutely! As we have said many times throughout this book, behavior does not occur in a vacuum. Because of this, we must look at the behavior of others in the student's environment to determine the reciprocal relationship between each of these variables. We know that what a teacher does in the classroom impacts his/her students. We also know that the behavior of students impacts the teacher's behavior. The better we can understand this ongoing interactive cycle, the better we will understand a particular interfering behavior.

13. Each time I design an intervention for a student, it seems that one of the primary components is the need for the teacher to change his/her behavior. Shouldn't the focus be on making the student more responsible for his/her own behavior instead of asking the teacher to do something different?

In an ideal world, this would be the case. Simply tell Liza which behavior was interfering with her ability to perform optimally academically and/or socially, tell her why she was engaging in that behavior, give her an alternative behavior to use, and let her get at it. However, the real world just does not work this way. Because of the reciprocal nature of behavioral interactions, it is imperative that in order to change a student's behavior, the teacher must usually change some aspect of his/her behavior. It may be as subtle as saying things in different ways (an antecedent manipulation) or responding differently to the interfering behavior (a consequence manipulation), or modifying the curriculum. In any case, programming teacher change is an integral part of most all positive behavior interventions.

14. What should I do when observing a behavior is difficult or nearly impossible?

We have emphasized the importance of conducting observations to directly gather information about the interfering behavior and related variables. However, what do you do when you are unable to observe behavior due to either of the following instances:

- The behavior does not occur during scheduled observations
- The student is unavailable for observation (i.e., frequently truant, chronically ill, or suspended for disciplinary reasons)

In those cases in which observations are scheduled and the behavior does not occur, one needs to determine if behavior is occurring at a very low rate (i.e., one or two times per month) and therefore the probability of ever observing the interfering behavior is quite low. In these cases, we have found that while observations of the target behaviors by the school psychologist are highly unlikely, other types of direct descriptive FBA procedures such as A-B-C recordings or modified scatterplots can be used. We have also found video recording of behaviors to be a very powerful tool when conducting FBAs in these types of situations. With video recordings, one is able to review and re-review the recordings to analyze the target behavior and associated variables.

There are other situations in which the presence of an observer influences the behavior of the referred student in such a way that she changes her behavior whenever she is aware that she is being observed. This is referred to as the *reactivity effect*. Reactivity is related to several variables such as the personal attributes of the observer, conspicuousness of the observer, and the rationale provided for the observations (C. H. Skinner, Dittmer, & Howell, 2000). Skinner et al. (2000) suggested the following strategies for reducing a student's reactivity during a classroom observation:

- Provide the student with a vague rationale regarding the presence of the observer.
- During observation, avoid staring directly at the referred student.
- During observation, avoid direct contact with the student.
- Utilize techniques such as one-way mirrors or video recordings.
- During observation, sit in an inconspicuous area of the room.
- Position yourself in the classroom before the students enter.

We have found that by through careful attention to these types of variables, reactivity is typically minimized.

Finally, in the case of students who are unavailable for observation due to truancy, illness, or suspension, one simply is not going to be able to conduct direct descriptive FBAs. In these cases, one needs to rely on indirect FBA procedures. Remember, FBA is a process. Also, FBA is part of the larger collaborative problem-solving process. In those cases in which direct observation is compromised or minimized, whenever conflicting data are found throughout the assessment process, whenever one questions the validity of the assessment results, or whenever one just needs more time to conduct a more thorough evaluation but the team is pressing for a report, we suggest that the report be titled "Preliminary Functional Behavioral Assessment." One of the first recommendations of such a report might well be for more comprehensive FBAs. Also, ultimately, the utility of the FBA is the degree with which the results of assessments are used in the design of effective interventions.

References

Ayllon, T. (1960). The application of reinforcement theory toward behavior problems: The psychiatric nurse as a behavioral engineer. *Dissertation Abstracts, 20,* 3372.

Ayllon, T., & Azrin, N. H. (1965). The measurement and reinforcement of behavior of psychotics. *Journal of the Experimental Analysis of Behavior, 7,* 327–331.

Ayllon, T., & Azrin, N. H. (1968). Reinforcer sampling: A technique for increasing the behavior of mental patients. *Journal of Applied Behavior Analysis, 1,* 13–20.

Azrin, N. H. (1960). Use of rests as reinforcers. *Psychological Reports, 7,* 240.

Azrin, N. H. (1961). Time-out from positive reinforcement. *Science, 133,* 382–383.

Azrin, N. H., & Lindsley, O. R. (1956). The reinforcement of cooperation between children. *Journal of Abnormal and Social Psychology, 52,* 100–102.

Azrin, N. H., & Powell, J. (1968). Behavioral engineering: The reduction of smoking behavior by a conditioning apparatus and procedure. *Journal of Applied Behavior Analysis, 1,* 193–200.

Baer, D. M., Peterson, R. F., & Sherman, J. A. (1967). The development of imitation by reinforcing behavioral similarity to a model. *Journal of Experimental Analysis of Behavior, 10,* 405–416.

Baer, D. M., & Sherman, J. A. (1964). Reinforcement control of generalized imitation in young children. *Journal of Experimental Child Psychology, 1,* 37–49.

Bijou, S. W., & Baer, D. M. (1961). *Child development. Vol. 1. A systematic and empirical theory.* East Norwalk, CT: Appleton-Century-Crofts.

Bijou, S. W., Peterson, R. F., & Ault, M. H. (1968). A method to integrate descriptive and experimental field studies at the level of data and empirical concepts. *Journal of Applied Behavior Analysis, 1,* 175–191.

Carr, E. G. (1977). The motivation of self-injurious behavior: A review of some hypotheses. *Psychological Bulletin, 84,* 800–816.

Carr, E. G., & Durand, V. M. (1985). Reducing behavior problems through functional communication training. *Journal of Applied Behavior Analysis, 18,* 111–126.

Corte, H. E., Wolf, M. M., & Locke, B. J. (1971). A comparison of procedures for eliminating self-injurious behavior of retarded adolescents. *Journal of Applied Behavior Analysis, 4,* 201–213.

Daly, E. J., III, Witt, J. C., Martens, B. K., & Dool E. J. (1997). A model for conducting a functional analysis of academic performance problems. *School Psychology Review, 26,* 554–574.

Dieterich, C. A., & Villani, C. J. (2000). Functional behavioral assessment: Process without procedure. *Brigham Young University Education and Law Journal, 2*, 209–219.

Dittmer-McMahon, K. I. (2001). *An evaluation of functional behavior assessments as implemented by teacher support teams after training.* Unpublished doctoral dissertation, Mississippi State University.

Drasgow, E., & Yell, M. L. (2001). Functional behavioral assessment: Legal requirements and challenges. *School Psychology Review, 30*, 239–251.

Drasgow, E., Yell, M. L., Bradley, R., & Shriner, J. G. (1999). The IDEA Amendments of 1997: A school-wide model for conducting functional behavioral assessments and developing behavior intervention plans. *Education and Treatment of Children, 22*, 244–266.

Edwards, R. P. (2002). A tutorial for using the Functional Assessment Informant Record—Teachers (FAIR-T). *Proven Practice: Prevention and Remediation Solutions for Schools, 4*, 31–38.

Ervin, R. A., & Ehrhardt, E. K. (2000). Behavior analysis in school psychology. In J. Austin & J. E. Carr (Eds.), *Handbook of applied behavior analysis* (pp. 113–135). Reno, NV: Context Press.

Flanagan, B., Goldiamond, I., & Azrin, N. H. (1959). Instatement of stuttering in normally fluent individuals through operant procedures. *Science, 130*, 979–981.

Gardner, W. I., Cole, C. L., Davidson, D. P., & Kavan, O. C. (1986). Reducing aggression in individuals with developmental disabilities: An expanded stimulus control, assessment, and intervention model. *Education and Training of the Mentally Retarded, 21*, 3–12.

Gewirtz, J. L., & Baer, D. M (1958a). The effect of brief social deprivation on behaviors for a social reinforcer. *Journal of Abnormal and Social Psychology, 56*, 49–56.

Gewirtz, J. L., & Baer, D. M (1958b). Deprivation and satiation of social reinforcers as drive conditions. Journal of Abnormal and Social Psychology, 57, 165–172.

Gresham, F., Watson, T. S., & Skinner, C. H. (2001). Functional behavioral assessment: Principles, procedures, and future directions. *School Psychology Review, 30*, 156–172.

Hacienda La Puente Unified School District v. Honig, 976 F. 2d 487, 491 (9th Cir. 1992).

Holz, W. C., Azrin, N. H., & Ayllon, T. (1963). Elimination of behavior of mental patients by response-produced extinction. *Journal of the Experimental Analysis of Behavior, 6*, 449–456.

Horner, R. H. (1994). Functional assessment: Contributions and future directions. *Journal of Applied Behavior Analysis, 27*, 401–404.

Individuals with Disabilities Education Act, 20 U.S.C. § 1400 *et seq.* (1997).

Iwata, B., Dorsey, M. F., Slifer, K. J., Bauman, K. E., & Richman, G. S. (1982). Toward a functional analysis of self-injury. *Analysis and Intervention in Developmental Disabilities, 2*, 3–20. Reprinted in *Journal of Applied Behavior Analysis, 27*, 197–209 (1994).

Iwata, B., Pace, G., Kissel, R., Nau, P., & Farber, J. (1990). The Self-Injury Trauma (SIT) Scale: A method for quantifying surface tissue damage caused by self-injurious behavior. *Journal of Applied Behavior Analysis, 23*, 99–110.

Jones, V., & Jones, S. (1998). *Comprehensive classroom management: Creating communities of support and solving problems* (5th ed.). Boston: Allyn & Bacon.

Kantor, J. R. (1959). Evolution and the science of psychology. *Psychological Record, 9*, 131–142.

Kazdin, A. E. (2001). *Behavior modification in applied settings* (6th ed.). Belmont, CA: Wadsworth/ Thomson Learning.

Kennedy, C. H., & Itkonen, T. (1993). Effects of setting events on the problem behavior of students with severe disabilities. *Journal of Applied Behavior Analysis, 26*, 321–327.

Kennedy, C., Meyer, K., Knowles, T., & Shukla, S. (2000). Analyzing the multiple functions of stereotypical behavior for students with autism: Implications for assessment and treatment. *Journal of Applied Behavior Analysis, 33*, 559–571.

Koegel, L. K., Koegel, R. L., & Dunlap, G. (Eds.). (1996). *Positive behavioral support: Including people with difficult behavior in the community.* Baltimore: Brookes.

Kolko, D. J., & Milan, M. A. (1983). Reframing and paradoxical instruction to overcome "resistance" in the treatment of delinquent youths: A multiple baseline analysis. *Journal of Consulting and Clinical Psychology, 51*, 655–660.

Krantz, P. J., & Risley, T. R. (1977). Behavioral ecology in the classroom. In K. D. O'Leary & S. G. O'Leary (Eds.), *Classroom management: The successful use of behavior modification* (2nd ed., pp. 349–360). New York: Pergamon Press.

Lalli, J. S., Browder, D. M., Mace, C. F., & Brown, K. D. (1993). Teacher use of descriptive analysis data to implement interventions to decrease students' problem behaviors. *Journal of Applied Behavior Analysis, 26*, 227–238.

LIH v. New York City Board of Education, 103 F. Supp. 658 2d (E.D.N.Y. 2000).

Mace, C. F., & Lalli, J. S. (1991). Linking descriptive and experimental analyses in the treatment of bizarre speech. *Journal of Applied Behavior Analysis, 24*, 553–562.

Mace, C. F., & Roberts, M. L. (1993). Developing effective interventions: Empirical and conceptual considerations. In J. Reichle & D. P. Wacker (Eds.), *Communicative alternatives to challenging behavior: Integrating functional assessment and intervention strategies* (pp. 113–133). Baltimore: Brookes.

McAfee, J. K. (1987). Classroom density and the aggressive behavior of handicapped children. *Education and Treatment of Children, 10*, 134–145.

McComas, J. J., & Mace, C. F. (2000). Theory and practice in conducting functional analysis. In E. S. Shapiro & T. R. Kratochwill (Eds.), *Behavioral assessment in schools: Theory, research, and clinical foundations* (2nd ed., pp. 78–103). New York: Guilford Press.

McComas, J. J., Wacker, D. P., & Cooper, L. J. (1998). Increasing compliance with medical procedures: Application of the high-probability request procedure to a toddler. *Journal of Applied Behavior Analysis, 31*, 287–290.

Michael, J. (1982). Distinguishing between discriminative and motivational functions of stimuli. *Journal of Experimental Analysis of Behavior, 37*, 149–155.

Miltenberger, R. G. (1997). *Behavior modification: Principles and procedures.* Pacific Grove, CA: Brooks/Cole.

Miltenberger, R. G. (2001). *Behavior modification: Principles and procedures* (2nd ed). Belmont, CA: Wadsworth/Thomas Learning.

O'Neill, R. E., Horner, R. H., Albin, R. W., Sprague, J. R., Storey, K., & Newton, J. S. (1997). *Functional assessment and program development for problem behavior: A practical handbook* (2nd ed.). Pacific Grove, CA: Brooks/Cole.

O'Neill, R. E., Horner, R. H., Albin, R. W., Storey, K., & Sprague, J. R. (1990). *Functional analysis of problem behavior: A practical assessment guide.* Sycamore, IL: Sycamore.

O'Reilly, M. F. (1995). Functional analysis and treatment of escape-maintained aggression correlated with sleep deprivation. *Journal of Applied Behavior Analysis, 28*, 225–226.

Pace, G. M., Ivancic, M. T., & Jefferson, G. (1994). Stimulus fading as treatment for obscenity in a brain-injured adult. *Journal of Applied Behavior Analysis, 27*, 301–305.

Pace, G. M., Iwata, B. A., Cowdery, G. E., Andree, P. J., & McIntyre, T. (1993). *Journal of Applied Behavior Analysis, 26*, 205–212.

Pierce, W. D., & Epling, W. F. (1995). *Behavior analysis and learning.* Upper Saddle River, NJ: Prentice-Hall.

Powell, J., & Azrin, N. H. (1968). The effects of shock as a punisher for cigarette smoking. *Journal of Applied Behavior Analysis, 1,* 63–71.

Radford, P. M., Aldrich, J. L., & Ervin, R. A. (2000). An annotated bibliography of 102 school-based functional assessment studies. *Proven Practice: Prevention and Remediation Solutions for Schools, 3,* 24–43.

Ray, K. P., & Watson, T. S. (2001). Analysis of the effects of temporally distant events on school behavior. *School Psychology Quarterly, 16,* 324–342.

Rodiriecus L. v. Waukegan School District No. 60, 90 F. 3d 249 (7th Cir. 1996).

Sattler, J. M. (2001). *Assessment of children: Behavioral and clinical applications* (4th ed). La Mesa, CA: Author.

Shapiro, E. S., & Kratochwill, T. R. (Eds.). (2000). *Behavioral assessment in schools: Theory, research, and clinical foundations* (2nd ed.). New York: Guilford Press.

Shriver, M. D., Anderson, C. M., & Proctor, B. (2001). Evaluating the validity of functional behavior assessment. *School Psychology Review, 30,* 180–192.

Shriver, M. D., & Watson, T. S. (2001). A survey of behavior analysis and behavioral consultation courses in school psychology: Implications for training school psychologists. *Journal of Behavioral Education, 9,* 211–221.

Skinner, B. F. (1938). *The behavior of organisms: An experimental analysis.* New York: Appleton-Century.

Skinner, B. F. (1953). *Science and human behavior.* New York: Macmillan.

Skinner, C. H., Dittmer, K. I., & Howell, L. A. (2000). Direct observation in school settings: Theoretical issues. In E. S. Shapiro & T. R. Kratochwill (Eds.), *Behavioral assessment in schools: Theory, research, and clinical foundations* (2nd ed., pp. 19–45). New York: Guilford Press.

Skinner, C. H., Rhymer, K. H., & McDaniel, C. E. (2000). Naturalistic direct observation in educational settings. In E. S. Shapiro (Ed.), *Conducting school-based assessments of child and adolescent behavior* (pp. 21–54). New York: Guilford Press.

Steege, M. W., Brown-Chidsey, R. B., & Mace, C. F. (2002). Best practices in evaluating interventions. In A. Thomas & J. Grimes (Eds.), *Best practices in school psychology—IV* (pp. 517–534). Washington, DC: National Association of School Psychologists.

Steege, M. W., Davin, T., & Hathaway, M. (2001). Reliability and accuracy of a performance-based behavioral recording procedure. *School Psychology Review, 30,* 252–261.

Steege, M. W., & Northup, J. (1998). Brief functional analysis of problem behavior: A practical approach for school psychologists. *Proven Practice: Prevention and Remediation Solutions for Schools, 1,* 4–11, 37–38.

Steege, M. W., Wacker, D. P., Berg, W. K., Cigrand, K. C., & Cooper, L. J. (1989). The use of behavioral assessment to prescribe and evaluate treatments for severely handicapped children. *Journal of Applied Behavior Analysis, 22,* 23–33.

Steege, M. W., Wacker, D. P., Cigrand, K. C., Berg, W. K., Novak, C. G., Reimers, T. M., Sasso, G. M., & DeRaad, A. (1990). Use of negative reinforcement in the treatment of self-injurious behavior. *Journal of Applied Behavior Analysis, 23,* 459–467.

Sterling-Turner, H. E., Watson, T. S., & Moore, J. W. (2002). The effects of direct training and treatment integrity on treatment outcomes in school consultation. *School Psychology Quarterly, 17,* 47–77.

Talkington, L. W., & Riley, J. B. (1971). Reduction diets and aggression in institutionalized mentally retarded patients. *American Journal of Mental Deficiency, 76,* 370–372.

Thorndike, E. L. (1898). Animal intelligence: An experimental study of the associative processes in animals. *Psychological Monographs, 2,* 1–109.

Touchette, P. E., MacDonald, R. F., & Langer, S. N. (1985). A scatter plot for identifying stimulus control for problem behavior. *Journal of Applied Behavior Analysis, 18,* 343–351.

Wacker, D. P., Steege, M., Northup, J., Reimers, T., Berg, W. K., & Sasso, G. (1990). Use of functional analysis and acceptability measures to assess and treat severe behavior problems: An outpatient clinic model. In A. C. Repp, C. Allen, & N. N. Singh (Eds.), *Perspectives on the use of nonaversive and aversive interventions for persons with developmental disabilities* (pp. 349–359). Sycamore, IL: Sycamore.

Walker, H. M., Block-Pedego, A. E., Todis, B. J., Severson, H. H., & Pedego, A. (1991). *School archival records search.* Longmont, CA: Sopris West.

Watson, J. B., & Rayner, R. (1920). Conditioned emotional reactions. *Journal of Experimental Psychology, 3,* 1–14.

Watson, T. S., & Kramer, J. J. (1995). Teaching problem solving skills to teachers-in-training: An experimental analysis of three methods. *Journal of Behavioral Education, 5,* 281–293.

Watson, T. S., Ray, K. P., Sterling, H. E., & Logan, P. (1999). Teacher implemented functional analysis and treatment: A method for linking assessment to intervention. *School Psychology Review, 28,* 292–302.

Witt, J. C., & Beck, R. (1999). *One minute academic functional assessment and interventions.* Longmont, CO: Sopris West.

Zarcone, J. R., Iwata, B. A., Vollmer, T. R., Jagtiani, S., Smith, R. G., & Mazaleski, G. L. (1993). Extinction of self-injurious escape behavior with and without instructional fading. *Journal of Applied Behavior Analysis, 26,* 353–360.

WEB SITES ON FBA AND PBS

The following web sites are offered as resources for practitioners seeking additional information about the FBA-PBS process.

http://cecp.air.org/fba/default.htm
http://www.pbis.org/english
http://www.childpsychologist.com/fba_bip/
http://nasponline.org/publications/cq263funcassessbibl.html
http://www.nasponline.org/publications/cq277fba.html

Author Index

243